MATTHEW SARDON

Breath of the eternal

The Holy Spirit in Scripture, the Church, and the Soul

Copyright © 2025 by Matthew Sardon

All rights reserved. No part of this publication may be reproduced, stored or transmitted in any form or by any means, electronic, mechanical, photocopying, recording, scanning, or otherwise without written permission from the publisher. It is illegal to copy this book, post it to a website, or distribute it by any other means without permission.

Matthew Sardon asserts the moral right to be identified as the author of this work.

First edition

This book was professionally typeset on Reedsy. Find out more at reedsy.com

Through the Spirit we become God's dwelling, His living temple.

St. Basil the Great

Contents

Prologue   1

I   The Spirit Who Creates (Purgation)

1. Breath Over the Waters: The Spirit in Creation   7
2. Spirit and Image: The Human Person as Spirit-Bearer   21
3. Fire in Israel: The Spirit in the Old Testament   35
4. Promise of a New Heart: The Spirit Who Purifies   47
5. The Spirit of Repentance: Purification and the Ascent of the...   61
6. From Purification to Illumination   74

II   The Spirit Who Anoints (Illumination)

7. The Spirit of the Messiah: Christ's Anointing   81
8. The Spirit Who Illuminates: Jesus Teaching in the Spirit   94
9. The Spirit and the Cross: The Fire of Love   108
10. The Spirit of Resurrection: New Creation Begins   122
11. Pentecost: The Descent of Fire   136
12. From Illumination to Indwelling   150

III	The Spirit Who Indwells (Union)	
13	The Spirit Who Makes the Church: Body, Temple, Bride	159
14	The Fire of the Sacraments	173
15	The Spirit in Scripture: Inspiration and Illumination	186
16	The Spirit in Prayer: The Breath Within Us	200
17	The Spirit Who Divinises: Virtue, Holiness, Glory	214
18	The Spirit Who Heals: Wounds, Passions, Conscience	228
19	From Union to Glory	245

IV	The Spirit Who Consummates (Glory)	
20	The Spirit and Mission: Love to the Ends of the Earth	255
21	The spirit in suffering: Consolation and martyrdom	269
22	The Spirit and the Last Things: Judgment and Mercy	287
23	The Spirit of the New Creation: All Things Made New	304

24	Conclusion	323
	About the Author	335

Prologue

From the first pages of Scripture to the final cry of the Bride in Revelation, there is a presence who moves quietly through the story of salvation—a presence as essential as breath and often just as unnoticed. The Fathers sometimes called the Holy Spirit the "shy person of the Trinity," not because He lacks power or glory, but because His work is to draw attention away from Himself so that the face of Christ may be seen. Basil of Caesarea, with his usual clarity, writes that the Spirit is the One who "makes known the Son," illuminating Him the way light illuminates a face in a darkened room. Augustine, centuries later, would echo this, describing the Spirit as the Love by which the Father and Son are united—and by which we are drawn into that same union. The Spirit reveals Christ, and Christ reveals the Father, and in this divine circulation of love humanity discovers its true home.

Yet if the Spirit reveals Christ so gently, almost imperceptibly, it should not surprise us that the Spirit is also the most forgotten Person of the Trinity. In many Christian hearts today, He is not denied so much as overlooked—spoken of in hurried phrases, reduced to a feeling, or confused with vague spiritual energy. This is not merely a theological oversight. It is a spiritual wound. When the Spirit is forgotten, Christianity collapses into moral effort, religious habit, or intellectual theory. The Father feels distant. Christ feels historical. Prayer becomes burden instead of breath. Faith becomes idea instead of life. The heart begins to feel spiritually thin, as though something essential is missing—because something is missing. The very life of

God meant to dwell within us lies unwelcomed at the door of the soul.

This forgetting has consequences. A Christianity without the Spirit becomes dry, anxious, and self-referential. It knows the commandments but not the fire that makes obedience possible. It studies Scripture but does not see the light shining behind the words. It believes in Christ but does not feel His indwelling presence. It prays but feels as though its voice remains unheard. Modern Christians often describe this interior dryness with painful honesty. They feel as though they stand before a silent heaven, as though their spiritual life is effort without encounter. They ask, sometimes with trembling hearts, why their faith feels hollow. The tragedy is that many have simply never been taught how near the Spirit truly is.

For Scripture reveals a world soaked in the Spirit's presence. Before light itself exists, the Spirit hovers over the waters. Before Adam rises from the dust, the Spirit is breathed into his nostrils. Before Israel speaks prophecy, wisdom, or praise, the Spirit overshadows the prophets. Before Christ begins His mission, the Spirit descends upon Him. Before the Church utters her first word of witness, the Spirit comes as fire. Before any human soul can cry "Abba," the Spirit has already made His home in its depths. The Spirit is present at every beginning: the beginning of creation, the beginning of Israel, the beginning of Christ's mission, the beginning of the Church, the beginning of prayer, the beginning of holiness. Wherever God begins something new, the Spirit is there first.

This is why the Fathers taught that the Spirit is not an optional dimension of the Christian life but its foundation. Without the Spirit, we may know about God, but we do not know God. We may admire Christ, but we do not become like Him. We may hear Scripture, but we do not encounter the Word living beneath the words. We may attempt virtue, but we do not taste transformation. Human nature, left to itself, cannot ascend. Only the Spirit can lift it. Only the Spirit can ignite it. Only the Spirit can draw it into the very life of God.

This book was born from the conviction that the forgetting of the Spirit is one of the quiet tragedies of modern Christianity—and that the recovery of the Spirit is its greatest need. Too many believers live weary, anxious, guilt-laden lives because they have been taught how to strive but not how to breathe. They have been told to imitate Christ but not how the Spirit forms Christ within them. They have been invited to prayer but not shown how the Spirit prays in them when their own words fail. They have been taught doctrines about God but not introduced to the Spirit who makes God present in the soul. A Christianity without the Spirit is a Christianity without warmth, without wonder, without inner fire.

The purpose of this book is simple: to make the Spirit known again—not as an abstract doctrine, but as the living Breath of God moving through Scripture, through the Church, and through the depths of the human soul. We will follow the path of salvation history, for the Spirit's identity is revealed through the great works of God: creation, promise, prophecy, incarnation, cross, resurrection, and glory. But we will also follow the path of the soul, for the Spirit's mission is not only cosmic but personal: to purify, illumine, and unite the human person to the life of Christ. These two paths—history and interiority—are not parallel stories. They are one story unfolding at two levels, the great and the small, the cosmic and the intimate. The Spirit who hovered over the waters is the same Spirit who hovers over the wounded places of the human heart.

This is the Spirit who creates order out of chaos, both in the world and in the soul. This is the Spirit who anoints the Messiah and makes His life radiant. This is the Spirit who indwells the Church so that Christ may be present in every age. This is the Spirit who carries suffering toward redemption and death toward resurrection. This is the Spirit who completes what the Father wills and the Son accomplishes. This is the Spirit who makes us sons and daughters in truth, who whispers "Abba" when our own strength fails, who prays within us with groans deeper than words, who carves the likeness of Christ into the clay of our humanity, who makes holiness possible, who makes union real, who makes glory our destiny.

To know the Spirit is to rediscover the heart of Christianity—not as a system, but as a life; not as an idea, but as communion; not as effort, but as grace. May every page that follows draw the reader more deeply into the presence of the One who hides Himself not to avoid us, but to lead us gently into the light of the Son. The Spirit is shy only because His humility is infinite. His love is not.

And if we learn to listen, we will hear Him breathing.

I

The Spirit Who Creates (Purgation)

1

Breath Over the Waters: The Spirit in Creation

In the beginning, before light fractured the darkness or form emerged from the deep, there was movement. Scripture does not begin with a shout of creation but with a whisper, a breath passing over the waters. The world's first image is not of stars or mountains or living creatures, but of the Spirit hovering—*ruach Elohim*, the breath of God drifting like a living wind across a world still steeped in unshaped possibility. Before a single word is spoken, the Spirit is already there, hovering with a presence both tender and immense, as though creation itself waited for His touch before daring to exist.

The ancient world imagined primordial waters as symbols of disorder—vast, formless, untamed. The biblical authors take this image not to frighten the reader but to prepare them for revelation. Chaos is not a rival to God. Darkness is not an opposing kingdom. The waters tremble not because they are strong, but because the Spirit is near. What terrifies us—emptiness, darkness, confusion—is the very place where the Spirit begins His work. Genesis reveals this with astonishing simplicity: the Spirit does not flee the chaos; He hovers over it. He leans into the void the way an artist leans over a blank canvas, not intimidated by its emptiness but moved by the desire to bring beauty out of nothing.

St. Basil the Great, reading Genesis with the eyes of wonder, calls the Spirit the "Perfecting Cause" of creation—the One who brings the divine plan to completion, who moves the Father's will and the Son's Word toward their final harmony. For Basil, creation is a Trinitarian symphony: the Father wills, the Word speaks, and the Spirit makes radiant. The Spirit is the divine artist who breathes order into the cosmos, shaping what is formless, illuminating what is dark, bringing life where there is none. The Fathers loved this image: the Spirit as the One who adorns creation with beauty, who gives matter its purpose, and who sets every element in its proper place. In the Spirit's presence, the world is not merely assembled—it is transfigured.

This first movement of the Spirit—hovering over the waters—is not a small detail in Scripture. It is the unveiling of His identity. He is the One who comes before the beginning, the One who prepares everything for the Word, the One who transforms chaos into cosmos. The first thing the Bible tells us about the Spirit is that He brings order out of disorder. And this is not a distant cosmic fact. It is the pattern by which He continues to work in every human soul.

The creation narrative unfolds like the slow rising of a hymn. Light bursts forth, not in violence, but in sheer generosity. Distinctions appear—day from night, waters above from waters below, land from sea. Life erupts in abundance: seeds, fruit, creatures that fill the earth and sky. All of this happens because the Spirit's hovering presence makes creation receptive to the Word. Without the Spirit, the Word is unheard; without the Word, the Spirit is unmanifested. Together, they bring forth a world that reflects the glory of the Father.

Genesis 2 brings the mystery closer. Humanity enters the story not as an afterthought but as the pinnacle of creation, formed with deliberate intimacy. "The Lord God formed man from the dust of the ground and breathed into his nostrils the breath of life." This breath is not mere animation. It is communion. It is the Spirit Himself, the divine breath that gives humanity more than existence—it gives humanity the capacity for God. Basil and Gregory of Nyssa insist that the image of God is not a static imprint but a capacity: the capacity to receive the Spirit, to be shaped by Him, to reflect His life. We were made for breath, made for indwelling, made to become luminous with the life of the one who formed us.

This is why the Fathers say humanity was made "in the image" but called to grow "into the likeness." Image refers to the structure of the human person—reason, freedom, desire for the good. Likeness refers to the destiny offered: to be filled with the Spirit, to be shaped into the pattern of divine love. Humanity without the Spirit is like a lamp without flame, a temple without glory, clay without breath. We possess the form of life but not its radiance.

And this is where the tragedy of the Fall takes its full theological weight. Humanity did not lose its nature; it lost its indwelling. The image remained but the likeness cracked. The clay endured but the breath withdrew. The Fathers describe this not as annihilation but as collapse: Adam and Eve, turning from God, collapse inward, becoming opaque where they were meant to be transparent, heavy where they were meant to be lifted, confused where they were meant to be illumined. Athanasius says humanity fell "back into corruption," not because God abandoned His creation, but because the Spirit no longer found a welcoming home within the human heart. The world outside remained ordered, but the world within became disordered.

The creation narrative now becomes a mirror of the soul. The same Spirit who once hovered over the cosmic waters now hovers over the waters of the human heart, longing to bring order out of the confusion that sin introduces. The interior life, like the primordial deep, can feel formless, dark, and restless. Desires collide. Thoughts multiply without purpose. Fears rise like waves. All of this is the echo of that ancient rupture. Yet Scripture insists that the Spirit does not avoid such places. He hovers over them. He waits for the moment we allow Him to speak light into our darkness.

To read Genesis rightly is to see that creation is not only a past event; it is a present pattern. The Spirit who breathed upon the first waters breathes upon us still. The Spirit who brought order to the cosmos brings order to the conscience. The Spirit who filled the world with light fills the soul with illumination. The Spirit who shaped creation into a temple shapes humanity into a dwelling-place for God. Creation is not merely the world we see; it is the world God is continually forming within those who open themselves to His breath.

The Fathers often paused at this point in Genesis to contemplate what it means for the Spirit to "hover." The Hebrew verb *rachaph* suggests a movement like a bird brooding over its nest, warming the unformed world with expectant love. It is not the image of a distant observer but of intimate, nurturing presence. Basil imagines the Spirit as the divine warmth that causes creation to blossom, the gentle fire that awakens potential into reality. Gregory of Nazianzus speaks of the Spirit as the One who "moves upon the waters, preparing the harmony of the world." For the Fathers, the hovering is already the promise of indwelling. The Spirit does not merely shape creation from the outside; He prepares it to hold God within itself.

This imagery carries profound anthropological weight. The Spirit's relationship to the world is not mechanical but maternal, not efficient but personal. If the Spirit hovers over chaos with such care, then the human experience of interior chaos—confusion, darkness, emptiness—is not a sign of divine absence but an invitation for the Spirit to do again what He did in the beginning. Genesis is not simply cosmology; it is spiritual psychology. The creation story is the grammar of the soul. Every time a person turns to God in the midst of inner disorder, the Spirit hovers again, breathing over the waters, waiting to bring forth light.

This movement continues through the first days of creation. The divine words—"Let there be"—do not shatter the darkness but illuminate it. Creation unfolds gently, almost liturgically, as though each day were a stanza in a great hymn. The Spirit's presence tethers the emerging world to the divine will. Light appears in response to the Word, but it is the Spirit who makes light able to shine. Land emerges from the waters, not by its own force but because the Spirit brings distinction where there was none. Life appears in profusion—seeds, fruit, creeping things, great sea creatures—because the Spirit, the Giver of Life, breathes vitality into every fibre of creation. Even the rhythms of day and night, seasons and years, show the Spirit's delight in order and harmony. Creation is intelligible because the Spirit makes it so.

The Fathers saw in this order not a cold structure but beauty—beauty as the signature of the Spirit. Augustine argues that the splendour of creation reflects the Spirit's gift of unity, that the harmony of all things hints at the Spirit's hidden governance. To contemplate the natural world is to sense the Spirit's artistry: the elegance of mathematical laws, the intricacy of living organisms, the vastness of the heavens—all of this is the Spirit's choreography. If the Son is the Word containing all the divine ideas, the Spirit is the breath that sings them into being. Creation is revelation: it reveals the Spirit's love for form, clarity, and radiant order.

This pattern reaches its peak in the creation of humanity. The biblical author slows the narrative dramatically when Adam enters the scene, as if the entire cosmos were holding its breath for this moment. Humanity is not spoken into existence like the rest of creation. Humanity is shaped. Formed. Fashioned from the dust by the hands of God. And then, in an act that eclipses all others, God breathes into this clay the breath of life. The Fathers read this breath as the Spirit Himself—the divine life that lifts humanity beyond the level of mere creature and into communion with God.

This is the foundation of Christian anthropology: we are dust touched by breath. Clay raised by grace. Matter infused with divine purpose. Basil writes that humanity was created "capable of receiving the Spirit," and Gregory of Nyssa adds that our likeness to God is "rooted in participation." This participation is not automatic; it is a gift meant to grow. Humanity begins in the image but is destined for likeness—destined for the fullness of the Spirit's indwelling, destined to reflect divine beauty not merely by nature but by communion.

To say humanity is the "image of God" is not to say humanity is a static replica. It is to say humanity is made with spiritual faculties—reason, freedom, desire—that open toward God, faculties that only find harmony when animated by the Spirit. Without the Spirit, these faculties turn inward and collapse on themselves, just as creation would collapse into chaos without His hovering presence. This is why the Fathers maintain that the Fall did not erase the image; it obscured it. The structure remained, but the radiance dimmed. The capacity endured, but the communion broke. Gregory of Nyssa compares fallen humanity to a tarnished mirror: the form is intact, but the light is no longer reflected clearly.

The consequence is spiritual disintegration. The heart becomes divided, the mind scattered, the desires disordered. Humanity experiences in its interior world what the primordial waters symbolize: chaos, restlessness, lack of form. This is not merely moral disorder; it is metaphysical impoverishment. We are creatures made for breath living as though breath were absent. The ache we carry—the sense that something essential is missing—is the memory of Eden, the memory of a time when the Spirit's indwelling animated every desire and illuminated every thought.

Yet even in this wounded state, the Spirit does not withdraw from creation entirely. The world remains sustained by His presence, and humanity remains haunted by His nearness. The Fathers insist that every longing for truth, every desire for the good, every movement of the heart toward beauty is already a whisper of the Spirit. Even fallen humanity is not abandoned; it is beckoned. The Spirit who hovered over the waters hovers over the fallen world still, drawing it slowly toward renewal. The first creation is the promise of a new creation yet to come. The Spirit who shaped the world will one day reshape the human heart.

It is precisely here that the theological meaning of "hovering" becomes most personal. The Spirit's first action in Scripture is the same action He performs in every soul that turns toward God. He does not begin by accusing or overwhelming; He begins by hovering—by surrounding the heart with the possibility of grace, by softening what is hardened, by awakening what is dormant. The Spirit's purifying work does not begin with judgment but with presence. The Spirit begins where we least expect Him: in the waters of our own confusion and weakness. Where we see darkness, He sees the possibility of light.

This pattern—order emerging from disorder through the Spirit's gentle movement—becomes the template for spiritual life. The soul, like creation, contains depths that are not yet shaped, places where shadow lingers, places where desire has not yet found its true form. We often experience ourselves as fragmented: our thoughts scattered, our choices inconsistent, our longings divided. The human heart can feel as restless as the primordial waters, pulled by currents we scarcely understand. Yet this restlessness is not the sign of divine absence. It is the surface trembling beneath the Spirit's hovering presence. What creation reveals outwardly, the spiritual life reveals inwardly: the Spirit is the One who moves before the dawn.

The Fathers insist that the Spirit's first work in the soul, as in creation, is the gift of clarity. Before there is holiness, there is light. Before there is virtue, there is distinction. The Spirit separates truth from illusion, good desire from disordered desire, authentic love from its counterfeits. Basil describes this as the Spirit "bringing the hidden things to light," not to shame the sinner but to free the heart from confusion. Just as the Spirit separated the waters to reveal land, the Spirit separates the tangled strands of the human heart so that true freedom can emerge. Without the Spirit, the soul remains opaque to itself; with the Spirit, it becomes transparent, capable of seeing and being seen.

This transparency is not merely psychological but theological. To become transparent is to reflect the light of God more clearly, to become once again what we were made to be: living icons. Humanity is not simply created by God but created to reveal God. The image of God is not decorative; it is participatory. Basil insists that the human person is "a creature that has received the order to become divine," not in essence, but in communion. The Spirit is the One who makes this possible, who draws the human person beyond natural limits and into the life of God. The movement from chaos to order in creation becomes the movement from sin to holiness in the soul.

The Fathers loved to read creation with this mystical lens. Gregory of Nyssa, in his contemplations on the making of man, suggests that the soul's journey back to God is nothing less than a re-creation—a second Genesis. The Spirit who hovered at the beginning now hovers over baptismal waters, over the Eucharistic gifts, over the heart in prayer. Every sacrament echoes Genesis: the Spirit descends, breathes, moves, and brings life. When the Church invokes the Spirit in the epiclesis—"Send down your Holy Spirit upon us and upon these gifts"—she is repeating the first words spoken over the world. The altar becomes a new Eden, the believer a new Adam, the bread and wine a new creation.

This is why the early Church spoke of the Spirit as the "Giver of Life." Not only because He animates physical existence, but because He awakens the capacity for divine life within humanity. Life, in the biblical sense, is not mere survival. Life is communion with God. Death, in Scripture, is not merely the cessation of biological function; it is separation from the Breath that makes us alive. When Adam turns from God, he does not die immediately in the flesh, but he dies in the Spirit. The Breath retreats; the clay remains. The tragedy of sin is not that humanity becomes less human, but that humanity becomes less luminous. The heart, created to hold light, becomes shadowed. The mind, created to behold truth, becomes clouded. The will, created to choose the good, becomes conflicted.

Yet Scripture never speaks of this condition without also hinting at its remedy. The Breath that withdrew will one day return. The Spirit who hovered at the beginning will hover again over the waters of Jordan, over the womb of Mary, over the apostles at Pentecost, over every soul who consents to His presence. Creation is not simply a past event but a promise. The Spirit does not abandon what He has formed. He completes it.

This continuity between the first creation and the new creation becomes even clearer when we turn to the figure of Christ. The New Testament describes Jesus not only as the incarnate Word but as the One upon whom the Spirit rests in fullness. If Adam is clay lifted by the Breath, Christ is humanity fully alive in that Breath. The Spirit who hovered over the waters hovers over the waters of Mary's womb; the Spirit who gave life to Adam gives life to the second Adam in a way that reveals His divine origin. The Gospel of Luke describes Jesus' entire mission as Spirit-saturated: conceived by the Spirit, anointed by the Spirit, led by the Spirit, teaching in the Spirit, sacrificing Himself through the Spirit, and raised from the dead by the Spirit. Christ is the revelation of what humanity looks like when fully shaped by the Breath of God.

This Christological horizon gives creation its deepest meaning. The purpose of the first creation is not merely to display God's power or beauty. It is to prepare the world for Christ and, through Christ, for the giving of the Spirit. The cosmos exists so that God may dwell within His creatures. The world begins with the Spirit hovering over waters because humanity will one day be reborn from water and Spirit. The clay receives breath because the clay will one day become the Body of Christ. The order and harmony of creation are not ends in themselves; they are icons of the divine communion into which humanity is called.

If this is true, then the Spirit's first mission—to bring order out of chaos—is also His ongoing mission in the life of every believer. The spiritual life is not primarily about self-improvement but about re-creation. The Spirit does not renovate the soul; He resurrects it. He does not rearrange the furniture of the heart; He begins a new creation within it. And just as the first creation unfolded gradually, with days and rhythms and stages, so does this spiritual creation. The Spirit does not overwhelm. He illumines. He purifies. He orders. He beautifies. He prepares the heart to bear the likeness of Christ.

This is why the mystics insist that purification is not a punishment but a promise. To be purified is to have one's chaos touched by the Spirit's hovering presence, to have the formless parts of the heart shaped by divine hands. The Spirit's purifying fire is the continuation of the light that first shone in Genesis. The wounds and confusions we bring to God are not obstacles to the Spirit but invitations for Him to do again what He did at the beginning: to breathe, to shape, to awaken, to create.

The same Spirit who moved over the primordial deep now moves with equal tenderness over the hidden depths of the human heart.

BREATH OVER THE WATERS: THE SPIRIT IN CREATION

What He accomplished in the cosmos He desires to accomplish in us: to transform darkness into light, restlessness into peace, chaos into communion. Yet unlike creation, the human soul possesses freedom—the sacred space where the Spirit waits to be welcomed. The Spirit does not force His way into the heart. He hovers. He invites. He stirs desire. He awakens longing. The entire drama of salvation begins not with compulsion but with breath, and in this breath the soul discovers that God's gentleness is more powerful than any force the world can wield.

This hovering presence explains why the first stage of the spiritual life is called *purification*. Purification is not moral scrubbing or divine reprimand. It is the Spirit's ordering love, renewing in the soul the same clarity and beauty He once brought to the cosmos. The early Church understood this deeply. Catechumens preparing for baptism were not merely instructed intellectually; they were purified. Their desires were re-ordered, their attachments loosened, their interior waters calmed. The Spirit prepared them the way He prepared creation: by hovering over the deep until light could be spoken into existence.

This process unfolds gently but decisively. The Spirit begins by revealing truth—not abstract truth, but personal truth. He shows us who we are, where we are wounded, where our desires have become tangled, where sin has obscured the image of God. This revelation is not meant to shame but to heal. Without the Spirit, we hide from ourselves; with the Spirit, we see ourselves truthfully and tenderly. The Spirit's light is warm, not harsh. It illuminates without destroying. It reveals without condemning. To be purified is to stand before this divine light and allow it to bring order to the chaotic interior landscape we often fear.

The Fathers saw this ordering work as a restoration of the image. The human heart, meant to reflect the beauty of God, becomes like a surface clouded by dust. Purification wipes the surface clean so that light may be reflected once more. Gregory of Nyssa describes this as "the polishing of the soul," a slow and deliberate work by which the Spirit makes us capable of receiving divine radiance. Basil speaks of the Spirit "shaping the soul as an artist shapes a work of beauty," not by violence but by touch, by presence, by illumination. The Spirit does not erase our nature; He perfects it. He does not replace our human faculties; He restores them.

This restoration touches every part of the human person. The intellect, once clouded by confusion, begins to perceive truth with greater clarity. The will, once divided, begins to choose the good with steadiness. The emotions, once unruly, begin to harmonise around love. The passions, once tools of sin, become instruments of virtue. The entire interior world undergoes a kind of Genesis. Old patterns break, new life emerges, and the soul becomes a place where God can dwell. This does not happen in a moment. It unfolds with the same patience and order as creation itself. Day follows day. Light grows gradually. Darkness recedes in stages. The Spirit works at a pace that respects the mystery of human freedom.

Yet this new creation within us is not merely a restoration of what Adam lost. It is preparation for what Christ will give. The Spirit who hovers, orders, and purifies is also the Spirit who anoints, illumines, indwells, and glorifies. Purification is the first movement of a larger symphony—a symphony that leads from creation to Christ, from Christ to the Church, from the Church to the final glory of the new heaven and new earth. The beginning of Genesis is already oriented toward the end of Revelation, where the Spirit cries out with the Bride, "Come." The Breath of God that moved at the beginning is the same Breath that will renew all things at the end.

This cosmic horizon reminds us that the spiritual life is not a private project but participation in the Spirit's universal work. The Spirit who creates the world also creates the Church; the Spirit who orders the cosmos orders the communion of believers; the Spirit who brings life to dust brings divine life to humanity in Christ. When we speak of purification, illumination, and union, we speak of the same Spirit who has been at work since before light existed. To become holy is to allow that Spirit to finish in us what He began in creation.

The beauty of Genesis lies not only in what it reveals about the world but in what it reveals about God. The first image Scripture gives us is of a God who draws near to what is formless, who hovers over what is dark, who prepares what is empty for fullness. The Spirit's presence at the beginning is the definitive sign that God does not fear disorder; He transforms it. He does not recoil from what is chaotic; He speaks into it. He does not abandon what is unformed; He brings it into being. This is why the spiritual life begins not with self-mastery but with surrender. The soul does not have to make itself worthy of the Spirit; the soul has only to welcome Him.

To pray, "Come, Holy Spirit," is to repeat the first moment of creation. It is to invite the Breath that hovered over the primordial deep to hover over the depths of our own hearts. It is to trust that the Spirit who brought light from darkness can do so again within us. It is to believe that the God who breathes life into clay can breathe life into every place within us that feels lifeless. This is not poetry; it is the fundamental truth of our existence. We are creatures who live because God breathes. We are creatures who become whole because God breathes again.

The dawn of creation is the dawn of the soul. The Spirit who first moved over the waters is the Spirit who now moves within us, preparing us for the fullness of life found in Christ. The order, beauty, and radiance He once brought to the cosmos He now desires to bring to our humanity. The world began in breath, and the spiritual life begins in the same way—with the gentle, persistent movement of the

Spirit drawing us into a new creation.

2

Spirit and Image: The Human Person as Spirit-Bearer

Humanity enters the biblical story not as a fleeting detail but as the summit of creation, the place where the visible and invisible worlds meet. The narrative slows, the tone deepens, and the imagery becomes intimate. After the vast symphony of cosmic order—light splitting darkness, waters gathering into seas, stars scattered like jewels across the heavens—Scripture draws near to the earth, to the dust, to the clay that will bear the breath of God. Nothing in creation receives the attention that humanity receives. The universe is spoken into existence, but humanity is shaped. The cosmos is commanded into being, but humanity is embraced into being. Creation is the revelation of God's power; humanity is the revelation of God's desire.

The Spirit, who hovered over the waters at the dawn of time, now draws near to the dust. "The Lord God formed man from the dust of the ground and breathed into his nostrils the breath of life." These words carry a tenderness unlike anything in the surrounding verses. God does not simply will humanity into existence; He leans down, He draws close, He breathes. What is imparted in this breath is not merely animation but communion. The Fathers saw in this moment not only the origin of biological life but the origin of spiritual vocation. Humanity is fashioned as the one creature capable of receiving the Spirit. Basil speaks of the human person as the "creature commanded to become divine," not because humanity possesses divine essence, but because humanity is made capable of divine participation. The breath is the key. Breath signifies not only life but relationship, not only existence but invitation.

This is why Scripture says humanity is made "in the image and likeness of God." Across the centuries, theologians have pondered these two terms—image and likeness—with profound reverence. In the Hebrew text, the distinction is not sharp, yet the Fathers discerned a theological richness in holding them together. The image refers to the structure of the human person: reason, freedom, relational capacity, desire for the good. The likeness refers to the destiny of the human person: holiness, communion, the radiant participation in divine life that the Spirit alone can bestow. Image is gift; likeness is growth. Image is the seed; likeness is the fruit. Image is the capacity; likeness is the fulfillment. To be human is not only to be created by God; it is to be created for God.

Gregory of Nyssa, contemplating these mysteries with the stillness of a monk peering into the depths of God, teaches that the human person is an icon in motion—an image capable of ever-deepening resemblance to its Prototype. Humanity is not static but expansive. Made in the image, humanity moves toward likeness; made in beauty, humanity moves toward glory. This is the mystery of theosis. The human person becomes truly human only when filled with the Spirit, because humanity was designed as a vessel for divine life. Without the Spirit, humanity remains structurally sound but dynamically incomplete. Clay without breath. Path without destination. Seed without flowering.

Athanasius captures this truth with breathtaking simplicity: "The

Word became man that we might receive the Spirit." In one sentence, he reveals the entire arc of salvation history. The Incarnation is not merely the forgiveness of sins or the revelation of divine truth; it is the restoration of the human person to its original vocation. Christ takes on humanity so humanity may regain the Spirit. The Son becomes what we are so that we may share what is His. The Spirit we lost in the Fall returns to us through the humanity of Christ, breathed again into the world at Pentecost, poured into the heart of every believer, given as the very life of the new creation.

This is the tragedy of the Fall: humanity did not lose its nature, but it lost its likeness. The image remained, but the radiance dimmed. The structure endured, but the communion fractured. The human person became like a mirror cracked through the centre. Light still touches it, but the reflection is distorted. Augustine describes the fallen heart as "curved inward," turned toward itself in a spiral of confusion and self-protection. Desire becomes fragmented, the mind becomes clouded, the will becomes weakened. Humanity retains its capacity for God but loses its ordering toward God. The ache that every human being feels—the sense of incompleteness, the longing for love, the hunger for meaning—is the natural cry of a creature who remembers breath even when it no longer feels it.

Yet even this wounded state speaks of hope. A mirror that remembers light can desire the return of that light. The longing itself is evidence of the Spirit's nearness. Fallen humanity is not an empty vessel but a thirsting one. The desire for truth, beauty, goodness—for a love that does not collapse under the weight of our hope—reveals humanity's spiritual identity. We are not simply bodies that think; we are images that yearn. Every genuine longing is the echo of the Spirit's breath within us, faint but insistent.

The human person, then, is not defined by sin but by capacity— capacity for the Spirit, capacity for communion, capacity for the life of God. This capacity is the foundation of dignity. Psalm 8 marvels at this mystery: "You have made him little less than God, and crowned him with glory and honour." Humanity is simultaneously humble in origin—dust—and exalted in calling—breath. The greatness of humanity is not self-generated; it is bestowed. It is not autonomy but participation. The glory of the human person is not independence from God but nearness to God.

This is why the spiritual life begins not with effort but with recognition. To see oneself truthfully is to realise that we are creatures made for the Spirit. We are not self-made beings navigating a meaningless world. We are images awaiting restoration, icons awaiting illumination, mirrors awaiting light. The longing for God that rises within us in moments of beauty or sorrow or silence is not illusion; it is identity. We long because we are made for communion. We desire because we are made for likeness. We ache because the Spirit who once filled us now draws us back to Himself.

The Fathers never speak of this longing as a psychological quirk or an evolutionary by-product. They speak of it as memory—memory of the Spirit's original indwelling, memory of a harmony once known, memory of a likeness once shared. Humanity carries within itself a trace of Eden, a quiet remembrance of what it was meant to be. Augustine's famous confession, "Our hearts are restless until they rest in You," is not the romantic sigh of a mystic but the anthropological diagnosis of a bishop who understood human nature with luminous clarity. Restlessness is not a flaw; it is a sign. It reveals the vacuum left when the Spirit's breath is absent. It hints at the destiny for which the heart was shaped.

The image of God remains the foundation of this destiny, but the image alone is not enough. Image is structure; likeness is life. Image gives capacity; likeness gives communion. Image provides the vessel; likeness pours in the fire. The tragedy of sin is not only that it wounds the image but that it severs the ascent toward likeness. Humanity becomes trapped within its own capacities—able to reason but unable to see clearly, able to choose but unable to choose well, able to desire but unable to desire rightly. It is not that the faculties disappear; it is that they turn inward, bend back upon themselves, and lose the orientation that alone can give them harmony.

This is why early Christian anthropology describes fallen humanity as disintegrated. The faculties no longer work in unity. The mind pursues truth but often prefers illusion. The will seeks the good but often collapses under pressure. The emotions, instead of flowing toward love, zigzag between excess and deficiency. Desire, instead of lifting the soul toward God, disperses itself across countless lesser loves. Gregory of Nyssa writes that the soul, once luminous like a polished surface, becomes "covered with the dust of passions," unable to reflect divine beauty. Yet the dust does not destroy the surface; it conceals it. Beneath the dust, the image remains intact, waiting for the Spirit to restore its shine.

Here lies the heart of purification. Purification is not moral scrubbing, nor is it a grim exercise in self-control. It is the Spirit's gentle restoration of the image so that likeness can begin again. Purification is the clearing of the dust so the mirror can reflect light. It is the healing of the intellect so it can see truth, the strengthening of the will so it can choose good, the ordering of desire so it can move toward God with freedom. The Spirit does not crush the faculties; He resurrects them. He does not replace human nature; He heals it. Theosis does not bypass humanity; it fulfills humanity.

The Spirit's work begins in the intellect. Scripture describes the fallen mind as "darkened," "futile," or "clouded," not because it lacks intelligence but because it lacks illumination. Basil argues that only the Spirit can make the mind truly capable of perceiving divine realities. Without the Spirit, the mind becomes clever but confused, sharp but shallow, analytical but blind. With the Spirit, the mind becomes translucent, able to behold truth with serenity. This illumination is not the acquisition of new facts but the awakening of a new way of seeing—seeing reality as God sees it, perceiving the world through the light of communion rather than through the shadows of self.

Next the Spirit heals the will. The will is the faculty that chooses, directs, commits. It is the steering wheel of the soul. Yet after the Fall, the will becomes fractured—easily pulled toward the good, easily pulled away from it. Maximus the Confessor describes this as the "gnomic will," a will marked by indecision, conflict, and interior division. The Spirit restores unity to the will by aligning it with divine desire. Strength and constancy return. The soul begins to choose the good with increasing freedom because the good now appears beautiful, luminous, desirable. The Spirit does not overpower the will; He frees it from confusion.

Finally, the Spirit reorders desire. Desire is the engine of the soul, the flame that propels the human person toward meaning. Yet when disordered, desire loses its direction—burning for things that cannot satisfy and growing cold toward the One who alone gives life. Disordered desire is not a sign of corruption but of misdirection. It is the natural power of the soul seeking eternity in temporal things. The Spirit does not extinguish desire; He purifies it, clarifies it, focuses it. The Spirit teaches the heart to long for what it was made to hold. The Fathers call this "eros transfigured"—love set ablaze not by earthly longing but by divine fire.

Through this restoration of intellect, will, and desire, the Spirit draws the image back toward likeness. The human person begins to resemble God again—not merely in capacity but in communion. The soul becomes orderly, harmonious, beautiful. Virtue arises not as grim duty but as the natural flowering of a life touched by breath.

Love becomes possible, then natural, then joyful. The Spirit does not impose holiness from outside; He awakens it from within. Holiness is humanity burning with the fire of likeness.

All of this is made possible by Christ, the true Image. Christ does not merely show us what humanity should be; He restores humanity from within. The New Testament calls Him "the image of the invisible God," not because He resembles the Father superficially, but because He reveals divine life perfectly in human form. In Christ, humanity reaches its fullness because humanity becomes fully Spirit-filled. The Spirit rests upon Him without measure, flows through His teaching, strengthens His obedience, and raises Him from the dead. To look at Christ is to see humanity as God intended it: a living temple where the Spirit dwells in glory.

This is why salvation cannot be reduced to forgiveness or moral improvement. Salvation is the restoration of the image and the recovery of likeness. It is the Spirit conforming us to Christ, re-creating the human person from within. Paul captures this movement with a phrase of astonishing beauty: "We all, beholding the glory of the Lord, are being transformed into the same image from glory to glory, as by the Spirit of the Lord." Glory to glory—this is likeness. This is theosis. This is humanity fulfilled.

The Fathers speak of Christ as the new Adam because they sensed a profound continuity between the first breath in Eden and the breath Christ gives in the upper room. Adam receives life from the Spirit; Christ, risen from the grave, breathes the Spirit back into humanity. What was lost through disobedience is restored through obedience. Where the first Adam allowed the likeness to fade, the second Adam radiates it in fullness. Salvation, therefore, is not accomplished at a distance. God steps into the very fabric of human existence so that the Spirit may dwell once again in the creatures made for divine life. Athanasius never tires of insisting that the Incarnation is oriented toward Pentecost. The Son descends so humanity might rise. The Word takes flesh so the Spirit may take up residence in the heart.

Union with Christ is the beginning of this restoration. The Spirit does not repair the human image from beyond; He works from within Christ's humanity, the one place where the image shines without distortion. When the Son assumes human nature, He assumes the wounded faculties of the race—an intellect vulnerable to ignorance, a will susceptible to hesitation, a heart prone to disordered longing. Yet in Him these faculties remain unbroken, luminous, entirely transparent to the Father. The healing of human nature occurs because Christ carries our nature into perfect communion. What sin fractured, Christ binds together. What weakness exposed, Christ strengthens. What desire misdirected, Christ purifies. The Spirit's work in us begins with Christ's work in Himself.

Paul's testimony makes this union clear: "It is no longer I who live, but Christ who lives in me." Such a statement is not mystical exaggeration but the very logic of redemption. Through the Spirit, the believer enters into Christ's mind, Christ's dispositions, Christ's vision of the Father. Christian virtue cannot merely be the copying of an external example; it must be the emergence of an internal life. The Spirit does not ask us to imitate Christ the way a student imitates a teacher. The Spirit enables us to share in Christ the way a branch shares in the life of the vine. The virtues that blossom are not human achievements polished by effort; they are fruits of divine life flowing through a healed humanity.

Every icon bears this truth. An icon is painted by contemplating the original face. Humanity is restored in the same way: by contemplating the true Image. The Fathers call this contemplative gaze *theoria*, a seeing that opens the soul. To behold Christ is to open oneself to the Spirit's artistry. The one who looks upon the Son with love finds that the Spirit slowly engraves the likeness of the Son within. Paul captures this mystery with rare precision: "We behold… and are being transformed." This pattern—beholding leading to becoming—lies at the heart of the Christian life. The Spirit fills the vision with light, and that light reshapes the one who sees. Christ stands not only as our goal but as the very pattern of our renewal.

Athanasius offers a memorable image for this work of restoration. Fallen humanity resembles a portrait marred by stains and scratches. The outlines remain, but the clarity is gone. The artist does not discard the damaged icon; he brings the original subject back into view and repaints the image according to the living model. Christ is that model. Scripture, liturgy, prayer, and contemplation serve as the workshop where the Spirit gradually repaints the soul. Nothing in this process is mechanical. Every stroke is relational, every refinement shaped by intimacy with the One whose face bears the fullness of divine light.

Purification unfolds in this relationship. The tangled loves within the heart begin to loosen. Confusions in the mind clear away like mist lifted by dawn. The will, once fragile, finds a renewed firmness. Fragmentation gives way to harmony. None of this resembles perfectionism. Purity does not mean flawlessness; it means orientation. A purified soul is one that faces God. Even if the steps are small and the progress slow, the direction is true. Light draws the heart forward, and the Spirit sustains the movement.

The ancient tradition names this reorientation *metanoia*—a turning of the whole self toward God. Repentance, in its deepest sense, is not gloom or self-accusation; it is the image leaning toward its likeness. The Spirit bends the heart back to its natural posture. Without Him, repentance sinks into regret or despair. In His presence, repentance becomes the doorway of new life. The first breath of the Spirit in the soul is often felt as a turning—a gentle but decisive shift toward the face of Christ.

As this new orientation grows, the faculties of the soul awaken. The intellect begins to perceive truth not merely as correct information but as communion with reality. The will discovers a strength it did not know it possessed, because love now empowers choice. Desire stirs with a new hunger—not for passing satisfactions, but for the One who breathed life into the dust. The mystics speak in the language of fire because fire conveys what words fail to capture. Fire purifies by consuming only what is unworthy; fire illumines by revealing what was hidden; fire warms by drawing the heart near. The Spirit is the flame that does all three. Nothing in the soul is destroyed except what is not love.

No two souls experience this transformation identically. Each human life bears a distinct imprint of the divine image, and each is restored in its own way. The Spirit respects the contours of every heart. He heals without flattening, sanctifies without erasing personality, glorifies without making replicas. The saints reveal this diversity: one reflects Christ's compassion, another His courage; one His silence, another His proclamation; one His contemplation, another His zeal. Divine beauty refracts through each life in a particular hue. Holiness does not produce uniformity; it reveals individuality transfigured.

Within this diversity lies vocation. Every person carries a unique way of manifesting the likeness of Christ. The Spirit animates that vocation, shapes it, unfolds it across the years. What begins as a fragile impulse becomes, under His touch, a path toward glory. A person discovers not only who they are but who they are meant to become. The Spirit crafts saints, not duplicates—each a living icon displaying a facet of Christ's inexhaustible beauty.

To speak of humanity as created for the Spirit, then, is not poetic exaggeration. It is the deepest truth of the human person. We are fashioned to bear the fire of God. Without the Spirit, we remain capable but unfulfilled—like an altar with no flame or a lamp with no oil. With the Spirit, the image finds its clarity and the likeness begins its ascent. Humanity becomes what it was always intended to be: alive with divine life, ordered toward love, radiant with the glory of the One who breathed into clay and made it capable of God.

Humanity's capacity for the Spirit does not reveal itself only in virtue or contemplation; it reveals itself even more profoundly in our longing. Every heart carries an ache that refuses to be silenced—a quiet insistence that life must hold more than survival, more than pleasure, more than self-expression. That ache is not a defect. It is the signature of the Spirit. We desire because we were made for communion. We search because we were created for vision. We hunger because the likeness has been obscured and we yearn for its return. No animal wrestles with meaning. No bird writes psalms. No river cries out for redemption. Only humanity searches the horizon for Someone who can answer its restlessness. That search is proof of design.

The Fathers often spoke of this longing as evidence that the soul is "stretched toward God." Even fallen, the human person retains a direction, a gravitational pull, a sacred orientation. Sin may distort desire, but it cannot erase the deeper yearning that shapes the soul from within. When Augustine says, "You made us for Yourself," he is naming the deepest truth of anthropology: the human heart is structured for the Spirit. Our restlessness is the echo of an ancient life, the memory of breath, the whisper of a likeness we have not forgotten.

Yet longing alone is not enough. Desire must be fulfilled, and only the Spirit can fill it. The Spirit does not descend into the human heart as a visitor but as the One for whom the heart was carved. When He enters, He does not come as a stranger but as a returning inhabitant, the long-awaited flame in the lamp, the long-absent breath in the lungs. A person touched by the Spirit often feels less like they have acquired something new and more like they have recovered something old—something they always should have had. The Spirit awakens what lies dormant, heals what lies wounded, restores what lies broken.

The early monastics understood this intuitively. When they retreated into the desert, they were not fleeing the world; they were seeking the One who could reorder the world within them. The spiritual struggle was not an escape from humanity but a return to true humanity. The desert exposed everything that was not the Spirit—every illusion, every attachment, every false love—so that the Spirit could reclaim the soul in its simplicity. Purification, illumination, union: the desert became the workshop where the image was restored and the likeness began to shine again.

Modern people sometimes imagine holiness as an optional ornament, something reserved for the spiritually gifted. The Fathers would find such an idea incomprehensible. Holiness is simply the human person functioning as designed. A holy person is not an exception; a holy person is a revelation. Holiness shows what humanity looks like when the Spirit indwells without resistance. The saint is not less human but more human. The saint reveals the faculties healed, the desires ordered, the intellect illumined, the heart ignited. The saint is the living proof that the Spirit still breathes in the world.

Even suffering takes on a new meaning in a Spirit-bearing life. The wounds of the soul—betrayals, disappointments, losses—do not vanish, but they are transfigured. The Spirit does not erase pain; He draws it into a larger horizon. Pain becomes a place of communion, a place where the likeness can grow. The Cross reveals this with piercing clarity: when Christ suffers in the Spirit, He transforms suffering into love. The same transformation begins to unfold in the one who shares His life. A purified image reflects divine compassion; a soul in likeness reflects divine endurance. Even the darkest experiences become places where the Spirit speaks, heals, and strengthens.

Ultimately, the Spirit's work is nothing less than the restoration of glory. Glory is not a poetic flourish; it is the destiny of the human person. Glory means the human being fully alive with divine life, radiant with a beauty that does not fade. The return of glory begins here and now, though its fullness belongs to the age to come. Paul describes the Christian life as a movement "from glory to glory," a continual ascent into deeper participation. Every act of virtue, every moment of prayer, every step of repentance is a brushstroke in the Spirit's masterpiece.

In this light, the anthropology of the image becomes the anthropology of hope. No human being is beyond restoration. No soul is too darkened to reflect light again. No desire is too tangled to be straightened by the Spirit's breath. The Spirit's patience is infinite because His love is infinite. The God who shaped the first human from dust does not abandon the work of His hands. He bends close once again. He breathes once again. He forms once again.

All of this leads to the final truth that binds the chapter together: humanity is incomplete without the Spirit. Our nature is not defective, but it is unfinished. We are created with the architecture of communion but require the Spirit for its completion. The image sets the stage; the likeness fulfills the drama. The Spirit descends not to make us something other than human but to make us truly human. What we call sanctity, Scripture calls life. What we call transformation, the Fathers call restoration. Christ opens the way; the Spirit brings us into it.

The human person, therefore, stands at a threshold—shaped from the earth yet destined for glory, wounded yet capable of healing, restless yet oriented toward rest. Every longing, every search for meaning, every cry in the night is the heart reaching for the One who once breathed into dust and made it shine. The Spirit who hovered over the waters now hovers over the soul, waiting to bring order out of chaos, beauty out of confusion, likeness out of loss. When the heart yields, the Spirit descends. When the Spirit descends, humanity awakens.

And when humanity awakens, the image begins to shine again.

3

Fire in Israel: The Spirit in the Old Testament

Israel enters the story of salvation with the sound of groaning. Before there is covenant, before there is law, before there is promised land, there is a people crushed beneath the weight of a world that has forgotten God. The opening chapters of Exodus present not heroes but slaves, not triumph but anguish. Into this darkness the Spirit begins to move once more—not hovering over primordial waters as in Genesis, but stirring within history, preparing a people to recognise the God who calls them His own. The drama of Israel is the first great revelation of the Spirit acting not simply upon creation, but within a people.

The Spirit's earliest manifestation in Israel's story is not gentle. It is flame. When Moses turns aside to behold the bush that burns without being consumed, he encounters a fire unlike earthly fire. This flame does not destroy; it reveals. It speaks. It summons. The Fathers saw in this moment the beginning of Israel's schooling in the Spirit. The burning bush, they said, is the sign of divine life—intense yet life-giving, purifying yet preserving. The One who spoke to Moses in fire would lead Israel by fire. The One whose presence blazed in the bush would soon blaze in the desert night.

When Israel crosses the threshold of deliverance, leaving Egypt behind, the Spirit appears as a pillar of cloud by day and a pillar of fire by night. These are not merely symbols of guidance; they are theophanies. The same Breath that hovered over the waters now descends to shepherd a people. The cloud shields, obscures, and protects; the fire illuminates, warms, and reveals. The Spirit becomes light for those who walk in darkness and shelter for those who wander through wastelands. Israel learns to trust the One who moves ahead of them—even when His presence is veiled, unpredictable, or overwhelming.

The climax of this desert revelation arrives at Sinai. There the mountain trembles with smoke and flame, not as a display of divine anger but as a manifestation of divine nearness. The God of Abraham, Isaac, and Jacob is no distant deity; He is the living God whose presence has weight, whose glory has substance. The Hebrew word for glory, *kavod*, signifies heaviness, density, reality. When the Spirit descends, Israel is confronted not with abstraction but with presence—overpowering, luminous, holy. It is here that Israel begins to learn that God's holiness is not an idea but an encounter. The Spirit is the God who draws near.

When the tabernacle is finally constructed, Scripture tells us that the cloud covered the tent and "the glory of the Lord filled the tabernacle." Moses himself cannot enter. The Spirit takes possession of the sanctuary, not to exclude Israel from His presence, but to dwell at the centre of their life. For the first time in the history of the world, the presence that hovered over the waters and burned in the bush now rests in a dwelling made by human hands. The tabernacle becomes the beating heart of Israel—the place where fire and cloud remain, the place where God lives among His people. Basil describes this moment as the Spirit "making His home" in the midst of the nation, preparing

Israel to understand that God desires communion, not distance.

But Israel's story is not only the story of a people led by pillar and cloud; it is the story of individuals filled with the Spirit for particular missions. In the age of the Judges, the Spirit does not yet rest permanently upon Israel, but He descends with sudden force upon chosen deliverers. "The Spirit of the Lord rushed upon Othniel," Scripture says. The same line appears again and again: upon Gideon, upon Jephthah, upon Samson. Each was raised from obscurity or weakness to accomplish deliverance. The Spirit uses unlikely vessels—timid men, flawed men, men without pedigree—to show that salvation is not born of human strength but of divine initiative. Israel learns to recognise the Spirit as the One who empowers, fortifies, and liberates.

This pattern intensifies with the rise of the monarchy. Saul, anointed by Samuel, receives the Spirit and becomes "another man." The Spirit transforms the reluctant into the capable. Yet when Saul turns from obedience, the Spirit departs, revealing that divine anointing is not magic but relationship. In David the revelation becomes clearer still. "The Spirit of the Lord rushed upon David from that day forward." Unlike Saul, David learns to live in the Spirit's presence. His courage, his poetry, his mercy, his repentance—all are fruits of a life overshadowed by divine breath. David's psalms are not merely songs of human genius; they are words breathed by the same Spirit who rested upon him. When he cries, "Take not Your Holy Spirit from me," he reveals what Israel has slowly come to understand: the Spirit is not a force but a companion, not an influence but a presence.

Through these encounters, Israel discovers that the Spirit is not confined to sanctuary or symbol. The Spirit speaks. The Spirit calls. The Spirit anoints. The Spirit convicts. And gradually, through the centuries, Israel begins to recognise that the Spirit who descended as fire and cloud is the same Spirit who inspires prophets to speak words that burn with divine truth.

Prophecy is the moment when the Spirit's fire becomes voice. The prophets do not speak from imagination or reaction; they speak from encounter. Their words surge with a power that exceeds human eloquence because they carry the weight of the Breath who formed the world. When Isaiah declares, "The Spirit of the Lord is upon me," he is not describing a feeling. He is announcing a divine commission. The Spirit does not merely inspire thought; He seizes the entire person—mind, will, imagination, memory—and aligns them to the rhythm of God's own heart. The prophet becomes transparent, a vessel through whom the Spirit reveals the divine will.

Among the prophets, Isaiah stands as the towering figure who most clearly reveals the Spirit's future work. In him, the Spirit is no longer confined to the margins of national life or restricted to kings and judges. Isaiah announces a coming age when the Spirit will rest upon the Messiah in fullness. "The Spirit of the Lord shall rest upon Him—the Spirit of wisdom and understanding, the Spirit of counsel and might, the Spirit of knowledge and the fear of the Lord." Here the Spirit is named not as power alone but as wisdom, counsel, insight, piety. The Messiah will not simply be empowered by the Spirit; He will be permeated by the Spirit. The gifts named in Isaiah 11 will later become the seven gifts of the Spirit in Christian tradition. It is in Isaiah that the Spirit ceases to be seen primarily as force and becomes understood as divine communion.

Isaiah deepens this revelation in chapter 42, where the Lord speaks of His Servant: "I have put My Spirit upon Him; He will bring forth justice to the nations." Justice is not political strategy or military conquest but fidelity to the covenant, restoration of righteousness, the healing of creation. The Spirit is the One who accomplishes this justice through the Servant. The prophet begins to unveil that the Spirit will one day animate not merely individuals, but One who embodies Israel itself. And when Isaiah finally proclaims, "The Spirit of the Lord God is upon me, because the Lord has anointed me to bring good news to the poor," the line between prophecy and future fulfillment becomes almost translucent. Centuries later, Christ will take these words upon His lips, declaring them fulfilled. Isaiah becomes the bridge between the age of longing and the age of arrival.

Ezekiel, by contrast, reveals the Spirit's power to resurrect what has died within a people. He speaks to a nation in exile, cut off from land, temple, identity, and hope. To this devastated people the Spirit gives a vision of a valley filled with dry bones. No image in the Old Testament more vividly portrays the condition of fallen humanity. The bones are scattered, devoid of life, severed from their purpose. Yet when the prophet speaks the word commanded by God, the Spirit begins to move. As wind, as breath, as life-giving force, the Spirit enters the bones and knits them together, raises them up, and fills them with breath. The Spirit who brought order out of chaos in Genesis now brings life out of death in exile. Ezekiel's vision reveals that the Spirit's mission is resurrection—resurrection of nations, resurrection of hope, resurrection of humanity's true identity. Later the prophet announces the promise that stands at the centre of Israel's hope: "I will put My Spirit within you, and you shall live." The Spirit is not content to act around Israel; He intends to act within Israel.

Joel moves this revelation to its climax. In the last days, he proclaims, God will pour out His Spirit on all flesh—sons, daughters, young, old, even servants. This is seismic. Nothing in Israel's past prepares for such universality. Until this point, the Spirit rested upon particular individuals for particular tasks. Joel declares that the age of limitation will end. The Spirit will be poured out without distinction. Prophecy will no longer be reserved for the select few. The presence once confined to the tabernacle and temple will saturate the entire people. The fire that descended at Sinai will one day descend upon hearts. Joel expands Israel's imagination, teaching the nation to expect a future in which the Spirit becomes the inheritance of all God's children.

Through the prophets, Israel slowly comes to perceive that the Spirit is not a symbol or poetic device. The Spirit possesses intellect, intention, and will. The Spirit grieves. The Spirit instructs. The Spirit calls. Such personal qualities reveal that Israel is not dealing with an impersonal energy but a divine Person whose identity is unveiled only gradually. Gregory Nazianzen will later speak of this long unveiling as a pedagogy of God: the Father made Himself known clearly, the Son more dimly; in the fullness of time the Son was revealed, and the Spirit began to shine forth; now, in the age of the Church, the Spirit is known intimately. But the seeds of that knowledge were planted in Israel's story.

Beyond law and prophecy lies an entire stream of Israel's reflection where the Spirit appears under another name: Wisdom. In the books of Proverbs, Sirach, and the Wisdom of Solomon, Wisdom stands as God's delight, God's ordering presence, God's companion in creation. "She is a breath of the power of God," says the Wisdom of Solomon, "a pure emanation of the glory of the Almighty." Though the language is poetic, the Fathers recognised that this description resembles the Spirit's activity. Wisdom grants discernment, clarity, right judgment, and harmony. Wisdom brings order to chaos, peace to conflict, stability to the heart—exactly what the Spirit accomplishes throughout salvation history. As Israel learns to recognise Wisdom, it learns to recognise the Spirit.

As the wisdom tradition unfolds, the presence of the Spirit becomes increasingly interior. No longer is divine wisdom seen merely in the order of creation or the justice of Israel's kings; it is discovered within the depths of the human heart. "The spirit of man is the lamp of the Lord," Proverbs declares, suggesting that the human person possesses an inner space where divine light can dwell. The Wisdom of Solomon goes further still, describing Wisdom as "the kindly spirit" who makes souls friends of God. Here the Spirit is not simply the power behind mighty deeds or prophetic utterance but the One who shapes moral vision, enlarges understanding, and draws the heart toward the good. The same Breath that brought cosmos out of chaos now brings clarity out of confusion within the soul.

Yet Israel also learns, painfully, that the Spirit can be resisted. When the prophets cry out that the people "stiffen their necks" or "harden their hearts," they are naming a tragedy: the Spirit desires to guide, but the people prefer the comfort of their own illusions. Isaiah laments, "They rebelled and grieved His Holy Spirit." That line marks one of the earliest moments in Scripture when the Spirit is spoken of with personal vulnerability. A force cannot be grieved. Only a person can suffer rejection. Israel's disobedience reveals not only the stubbornness of the human heart but the tenderness of the Spirit who longs for communion. The divine fire is not coercive; it is relational. It respects human freedom even when that freedom turns away.

The exile becomes the great furnace in which this relational truth is learned. When the temple falls and the land is lost, Israel confronts an unbearable question: Has God abandoned His people? The prophets answer with a deeper revelation. God has not withdrawn; God is preparing something greater. The loss of the physical sanctuary forces Israel to discover that the Spirit's dwelling place is not limited to stone or geography. Ezekiel sees the glory depart the temple, but he also hears the promise of a new heart and a new spirit. The same Spirit who once filled the sanctuary will one day fill the people themselves. Israel's catastrophe becomes the foundation for a more intimate communion. The Spirit will not merely rest upon leaders or overshadow sacred spaces. He will dwell within every believer.

This shift from external to internal presence becomes one of the defining movements in Israel's spiritual history. The prophets do not present it as a new idea but as the fulfillment of the covenant's deepest purpose. From the moment God declared, "I will be your God, and you shall be My people," the aim was communion, not proximity. The Spirit is the One who accomplishes that communion. The cloud and fire taught Israel reverence; the voice of the prophets taught Israel obedience; the wisdom tradition taught Israel discernment; but the promise of the new spirit teaches Israel intimacy. God intends to share His own life with His people.

Through all these centuries, the Spirit's revelation advances patiently, deliberately. Irenaeus describes this development with an image both simple and profound: God shapes humanity with two hands—the Word and the Spirit. In the Old Testament, these two hands work together to form a people who can recognise the Messiah when He comes. The Word speaks through the prophets; the Spirit prepares their hearts to understand the speech. The Word reveals God's will; the Spirit grants wisdom to discern it. The Word gives the law; the Spirit inscribes its meaning upon the heart. Salvation history is not a series of disconnected moments but the unfolding of a single divine artistry moving toward Christ.

Even the failures of Israel become part of this divine pedagogy. When kings fall into corruption, the people learn that political power cannot secure the covenant. When prophets are ignored, the nation discovers that human insight is insufficient. When exile shatters national pride, Israel confronts the truth that holiness is not guaranteed by heritage. These lessons are not punishments but preparations. They awaken a longing for a Spirit who will not merely descend for a moment but remain forever. They stir the hope for a king who will be perfectly Spirit-filled, a prophet whose word will never fail, a priest who will mediate not only ritual purity but interior transformation. In every disappointment, Israel is being shaped to recognise the One upon whom the Spirit will rest in fullness.

The Psalms offer a unique window into this longing. Many were born of David's own experience of the Spirit's nearness. In moments of triumph he sings, "By Your Spirit You guide me." In moments of sin he pleads, "Create in me a clean heart... take not Your Holy Spirit from me." The psalmist does not treat the Spirit as an optional aid but as the source of life itself. For David, the loss of the Spirit would be spiritual death, exile far worse than the Babylonian captivity. The Psalms therefore become Israel's prayerbook for recognising and desiring the Spirit. They are the interior counterpart to the historical narrative, teaching Israel to yearn for the Spirit as intensely as they once yearned for deliverance.

By the time the Old Testament draws toward its close, Israel stands on the threshold of a new era. Centuries of revelation have prepared the way: the fire that led them through the wilderness, the cloud that filled the sanctuary, the Spirit who rushed upon judges and kings, the voice that thundered through the prophets, the wisdom that illuminated the heart, the promise of a new creation within. Everything converges toward an expectation almost too daring to speak aloud: that the Spirit will one day descend not in temporary flashes but in permanent indwelling; not upon a chosen few but upon all; not for particular tasks but for the transformation of humanity itself.

Israel has learned that the Spirit is not a vague force but a divine Person who guides, teaches, corrects, consoles, and dwells. What remains is for the Spirit to reveal Himself fully in the One who is to come.

All the movements of Israel's history gather into a single, rising anticipation. From the fire in the bush to the fire in the temple, from the Spirit rushing upon judges to the Spirit whispering through prophets, from the breath that enters dry bones to the promise of an outpouring upon all flesh, the arc is unmistakable. The Spirit who once acted occasionally and selectively is preparing to act universally and permanently. Something is coming—someone is coming—through whom the Spirit will be given without measure.

Israel senses this even if it cannot yet articulate it fully. Every new revelation expands the horizon. The Messiah, in Israel's imagination, is no longer only a king who restores national glory or a prophet who speaks with divine authority. He is the One upon whom the Spirit rests in fullness, the One whose reign ushers in a new age of the Spirit. Isaiah's Servant, endowed with wisdom, counsel, understanding, and fear of the Lord, stands as the template. Ezekiel's promise of a new heart and new spirit becomes the longing. Joel's vision of Spirit poured upon all flesh becomes the hope.

By the close of the Old Testament, Israel has not only learned the identity of the Spirit; it has learned to long for Him. The Spirit is no longer merely the fire in the sky or the breath in the mouth of a prophet. He is the divine presence who makes God's people capable of communion. Everything in Israel's story presses toward this: a restored humanity animated from within by God's own life. What began in Eden as the breath given to the first human will one day be renewed in a humanity reborn.

This anticipation becomes especially vivid in the intertestamental writings, where the faithful remnant views history through a lens of longing. The oppression of foreign empires, the desecration of the temple, the apparent silence of prophecy—all of these sharpen Israel's awareness that something essential is missing. They have the law but lack the heart to keep it. They have the temple but lack the glory that once filled it. They have priests but lack the holiness that sustains the covenant. Underneath their worship lies an unspoken ache: *When will the Spirit return? When will God breathe again upon His people?*

The Spirit's absence becomes a kind of presence—a felt void that prepares the soul for fulfillment. Israel learns, painfully and deeply, that life with God is impossible without the Spirit. History becomes a spiritual pedagogy. The law teaches obedience, but only the Spirit can write it on the heart. Sacrifice teaches repentance, but only the Spirit can purify the conscience. The temple teaches reverence, but only the Spirit can make a person a living sanctuary. The entire Old Testament becomes a school of desire in which Israel is trained to yearn for the very gift it could not yet receive.

This yearning is not despairing; it is hopeful. The prophets refuse to let Israel think God has abandoned His people. Isaiah sees a day when the Spirit will be poured "until the wilderness becomes a fruitful field." Ezekiel promises that God Himself will cleanse, renew, and re-create. Joel foresees a dawn in which prophecy becomes the common language of the people of God. Even when the external markers of holiness fade, the prophetic word insists that God is preparing a greater revelation. The Spirit who once hovered over the waters will hover once more—this time over a humanity ready to be made new.

What emerges from this vast tapestry of longing is a striking unity. Across centuries, across genres, across triumph and exile, the Spirit acts with absolute coherence. The same Breath that brought form to formlessness in Genesis now brings hope to hopelessness in Israel. The same fire that burned in the bush now burns in the hearts of the prophets. The same presence that filled the sanctuary now begins to fill the imagination of a people awaiting redemption. The Old Testament is not the story of a different God but the unfolding revelation of the Spirit who will be fully unveiled in Christ.

By the time Israel reaches the threshold of the New Testament, its spiritual vocabulary has been prepared. It knows that the Spirit can rush upon a person and transform them. It knows that the Spirit can inspire prophecy, grant wisdom, reveal truth. It knows that the Spirit can purify, renew, and resurrect. It knows, above all, that the Spirit is holy—so holy that even the righteous fear to lose Him, so holy that David's deepest terror is the withdrawal of the Spirit's presence.

Yet Israel also knows that the Spirit has not yet come in fullness. Every revelation, every sign, every prophecy feels like a precursor. The fire has burned, but not yet erupted. The breath has stirred, but not yet filled. The promise has been spoken, but not yet fulfilled. The story ends with a sense of incompleteness, as though the Spirit is standing at the door, ready to step across the threshold into history in an unprecedented way.

And so the Old Testament concludes not with resolution but with expectation. The curtain closes on a people longing for the Spirit who hovered, who burned, who spoke, who called, who consoled, who convicted—and who promised to come again. Israel stands waiting for the One who will baptise not with water but with the Holy Spirit and fire. Waiting for the Messiah upon whom the Spirit rests without measure. Waiting for the moment when the divine breath will sweep through humanity once more, transforming creation from the inside out.

The fire in Israel has been lit. The breath has been promised. The glory has drawn near.

Everything now turns its gaze toward the One in whom the Spirit will dwell fully, and through whom the Spirit will finally be given to all.

4

Promise of a New Heart: The Spirit Who Purifies

Israel's history is a long lesson in the limits of human effort. The people return from exile, rebuild the temple, restore the priesthood, renew the sacrifices, and yet the deep wound within them remains untouched. They have the law, but lack the power to keep it. They have rituals, but lack the love that fulfils them. They have structure, but not the interior strength to live it. Over and over, Scripture shows a people who desire fidelity yet feel themselves slipping into infidelity, who long for holiness yet find themselves unable to sustain it. Their tragedy is not ignorance—it is impotence. They know what God commands, but the heart is unable to respond with consistent love.

This is where the prophets step in, naming the secret that Israel can sense but cannot articulate: the human heart is wounded, and no amount of external reform can heal it. The root of the problem lies deeper than behaviour, deeper than habits, deeper even than intention. Something at the centre of desire has been distorted. Israel confesses repeatedly, "Create in me a clean heart," because no human hand can do it. The law stands luminous and good, but the heart is weighed down, hesitant, divided. For all its beauty, the old covenant reveals a profound truth: humanity cannot heal itself.

Into this crisis God speaks a promise so unexpected that it transforms the spiritual imagination. Through Ezekiel, He declares, "I will sprinkle clean water upon you, and you shall be clean." The purification begins not with Israel's initiative, but with God's touch. Cleansing is gift, not achievement. Then comes the promise that shatters every prior category: "A new heart I will give you, and a new spirit I will put within you." The heart—which in biblical language means the whole interior person, the place where choices, loves, desires, and identity converge—will not be strengthened or trained. It will be re-created.

Humanity cannot remodel the heart; only God can give a new one. And God does not give it reluctantly. The verbs roll like waves: *I will cleanse... I will give... I will put within... I will remove... I will write... I will pour out...* Purification belongs to God's action. The prophets do not describe a moral improvement project. They describe a divine descent. God takes responsibility for shaping the heart He desires. What Israel cannot do from below, God will accomplish from above.

Ezekiel presses this point further when he records God's final promise: "I will put My Spirit within you, and cause you to walk in My statutes." Purification is not simply about removing sin; it is about making space for the Spirit. The Spirit is not given as a reward for moral progress; the Spirit *creates* the progress. Only the Spirit can orient the heart toward God. Only the Spirit can free desire from its distortions. Only the Spirit can empower the human person to love what God commands. Holiness, therefore, is no longer a burden placed upon the human will; it is the fruit of divine indwelling.

Jeremiah deepens this vision. He does not describe a new set of moral obligations or stricter commandments. He describes a new covenant written not on stone but on the heart. "I will write My law upon their hearts." The act is intimate—God Himself becomes the scribe, engraving His love into the centre of the person. The commandments are no longer external demands; they become the inner harmony of a healed heart. The law is not abolished; it is interiorised. Obedience becomes not the struggle of a fractured will but the natural rhythm of a purified heart.

Jeremiah's promise also includes a new kind of knowledge: "They shall all know Me." This knowledge is not conceptual but relational. It is the knowledge that comes from proximity, intimacy, communion. The heart is purified not to perform better, but to know God more deeply. Purification prepares the soul for encounter. The more the Spirit heals the heart, the more the heart becomes capable of God. The prophets show that sanctity is not an achievement but a capacity—the capacity to receive divine life.

Joel widens the horizon even further. His prophecy reveals that purification is not reserved for the elite, the learned, or the morally exceptional. "I will pour out My Spirit on all flesh." Sons and daughters, young and old, servants and free—all become potential vessels of divine fire. The Spirit is not given according to merit but according to God's generosity. This universality marks a decisive shift. The new heart is not a private gift but the beginning of a new humanity. The Spirit will not descend occasionally upon a prophet or a king. The Spirit will be poured out upon all who open themselves to the gift. Purification becomes the foundation of a new people, a new covenant community, a renewed world.

At the centre of these prophetic promises stands one unchanging truth: purification is a divine work. The human person cooperates, but the initiative is always God's. Israel had tried to obey, tried to believe, tried to keep covenant, and all its effort revealed the same truth: without the Spirit, the heart bends inward; with the Spirit, the heart bends toward God. Purification is not the result of greater willpower. It is the result of greater grace.

In this sense, purification is not punishment but liberation. The Spirit does not descend to wound; the Spirit descends to free. The new heart is not a burden but a restoration—the restoration of humanity's original capacity for communion. The new spirit is not an imposition but a gift—the gift of divine strength breathed into human weakness. God does not purify to make life harder; He purifies to make love possible.

And all of this points toward the One who will come. The prophets are preparing the world for Christ—not only as teacher or king, but as the One who brings the Spirit. Their promises form the doorway through which the Gospel will enter. Purification is not merely a stage of the spiritual life; it is the threshold of the Incarnation, the preparation for the descent of the Spirit who will dwell in humanity through the Son.

The more deeply one listens to the prophets, the clearer the pattern becomes: God is not demanding that humanity climb toward Him by sheer effort. He is descending to recreate the very capacity by which humanity receives Him. This is why the language of the prophets is filled with tenderness rather than threat. God does not say, "Try harder to love Me." He says, "I will give you a heart capable of love." The movement is entirely grace. Israel's repeated failures become the canvas upon which God reveals the surprising character of His mercy. He does not punish the weakness of the human heart; He heals it by replacing its centre.

Ezekiel's vision of the heart of stone becoming a heart of flesh expresses this with startling clarity. A heart of stone is not stubborn by choice—it is incapable of movement. It cannot yield, cannot respond, cannot turn. The tragedy is not rebellion but paralysis. When God promises to remove the heart of stone, He is naming the deepest truth about sin: it has not merely damaged the heart, it has immobilised it. Divine commands cannot revive stone. Only divine touch can. The gift of a heart of flesh is the gift of responsiveness restored. Grace does not augment human capacity; it resurrects it.

This movement from paralysis to responsiveness is the essence of purification. The Spirit does not impose holiness from outside; He awakens the interior freedom to desire holiness. He does not intimidate the heart into obedience; He reorders desire so that obedience flows from love. Sins fall away not because the will grows stronger, but because the Spirit opens the heart to a greater beauty. Under the old covenant, Israel feared the law but could not love it. Under the new heart, the law becomes not a threat but a delight. Purification reclaims the harmony between command and desire—something humanity has not known since Eden.

Jeremiah's vision reinforces this. When God says He will write His law upon the heart, He is describing something far more profound than moral instruction. The law becomes inscribed into the interior structure of desire. What God commands, the heart now wants. What God reveals, the heart now recognises as true. Purification is the re-alignment of the heart's loves—not the crushing of desire but its illumination. The law written on stone exposes sin; the law written on the heart enables holiness. Jeremiah's promise signals a theological shift from obligation to union.

This union is already hinted at in the way the prophets speak of knowledge. "They shall all know Me," says the Lord. In Scripture, knowledge always implies intimacy; it is the meeting of persons, not the memorising of propositions. A purified heart knows God because the Spirit clears away the false images of Him that sin creates. Fear gives way to trust. Distance gives way to nearness. The prophets describe purification in relational terms because the Spirit's work is relational. He heals the heart so the heart can love the One who made it. He restores the interior world so communion can flourish.

The universality of Joel's promise makes this dynamic even more striking. The Spirit will not be poured out in proportion to merit or sanctity. He will be poured out on "all flesh"—the weak and the strong, the learned and the unlearned, the young and the old. The Spirit does not descend because humanity has become worthy; humanity becomes worthy because the Spirit descends. Purification is therefore not the achievement of a select few but the invitation extended to the whole of humanity. When Joel imagines sons and daughters prophesying, he is envisioning a people whose hearts have been so opened by the Spirit that divine life overflows. Purification becomes the doorway to participation.

At this point it becomes clear that purification in the prophetic vision is not a matter of moral polishing—it is the preparation for indwelling. The human heart is being prepared to become the dwelling place of God. The prophets speak again and again of God living among His people, but the climax is Ezekiel's repeated declaration: "My Spirit within you." Not beside you. Not near you. Not around you. *Within you.* Israel was prepared for a Messiah, but the prophets prepare them for something more radical still: the Spirit who once hovered over creation will hover over the soul; the fire that once burned on Sinai will burn in the heart.

This interiorisation is the turning point. For Israel, holiness had always involved movement toward the presence—ascending the mountain, approaching the temple, entering the courts. But the prophets reveal that in the coming age, the presence will move toward them. The holy will no longer be a place to be reached but a life to be received. Purification is therefore not spatial but personal; not ritual but relational. God cleanses the heart in order to enter it. The new covenant is not humanity brought near to God—it is God making His home within humanity.

All of this leads naturally to the figure of John the Baptist. John inherits the entire prophetic tradition, and his message makes explicit what the prophets only implied: purification is preparation for a person. John does not call Israel to repentance as an end in itself; he calls them to repentance because "the One who is coming" will bring the decisive gift the prophets promised. John's water can wash the exterior; Christ's Spirit will cleanse the interior. John prepares the heart; Christ transforms it. John cries out in the wilderness because the wilderness represents the stripped, emptied place where the heart can finally receive the One who is coming. Repentance becomes readiness. Purification becomes openness.

And at the heart of John's message stands the essential claim: "He will baptise you with the Holy Spirit and fire." Fire in Scripture is almost always the sign of divine presence. It enlightens, warms, purifies, and transforms. The fire Christ brings is not the fire of destruction but the fire of love—the fire that burns away false loves so true love can take root. Christ does not simply fulfil the promise of purification; He *is* the fulfilment. Purification prepares for Him because He alone brings the Spirit who purifies.

Purification, then, is no longer Israel's attempt to fix itself. It is the heart's surrender to the One who alone can heal it. The prophets announce a future where God's people will finally be able to love Him—not because they have become strong, but because He has become near.

Once we grasp that purification is God's initiative rather than humanity's achievement, the entire spiritual landscape changes. The heart no longer stands at the centre as an exhausted labourer striving upward; the Spirit stands at the centre as the divine healer descending downward. This shift is not merely theological—it is existential. It means that the transformation of the human person does not depend on the intensity of one's will, the consistency of one's discipline, or the brilliance of one's understanding. It depends on the willingness to be opened, touched, and reordered by the Spirit who alone can heal what lies beneath the surface of behaviour.

The prophets return repeatedly to the same theme: the greatest obstacle to holiness is not ignorance but bondage. Sin binds the heart, not simply through guilt, but through distorted desire. A person may know the good and still be unable to choose it; may desire holiness yet feel pulled toward its opposite; may long for God yet remain trapped in attachments that suffocate that longing. The human will, left to itself, oscillates between aspiration and collapse. This is why purification cannot be a moral exercise. It must be a divine deliverance. Only the Spirit can free the heart from the interior gravity that draws it toward lesser loves.

This divine deliverance unfolds in subtle and profound ways. When Scripture speaks of the heart being cleansed or renewed, it is not describing external behaviour but the reconfiguration of desire itself. Purification touches the place where loves are formed. The Spirit purifies not by suppressing desire but by restoring its true direction. The heart begins to perceive the beauty of God more clearly and the allure of idols more honestly. A spiritual light dawns within, exposing false promises and awakening the capacity for true joy. What once seemed irresistible loses its hold. What once seemed distant becomes desirable. The Spirit creates a new interior landscape in which holiness becomes not a burden but a possibility.

This inner shift is often gentle, even imperceptible at first. The prophets describe the new heart not as something violently imposed but as something quietly given. Water sprinkled. Stone replaced with flesh. Law written softly within. Spirit breathed into dry bones. God works not with force but with patience. His fire purifies without consuming; His breath restores without overwhelming. The heart opens, slowly but surely, because the Spirit is not an intruder but a healer. He does not coerce holiness—He awakens it.

Yet purification is not only tender; it is also decisive. The Spirit does not merely soothe the heart but reclaims it. This reclaiming involves the unveiling of truth. One of the Spirit's most important roles in purification is revelation—He reveals the truth about God and the truth about the self. Without this revelation, the heart remains divided, clinging to illusions that promise pleasure but deliver emptiness. The Spirit cuts through these illusions with clarity. He convicts—not to shame, but to free. He shows the heart its false loves not to condemn, but to liberate it from them. The prophets describe this as God "removing idols from the land," because idols always begin in the heart before they appear in culture.

This unveiling of truth is the beginning of genuine repentance. Repentance is often misunderstood as a human achievement—a sorrow we generate, a resolve we muster. But in the prophetic vision, repentance is the fruit of purification, not its cause. The Spirit reveals the true state of the heart, and the heart, finally able to see itself, turns toward God with sincerity. Repentance is the heart awakening under the Spirit's touch. It is the heart saying "yes" to the purification already at work within it. This is why the prophets speak of repentance and renewal side by side: repentance is the heart's cooperation with divine healing, not the means by which healing is earned.

When purification is understood in this way, its relationship to freedom changes. Freedom is no longer the power to choose arbitrarily; it is the power to choose well. The purified heart is the free heart—not because it has acquired discipline, but because the Spirit has unbound it from the interior chains that once governed its choices. The Spirit does not override human freedom; He restores it. He does not bypass the will; He heals the will so it can move toward the good without inner sabotage. True freedom is born when the Spirit reorders the interior world so that desire and truth converge.

Joel's universal promise of the Spirit reveals another dimension of purification: its communal character. The new heart is given not only to individuals but to a people. Purification is the foundation of a community capable of bearing God's presence. When the Spirit purifies hearts, He does not create isolated saints but a holy communion. This is why the prophets speak of a renewed Israel, a people who will walk together in the Spirit's ways. Under the old covenant, the people were united by a law they could not fully keep. Under the new covenant, they will be united by the Spirit who writes the law within them. Purification becomes the source of ecclesial unity. The people of God are formed not by collective discipline but by shared indwelling.

This communal dimension also reveals why purification must precede union. The Spirit cannot dwell where the heart remains closed. He will not force entry. The new heart is His work, but the opening of that heart is a cooperation He invites. God purifies because He desires communion. The prophets make purification a necessary preparation for the Messiah because the Messiah will bring the Spirit in fullness. To receive Christ is to receive the Spirit. To receive the Spirit is to become capable of union with God. Purification is the clearing of the interior space where Christ will dwell.

Everything in the prophetic promise bends toward this reality: purification is preparation for Christ. Without purification, the heart cannot receive Him. With it, the heart becomes the place where divine life takes root. The prophets are not preparing Israel for a moral reformer; they are preparing Israel for a divine in dweller. The new heart will be the home of the One who comes.

The prophetic promises of purification gather into a single point of anticipation: someone is coming who will accomplish what Israel could never achieve. The prophets are unanimous. The new heart, the new spirit, the cleansing water, the interior law, the Spirit poured out—all of this depends on the arrival of a figure who will embody God's presence and mediate God's Spirit. That figure is the

Messiah. Purification is not a concept floating through Israel's hope; purification is preparation for a person.

John the Baptist stands at this threshold like a bridge between centuries. He embodies the ache of Israel's longing. His entire mission is to announce that the decisive moment has arrived. He does not offer new techniques of holiness or a stricter path of moral reform. He offers a warning and a promise. The warning exposes every illusion of moral self-sufficiency: "Do not say, 'We have Abraham as our father,' for God can raise children of Abraham from these stones." The promise exposes every false hope in human effort: "He will baptise you with the Holy Spirit and fire." John announces the end of religion built on human strength and the beginning of life made possible by divine gift.

John's baptism in water is symbolic, preparatory, provisional. It cleanses outwardly but cannot transform inwardly. It awakens desire but cannot fulfill it. It opens the heart but cannot heal it. John knows this. His greatness lies not in what he accomplishes but in what he anticipates. All purification before Christ is a door; Christ is the One who walks through it. John's water reveals the need; Christ's Spirit heals the wound.

And so when Jesus steps into the Jordan, the story shifts. The heavens open. The Spirit descends. The Father speaks. The moment reveals not only who Christ is but what He has come to give. The Spirit who hovered over the waters of creation now hovers over the humanity of Christ. The new creation has begun. Christ receives the Spirit in His humanity so He can pour the Spirit into ours. The prophets promised a new heart; Christ receives the Spirit so that His own heart—flawless, free, burning with filial love—can become the source from which every new heart is fashioned.

Purification, therefore, is inseparable from Christ's person. It is not an abstract spiritual process but a participation in His humanity.

The Spirit purifies not by operating beside Christ, but by grafting the believer into Christ. This is why the New Testament speaks of salvation as union. To be purified is to share the heart of Christ. To be healed is to be drawn into His obedience. To be cleansed is to receive His desires as one's own. Christ becomes the measure of the new heart—not only as example but as indwelling life.

The prophets spoke of the law written on the heart; Christ is the living law whose love becomes the heart's new rhythm. The prophets spoke of water sprinkled for cleansing; Christ offers the living water that flows from His side. The prophets spoke of the Spirit within; Christ breathes the Spirit upon His disciples. Everything the prophets promised, Christ embodies and gives.

This unveils the deepest meaning of purification: it is the preparation for communion. God cleanses the heart so the heart can receive God. The Spirit purifies desire so desire can cling to Christ without resistance. The Spirit removes the idols so the soul can love without divided loyalty. Purification is not about making the heart morally tidy; it is about making the heart spacious enough for divine indwelling. God does not aim to produce disciplined servants. He aims to produce lovers—people whose hearts have been freed from false loves so that they can receive the one true Love.

Because purification aims at communion, it is not completed in a single moment. It stretches across the entire spiritual life. The Spirit works patiently, continuously, often invisibly, purifying layer after layer of the heart's disorder, always moving toward union. What begins at baptism unfolds through a lifetime of grace. The new heart is given in seed, and the Spirit cultivates it through every circumstance of life—joys that expand the heart, trials that refine it, sufferings that deepen it, consolations that awaken it, dryness that strengthens it. Purification is not a stage to be passed through but a rhythm in which the Spirit continually returns the heart to its true orientation.

This dynamic makes sense only in light of Christ. The heart is purified because it is being prepared for union with Him. The heart is made new so that Christ may dwell within it. The Spirit cleanses so that He may remain. Every act of purification is an act of preparation for communion. Every layer of healing is a layer of readiness for deeper intimacy. This is why the prophets look forward not merely to forgiveness but to indwelling. Forgiveness removes barriers; indwelling completes communion. Purification is thus the first movement of deification—God preparing the human soul to participate in His life.

When the prophets proclaim, "I will give you a new heart," they are not announcing a moral improvement project. They are announcing the dawn of a new creation. They are announcing Pentecost. They are announcing that the Spirit who hovered over the primordial waters will soon hover over human souls. In this promise, purification becomes the hinge of salvation history: the Spirit who cleanses preparing the way for the Spirit who fills, the Spirit who unveils preparing the way for the Spirit who indwells, the Spirit who restores preparing the way for the Spirit who divinises.

The heart purified is the heart readied for God. It stands open, unburdened, capable of receiving the One who comes. The shadows that once clung to its desires give way to a quiet clarity; the barriers that once kept it divided fall away; the fears that once kept it closed loosen their hold. What remains is a heart made spacious for grace, a heart shaped for communion, a heart awakened to the possibility of God's own life.

Purification is the Spirit preparing a sanctuary.

Purification is desire returning to its source.

Purification is the beginning of union.

The prophets speak, and the promise rises like a flame in the darkness: a new heart, a new spirit, a new creation. The Spirit draws near. The soul begins to breathe again.

5

The Spirit of Repentance: Purification and the Ascent of the Soul

Repentance is often imagined as a human response—an act of will, a decision to turn, a sorrow produced by one's own conscience. But Scripture reveals something far more mysterious and tender: repentance is the first movement of the Spirit within the soul. Long before a person feels remorse or recognises sin, the Spirit has already approached with a quiet light, already touched the heart with a truth it can barely articulate. Repentance does not begin with human initiative. It begins with divine visitation.

The Spirit is the one who awakens the interior world. He is the lamp that searches the rooms of the heart, not to expose in order to shame, but to reveal in order to heal. When Proverbs declares that "the spirit of man is the lamp of the Lord," it points to this divine search—God illuminating the depths through the very faculty He sustains. Yet this illumination does not arise naturally. It is the Spirit who ignites the lamp. Conscience, in the biblical vision, is not an independent moral monitor. It is the place where the Spirit whispers truth with a gentleness that respects freedom and a clarity that calls the soul home.

John Henry Newman captured this with rare precision when he

described conscience as "the aboriginal Vicar of Christ." He meant that conscience is not self-generated; it is the echo of God's voice within the human person. But even this description reaches deeper when read through the lens of the prophets: conscience is the chamber where the Spirit breathes. When the Spirit moves, conscience awakens. When the Spirit withdraws, conscience grows dull. Repentance, therefore, is not the product of guilt but the fruit of God's presence.

Jesus Himself confirms this when He speaks of the Spirit's future work: "When He comes, He will convict the world of sin." The word *convict* is easily misunderstood. It does not mean to crush or condemn. The Greek *elenxei* means to illuminate, to reveal, to disclose what has been hidden. The Spirit does not accuse. The Spirit unveils. He reveals sin as something that does not belong to the beloved of God. He uncovers the lie so the heart can turn toward the truth. The Spirit's conviction feels different from guilt because guilt presses downward, while conviction draws upward. Guilt closes; conviction opens. Guilt isolates; conviction summons. The Spirit's work produces sorrow, yes—but a sorrow that frees rather than suffocates.

This is why genuine repentance is never despairing. It is hopeful. The Spirit does not reveal the wound to deepen the pain but to initiate the healing. The heart that begins to see its sin sees it only because the Spirit has already begun to draw near with mercy. Repentance is the recognition that grace is at the door. It is the moment when the soul feels itself awakened by Someone who knows it better than it knows itself. Even the desire to return is grace.

This grace often takes the form of tears in the lives of the saints. The Desert Fathers speak of tears not as emotional overflow but as the sign that the heart has been pierced by divine love. Compunction—*katanyxis*—literally means "to be punctured," to have the hardness of the heart softened by the touch of God. These tears are not born of fear but of clarity. They come when the soul sees the beauty of

God and recognises how far it has wandered. St. Isaac the Syrian calls compunction "a second baptism," the washing of the heart by the Spirit's fire and tenderness. Tears become the outward sign of an inward healing.

The Desert tradition teaches that repentance is not the humiliation of the sinner but the awakening of the beloved. A person grieves because they glimpse, even for a moment, the radiance of the One they long for. The tears arise from love, not self-loathing. They do not suffocate hope; they strengthen it. Compunction is the heart breaking open so that grace may enter. It is the Spirit loosening the knots of pride, fear, and illusion that prevent the soul from rising toward God. The tears burn, but they burn with cleansing fire.

This fire imagery is woven throughout the Scriptures because the Spirit purifies as fire purifies. Fire lightens by consuming what weighs down. Fire clarifies by removing what distorts. Fire warms by awakening what has grown cold. Divine fire burns away only what is not love. Basil the Great describes the Spirit's fire as the flame that makes the soul luminous, and Origen speaks of the fire that "saves," interpreting Paul's teaching that we pass "through fire" as a metaphor for purification. In this fire there is no cruelty—only healing. The Spirit is not a destroyer but a refiner. Repentance is the moment when this refining begins in earnest.

Yet the Spirit's fire does not annihilate desire; it transforms it. The passions—those movements of the heart that have been distorted by sin—are not enemies to be crushed but energies to be healed. Anger, when healed, becomes courage. Desire, when purified, becomes love. Sorrow, when touched by the Spirit, becomes compassion. Fear, when illumined, becomes reverence. The Spirit does not flatten the soul; He harmonises it. Repentance is the beginning of this harmonising, the moment when the passions begin their slow return to their rightful order.

In all of this, repentance is revealed not as punishment but as preparation. The Spirit purifies the heart because the heart is being drawn toward communion. The soul begins its ascent not by climbing but by being cleansed. The Spirit prepares the way. He loosens the chains. He opens the wounds to healing. Repentance is simply the heart consenting to be remade.

Repentance begins when the Spirit draws near; it deepens when the Spirit begins to reorder the interior world. The Fathers teach that the first sign of this reordering is the awakening of conscience—not as an inner scolding, but as an inner illumination. When the Spirit breathes upon conscience, the soul sees with new clarity. Behaviours once defended begin to appear hollow. Motives once hidden begin to surface. Attachments once cherished begin to loosen. This unveiling is gentle but piercing. The Spirit does not shame; He reveals. Shame turns the soul in on itself; revelation opens the soul toward God.

This unveiling marks the beginning of interior honesty. A person who once navigated life through distraction, noise, or denial suddenly finds themselves standing in a light that cannot be escaped but also does not condemn. It is the light of truth, and it feels both searching and safe. The Desert Fathers describe this moment as the heart "coming to itself," a phrase borrowed from the parable of the prodigal son. The boy does not return home because he is terrified of punishment; he returns because he recognises his hunger for the father's house. Repentance follows the same pattern. The Spirit reveals not only the emptiness of sin but the possibility of a different life. The heart sees what it has become and remembers what it was made to be.

This memory is crucial. Repentance is not nostalgia for an imagined innocence but the rediscovery of the image of God within the soul. The Spirit holds up the truth of who the person is—a truth obscured by fear, pride, and desire gone astray. When the Spirit reveals sin,

He does so in the same movement by which He reveals dignity. The two revelations are inseparable. A person feels contrition not because they have violated an impersonal rule but because they have wounded love. Tears appear when the soul realises it is loved even in its sin, and loved by One who desires not to discard the sinner but to restore the image.

This restoration begins with humility. Humility is often misunderstood as self-negation, but in the spiritual tradition it is something luminous: the heart standing unmasked before God. Humility is truth. Humility is transparency. Humility is the undoing of illusions that keep the soul at a distance from God. When the Spirit awakens humility, a person does not feel smaller—they feel more real. They see themselves without pretence and without despair. They recognise their poverty, yet this recognition does not crush them; it frees them. Humility is the ground on which the Spirit begins His ascent within the soul.

From humility flows compunction. Compunction is not the sorrow of self-disgust. It is the sorrow of love. The Desert Fathers describe compunction as a trembling of the heart before the beauty of God. It is the moment when the heart becomes soft again, when the layers of indifference melt, when the soul realises that it has been pursued by mercy even in its wandering. Compunction is always tender, never violent. It produces tears, but these tears are the tears of resurrection—water flowing where the soul felt dry, signs that the Spirit has touched places long sealed off.

This tenderness is often accompanied by an interior fire. The Spirit's fire is not experienced as destruction but as clarity. It burns through the excuses, the rationalisations, the self-protective mechanisms that keep the soul trapped in half-truths. Fire illuminates even as it purifies. Many saints describe this stage of repentance as the soul beginning to feel "warmth," an interior flame that both consoles and challenges. It is the flame of divine love drawing the soul toward truth, urging it to let go of what cannot coexist with God.

This movement naturally leads to the purification of the passions. The passions are not enemies; they are energies that have lost their direction. The Spirit does not crush them—He redirects them. Anger, when purified, becomes a holy determination to reject what harms the soul. Desire becomes yearning for God. Sadness becomes compassion. Fear becomes reverence. Even the intense passions that feel unruly in their fallen form carry within them a seed of virtue once the Spirit reclaims them. Repentance begins to unveil this hidden structure: the soul learns that it is not called to emotional sterility but to emotional transfiguration.

Purification of the passions is slow, patient work. The Spirit does not overwhelm the soul; He guides, strengthens, clarifies. Patterns of thought and behaviour that once seemed immovable begin to shift. The soul desires different things. Old temptations lose some of their force. Areas of life once dominated by compulsion begin to open toward freedom. These changes are often subtle and fragile, but they mark the beginning of the ascent. The Spirit is forming new instincts within the person—instincts ordered toward the good.

As this purification unfolds, the soul begins to understand repentance less as a moment and more as a way of life. Repentance becomes the posture of openness to the Spirit's work. It becomes the willingness to be led into deeper truth, deeper freedom, deeper communion. Repentance is not episodic but habitual. It is the ongoing "yes" to the Spirit's work of remaking the heart. This is why the Fathers insist that repentance is joy. Not because sin is taken lightly, but because grace is taken seriously. Repentance is the doorway into an ever-renewed encounter with God.

And at every stage, it is the Spirit who draws the soul forward. Repentance does not begin in human strength and it does not continue in human strength. The ascent into holiness begins with the Spirit cleansing desire, and it continues with the Spirit reshaping the heart. The soul cooperates, but the Spirit initiates. The Spirit sustains. The Spirit leads. Repentance is not the soul trying to climb out of a pit; it is the soul discovering that God has descended into the pit and is lifting it upward.

As the Spirit continues His quiet work, repentance deepens into something far more profound than sorrow for sin. It becomes the soul's reawakening to truth. Sin thrives in illusion—false narratives about God, the self, others, and the world. Repentance is the collapse of these illusions under the weight of divine light. The Spirit dispels shadows not by force but by revelation. He gives the soul the grace to see reality as God sees it. In this sense, repentance is the beginning of spiritual vision.

This vision reveals two things at once: the extent of the wound and the depth of the mercy. The Spirit shows the soul what it has clung to, what it has feared, what it has loved wrongly, not to humiliate but to free. He brings the heart to understand not only what it has done but what it has become, and what it can become again. This dual revelation—truth about the wound and truth about the remedy—prevents repentance from devolving into despair. The soul sees its poverty, but it sees it in a light that promises healing. The Spirit reveals sin in order to reveal God's desire to remove it.

When this revelation pierces the heart, the soul experiences a cleaving—a splitting between its old self and its emerging new self. The Desert Fathers describe this as the moment when the inner man awakens. It is the beginning of an inner journey that climbs from the depths of compulsion toward the heights of communion. The Spirit does not simply show the path; He becomes the path within the person, forming the desires that know the way toward God. Repentance becomes movement—slow, humble, but real.

During this movement, the passions undergo their first true refinement. The passions are the soul's energies—those interior movements that, in their fallen state, pull the person toward disorder. The Spirit does not eradicate them; He heals them at their roots. The healing begins by revealing their true purpose. Anger was designed to protect love. Desire was designed to draw the soul toward God. Sadness was designed to open the heart to compassion. Fear was designed to guard the soul against evil. In the fallen heart, these energies turn inward or sideways; in the repentant heart, they begin returning to their original orientation.

The Fathers speak of this process with remarkable psychological insight. Evagrius describes the passions as horses that have thrown their rider; the Spirit does not kill the horses—He places the rider back upon them. Cassian teaches that the passions must be re-ordered, not despised. Maximus the Confessor goes even further, insisting that the passions, when purified, become instruments of virtue. This purification is not the work of severity or repression but of light. The Spirit illumines each passion so that its true nature becomes visible again. The person begins to recognise their interior movements not as enemies but as energies that can be directed toward God.

This interior reorientation often produces a new kind of sorrow—the sorrow that longs for more of God. It is not grief over past actions but yearning for deeper communion. The Fathers call this "blessed sorrow." It is sorrow born of love, not fear. It is the ache of the heart that has tasted divine beauty and desires more. Augustine captures this when he writes, "Our hearts are restless until they rest in You." Restlessness becomes a sign of grace—the Spirit stirring the depths, refusing to let the soul settle for less than communion.

This restlessness is accompanied by a newfound tenderness. The repentant heart becomes gentler toward others, because it has seen its own fragility under the Spirit's light. Pride, which once masked insecurity, begins to dissolve. Harshness softens. The person recognises in others the same struggle, the same longing, the same wounds, and the compassion that flows from this recognition is itself the work of the Spirit. Repentance becomes the seed of mercy. The soul that knows its own need becomes a refuge for others.

At the same time, repentance awakens courage. The Spirit who reveals truth also strengthens the will to follow it. What once felt impossible begins to appear attainable. What once felt overwhelming begins to appear bearable. The soul experiences moments of clarity, moments of resolve, moments of deepening trust. These are not the achievements of the will; they are the infusions of grace. The Spirit gives courage not by shouting commands but by drawing the heart toward the good with a quiet but irresistible pull. Repentance becomes the soul's ascent into trust.

This ascent is not linear. The Spirit guides the soul through movements of light and darkness, consolation and dryness. These oscillations are not signs of failure but signs of deeper purification. The Spirit loosens attachments layer by layer, revealing what clings to the heart and what the heart clings to. In seasons of dryness, the soul is invited to trust the presence it cannot feel. In seasons of consolation, it is invited to believe that the love it feels is real. Both are necessary. Both are purifying. Both are movements of the Spirit drawing the soul toward God.

Through all of this, repentance becomes less an event and more a relationship. The soul begins to recognise the Spirit's presence in the subtleties of conviction, the gentleness of inner prompting, the warmth of compunction, the clarity of conscience, the strengthening of virtue. The Spirit becomes familiar. The soul learns the movements of grace the way one learns the nuances of a friend's voice. Repentance is the beginning of intimacy. It is the moment when God ceases to be a concept and becomes a presence.

And as this intimacy grows, the soul begins to ascend. This ascent is not the triumph of human discipline but the lifting power of the Spirit. The Spirit is the wind that rises from within, the fire that burns away what is not love, the light that guides the soul upward. Repentance reveals the true nature of the spiritual life: we rise because the Spirit lifts; we see because the Spirit illumines; we love because the Spirit transforms desire. Repentance is not the soul climbing toward God; it is the soul allowing itself to be drawn upward by the God who has descended.

As repentance matures under the Spirit's touch, the soul discovers a new way of inhabiting its own interior life. The heart that once felt scattered becomes gathered. The mind that once ran in anxious circles begins to rest. The desires that once pulled the person downward begin, almost imperceptibly, to rise. The Spirit never rushes this work. He moves with the patience of one who knows He is shaping eternity. The soul learns to cooperate, not by striving, but by yielding.

Yielding becomes the mark of the repentant life. Not passivity, but surrender. The surrender of false narratives, of cherished sins, of defensive postures, of wounded pride, of self-protective illusions. The Spirit loosens each of these not through force but through love. Love exposes what fear hides. Love unmasks what shame defends. Love draws the soul into truth and gives it courage to remain there. The soul that yields begins to experience repentance as liberation rather than loss.

In this freedom, humility takes root. Humility is not humiliation; it is clarity of being. The Spirit grants the soul a true vision of itself—beloved, wounded, dependent, capable of grace, in need of mercy. Pride cannot survive this clarity. Nor can despair. Humility grows where truth and love meet. It becomes the soil in which all other virtues are planted. The Desert Fathers saw humility as the foundation of the ascetical life because it is the first fruit of repentance. A humbled soul becomes a spacious soul, open to God.

As humility deepens, prayer changes. The soul that once approached God out of fear now approaches out of longing. Words become fewer. Listening becomes more natural. The Spirit teaches prayer not by giving techniques but by giving desire. Desire is prayer's true beginning. A single sigh toward God contains more theology than many pages of discourse. The Fathers often said that the Spirit gives the soul the tears that it cannot produce on its own—tears that cleanse, tears that soften, tears that reveal. These tears are not the mark of sorrow but the mark of awakening.

In this awakening, the conscience becomes keen. The Spirit sharpens its edge, not to wound, but to guide. Conscience is not a mere inner voice; it is the sanctuary where the Spirit instructs the heart. As sin loses its appeal, the soul becomes sensitive to its movements, not with scrupulosity but with clarity. What once seemed insignificant now reveals its roots. What once seemed overwhelming now appears conquerable. The Spirit trains the conscience as a master craftsman trains the hand—by repeated gentle pressure, by subtle correction, by forming instinct into virtue.

At the same time, the Spirit awakens gratitude. Repentance that matures always becomes thanksgiving. The soul begins to notice graces once ignored: a moment of calm, a softening of anger, an unexpected patience, a new tenderness, a restored desire for prayer, the quieting of an old temptation. Gratitude breaks the illusion of self-sufficiency. It reveals that every inch of progress is grace. Gratitude protects the heart from pride because it knows that the ascent is carried, not climbed.

As gratitude grows, the soul becomes more attentive. Attentiveness is the fruit of a purified heart. It is the ability to perceive God in the details of daily life—in interruptions, in burdens, in ordinary labour, in small joys, in unexpected encounters. The Spirit teaches the soul to recognise His movements beneath the surface of events. The repentant person begins to sense the divine nearness not as a feeling but as a quiet certainty. The heart becomes watchful, not anxious; alert, not tense. Attentiveness becomes a form of prayer.

This attentiveness makes obedience possible. Not the obedience of compulsion, but the obedience of love. The Spirit does not command from without; He inclines from within. What once felt like effort now feels like alignment. The will finds harmony with grace, like a sail finding wind. The soul discovers a new capacity for choosing the good—not through gritted teeth but through inner ease. The Fathers call this "the beginning of the spiritual life"—the moment when obedience is no longer experienced as constraint but as freedom.

Freedom becomes one of the clearest signs of the Spirit's presence. The repentant soul feels released from compulsions that once dominated it. Old patterns begin to lose their force. The imagination becomes less clouded. The emotions become more stable. The will becomes more steady. None of this arrives at once. It unfolds gradually, like dawn lighting the sky. The soul learns to trust this slow light. It realises that God heals in ways that are deliberate, personal, and often hidden until their fruits appear.

As the ascent continues, love becomes the true measure of repentance. Not sentimental affection, but love that is patient, steady, sacrificial, generous. The Spirit weaves this love into the heart as He purifies its desires. The person begins to love others with the same tenderness with which God has loved them. Old resentments soften. Judgments loosen. A new gentleness emerges. The repentant heart becomes a heart that carries others. The Spirit who convicts also consoles; He grants the capacity to console others.

Eventually, the soul understands that repentance is not the gate to the spiritual life but the life itself. Repentance becomes continuous conversion—a daily turning toward God, a daily loosening of attachment, a daily consent to grace. This is not exhausting but liberating. The more the soul turns, the more it beholds. The more it beholds, the more it loves. The more it loves, the more it rises.

The ascent is the Spirit's work from beginning to end. Repentance reveals the truth of the spiritual life: that God never asks the soul to lift itself. He asks only that it allow itself to be lifted. The heart that yields becomes the heart that rises. The Spirit cleanses desire so that desire may ascend. The Spirit wounds with truth so that truth may heal. The Spirit humbles so that love may grow. The Spirit awakens longing so that longing may find its rest in God.

In this way, repentance becomes the soul's first taste of union—union not yet full, but already real. The Spirit cleanses to make space, purifies to make room, softens to make the heart capable of love. The ascent begins here: in the quiet, hidden movements of grace that draw the soul upward into the life of God.

6

From Purification to Illumination

The story traced so far is the story of beginnings. Creation does not commence with light, but with the Spirit moving in silence over the deep. The Fathers delight in this image because it reveals the first truth about God's action: He draws near before He speaks. He hovers, broods, surrounds, enfolds. Nothing comes into being without His presence preparing it. The universe is born in the shadow of His wings.

This same movement repeats itself in the human heart. What God performs on the scale of galaxies, He performs again on the scale of the soul. The Spirit moves across the chaos within, not with reproach but with creative intention. He approaches the darkness not to condemn it but to summon light from it. Purification begins long before the person knows it is happening; the Spirit has already descended, already hovered, already breathed.

This descent is the keynote of the whole first movement: the Spirit is the One who prepares. He orders the disorder of the heart the way He ordered the primeval waters, and the result is the same—life becomes possible where previously nothing could grow. A soul untouched by the Spirit is like earth without light: fertile in potential, barren in practice. Only when the Spirit breathes does the soil come alive.

Humanity was shaped according to this breath. The image speaks of our capacity for God; the likeness speaks of our destiny in God. The image is the imprint of His fingers; the likeness is the imprint of His fire. When sin shattered the likeness, the image remained but dimmed, like a mirror clouded by smoke. The Spirit's first task is to clear that mirror. Not merely to return it to its original condition, but to make it capable of reflecting a greater brightness than Adam ever knew. Purification does not restore humanity to Eden; purification prepares humanity for Christ.

Israel's history reveals this with extraordinary clarity. Every act of God in the Old Testament carries the fragrance of preparation. The Spirit rests upon judges to secure the people, upon kings to shepherd them, upon prophets to call them back to fidelity. In the Temple His presence is veiled in cloud and fire, as if to teach the people that holiness cannot be approached without transformation. Holiness is not an atmosphere; it is a life. It demands hearts that can breathe its air.

Through the prophets, the Spirit unveils His intention: the heart must be remade. Stone must become flesh. Fear must become desire. Law must become communion. The purification God wills is not cosmetic—it is ontological. It is not the upgrade of moral behaviour but the re-creation of the interior world where desire, reason, memory, and will live and move. Only God can do this work. Only the Spirit can enter this depth.

When the prophets speak of a new heart, they are announcing nothing less than the beginning of a new creation. They proclaim that the same Spirit who moved over the waters will move again over humanity itself. The movement from formlessness to form, from void to fullness, from darkness to light, will unfold within the soul as surely as it once unfolded within the cosmos.

Yet this purification is not clinical. It is personal. The Spirit does not approach the soul as a surgeon approaches a wound, but as a lover approaches the beloved. He enters with patience, not interruption. He reveals with gentleness, not shock. He loosens attachments by making the soul desire something greater, not by tearing away what it clings to. The desert tradition is clear: it is love that frees, not fear. Tears flow because the heart has glimpsed beauty, not because it has been threatened with judgment.

Under His touch, the soul awakens to truth. It sees both its fragility and its dignity. It recognises its need and its calling. It becomes capable of repentance—not the shallow remorse that mourns consequences, but the profound turning that returns the soul to God. Repentance is the Spirit bending the heart back toward its source. It is the slow uncoiling of everything that has twisted desire away from the good.

This bending is the first step of ascent. The soul begins to rise as soon as it seeks God. Not because its effort is strong, but because the Spirit is already lifting. Divinity does not wait for perfection; it responds to longing. A single genuine movement of the heart initiates the ascent, because the ascent is not a human achievement but a divine drawing.

As the Spirit draws, the soul becomes integrated. The interior world that once felt divided begins to find harmony. The passions no longer run wild; they begin to serve love. Anger protects what is holy instead of defending ego. Desire reaches upward instead of spiralling inward. Sadness opens the heart to compassion instead of collapsing it in on itself. Even fear becomes wise, guarding the soul from sin rather than guarding sin from God. The Spirit does not destroy the passions; He transfigures them.

Transfiguration unfolds gradually, often quietly. The miracle is not in sudden ecstasies but in the steady reordering of the heart. What was impossible becomes possible. What was once resisted becomes welcomed. What once tasted bitter begins to taste sweet. The Spirit corrects not by violence but by attraction. Grace draws more effectively than force ever could.

This gradual transformation unfolds in light and darkness both. The Spirit sometimes grants consolations—moments when the soul senses His nearness with undeniable clarity. At other times He withdraws sensible warmth so that the soul may learn to cling to God Himself rather than to the feelings God gives. Both movements purify. Both teach. Both strengthen desire. The soul learns to love God in faith, which is the only way to love Him eternally.

Through this entire journey, purification continues to reveal its nature: it is not punishment but preparation. It prepares the soul for a glory it cannot yet receive. It removes the debris that would suffocate divine life. It clears the sanctuary where God intends to dwell. Its purpose is not destruction but enlargement. The soul becomes spacious—capable of God.

Once the soul is capable of God, a new horizon opens. The Spirit who has descended into the depths now begins to lift the heart toward heights it has never known. The movements of purification have created a hunger, a humility, a longing that can finally receive illumination. Illumination is not an abstract light; it is a personal light. It is the radiance of Christ, given through the Spirit, making the believer able to see with the eyes of the Son.

Christ stands at the centre of this transition, not as a distant exemplar but as the living fulfillment of everything the Spirit has prepared. His humanity is the first fully purified heart, the first fully illumined mind, the first fully Spirit-filled life. The Father reveals Himself through the Son, and the Spirit makes this revelation interior. Illumination is participation in Christ's own knowledge of the Father—His wisdom, His discernment, His compassion, His steadfastness, His obedience.

This is why the entire journey of purification bends toward the mystery of Jesus. Creation prepares for Him; Israel longs for Him; prophecy announces Him; repentance opens the heart to Him. The Spirit purifies so that Christ may be known. Not as an idea, but as a presence. Not as a memory, but as a life within. Purification clears the eyes; illumination lets the soul behold what those eyes were made to see.

The soul that has yielded to purification becomes capable of receiving the anointing of the Messiah. The Spirit who hovered over the waters now rests upon the humanity of Jesus. The Spirit who overshadowed the deep now overshadows the Virgin. The Spirit who moved the prophets now speaks through the Son. Everything the Spirit once prepared from afar He will now accomplish from within Christ's own flesh. Illumination is the discovery that the light of God has a human face.

This is the moment toward which all purification moves: the encounter with the Spirit-filled humanity of Jesus. The soul prepared by repentance becomes the soul capable of receiving His gaze, His word, His breath. The Spirit who cleansed now reveals. The Spirit who humbled now lifts. The Spirit who awakened longing now satisfies it.

Purification has led the soul to the threshold. Illumination is the crossing. The Spirit who worked in the depths of creation and the depths of the heart now reveals the depths of Christ. And the soul, made ready, begins to recognise the One for whom it was fashioned from the beginning.

II

The Spirit Who Anoints (Illumination)

7

The Spirit of the Messiah: Christ's Anointing

Israel waited for the Messiah with a longing that reached deeper than political hope and broader than national desire. What the people yearned for, often without fully grasping it, was the One upon whom the Spirit would rest. The prophets had spoken of Him with a clarity that sharpened with every generation. Isaiah described Him not merely as a future king, but as the man permeated by the Spirit: "The Spirit of the Lord shall rest upon Him, the Spirit of wisdom and understanding, the Spirit of counsel and might, the Spirit of knowledge and the fear of the Lord." The Messiah would not simply *have* the Spirit; He would be the One *in whom the Spirit dwells without measure*. Every anointing in Israel's history pointed beyond itself—toward the day when God would anoint a man not with oil, but with His own divine breath.

This expectation lived at the heart of Israel's Scriptures. Every judge empowered to rescue the people was a shadow of the true Deliverer who would act in the Spirit's strength. Every king anointed with oil was an imperfect sign of the One who would receive the Spirit's fullness. Every prophet who spoke with divine fire prefigured the One whose humanity would become the perfect instrument of revelation. The history of Israel was a procession of partial lights leading toward the One Light that would not fade. The Spirit touched many, rested on few, and filled none completely—until the Messiah came.

The longing was not only historical; it was existential. Israel experienced the limits of human strength, the fragility of human fidelity, the insufficiency of human wisdom. Kings failed. Priests became corrupt. Prophets were ignored or persecuted. The people oscillated between covenant faithfulness and idolatry. Beneath all these failures lay one deep truth: humanity could not save itself. The human heart, wounded and wandering, needed more than commandments or institutions. It needed the Spirit it had lost. The Messiah was awaited not merely as a ruler but as a vessel—the One through whom the Spirit would return.

The prophets sensed this intimately. They spoke of the Messiah's coming in the same breath as the return of God's Spirit. Isaiah 42 describes the Servant in words that shimmer with tenderness: "I have put My Spirit upon Him; He will bring forth justice to the nations." The Messiah will be gentle yet unbreakable, humble yet victorious, because He moves not by human calculation but by divine empowerment. Isaiah 61 brings this revelation to its crescendo: "The Spirit of the Lord God is upon me, because the Lord has anointed me." The Messiah's identity is inseparable from His anointing; His mission flows from His filling.

This is why Israel longed not simply for a saviour but for a Spirit-filled saviour. A merely political liberator would not satisfy the ache of the heart, nor cure the wound of sin, nor heal the disorder of desire. The one thing Israel lacked was the one thing it could not give itself: the indwelling Spirit. Without Him, the Law remained external, wisdom remained partial, and the heart remained divided. The Messiah was awaited as the turning point of all this—the moment when humanity would again breathe with the breath of God.

That longing reaches its mysterious fulfillment in the quietest of scenes, far from the centre of power, in a town forgotten by empires. The angel's greeting to Mary contains the first explicit revelation of the new creation: "The Holy Spirit will come upon you, and the power of the Most High will overshadow you." These words echo the poetry of Genesis. Once again the Spirit moves over a formless place. Once again He prepares the conditions for divine life. The overshadowing of Mary is the new hovering over the waters. The Spirit who shaped the cosmos now shapes the humanity of Christ.

This moment is the beginning of the Messiah's anointing—not at the Jordan, but in the womb. The humanity of Jesus is conceived, formed, and sustained by the Spirit. The Fathers insist on this: Christ does not receive the Spirit later as a gift foreign to Him. He receives the Spirit as the one whose human nature has been fashioned in the Spirit's fire from its first instant. What Adam lost, Christ receives; what Adam squandered, Christ fulfills. His humanity is the first fully Spirit-filled humanity in history. Not a borrowed anointing. Not a temporary empowerment. A permanent indwelling.

This is why the Incarnation is already Pentecost in seed. The Spirit does not come and go; He dwells and forms. The flesh of Christ is not a neutral vessel but a chalice filled with divine life. His mind, His desires, His affections, His human will are all movements of a humanity alive in the Spirit. There is no moment of His earthly life untouched by this mystery. He grows in wisdom and stature not through natural development alone but under the shaping presence of the Spirit. Every breath He draws is in communion with the One who overshadowed His conception.

Israel's longing, therefore, reaches its answer not in a spectacle of power but in the hidden sanctity of a young woman's assent. The Spirit who had prepared creation, prepared Israel, and prepared the human heart now prepares the humanity of God's own Son. This is the anointing before all anointings—the secret beginning of a mission that will one day break open in the Jordan. The Messiah does not become Spirit-bearing at baptism; baptism reveals the Spirit-bearing One to the world.

In this hidden beginning lies the key to understanding Christ's mission. He does not act as an isolated individual but as the man whose humanity is transparent to the Spirit. Everything He will later teach flows from the light the Spirit gives Him. Everything He will suffer is embraced through the strength the Spirit provides. Everything He will offer is offered "through the eternal Spirit." The Incarnation is the wellspring of this mystery.

The chapter now stands ready to unfold into the public unveiling of this anointing—when the Spirit who formed Christ in secrecy will descend upon Him in visible glory at the Jordan.

When Jesus emerges from Nazareth and walks toward the Jordan, the quiet fire that has filled His humanity from conception becomes ready to be disclosed. For thirty hidden years, the Spirit has fashioned His interior world—His affections, His discernment, His human freedom. Nothing in those years is wasted; nothing is incidental. The solitude of Nazareth is itself a work of the Spirit, preparing the heart of Christ to carry the weight of the world. The long silence surrounding His early life is not emptiness but gestation. The Spirit shapes Him in obscurity the way He shaped creation in darkness, and the hour of unveiling approaches with a gravity that creation itself seems to sense.

The baptism of Jesus is not an act of repentance—He has no sin to confess—but the moment in which the Spirit-bearing humanity of Christ is revealed. John the Baptist, standing in the river as the final prophet of the old covenant, senses the inversion of roles: "I need to be baptised by You." Yet Jesus steps into the waters, not to be cleansed, but to consecrate them. The One who will baptise "with the Holy Spirit and fire" descends into the depths to sanctify the waters that will one day sanctify humanity.

What happens next is the eruption of the hidden Trinity into visibility. As Jesus rises from the water, the heavens are opened—a phrase that echoes Isaiah's cry, "Oh, that You would rend the heavens and come down." The Spirit descends "in bodily form like a dove." This is not sentimental imagery. The Fathers see in the dove the sign of new creation, recalling Noah's flood and the olive branch carried back over waters washed clean. The dove is a symbol of peace, gentleness, and creative renewal. Its descent upon Christ reveals that the chaos of sin is about to be undone, and the new creation is beginning—not in the cosmos this time, but in the humanity of Jesus.

The descent of the Spirit in visible form is not for Christ's sake; it is for ours. It reveals to John, and to Israel, and to the world, that this man is the One long awaited. The Father's voice seals the revelation: "This is my beloved Son, in whom I am well pleased." These words do not bestow identity; they declare it. The Son is eternally beloved; the pleasure of the Father rests upon Him eternally. What is revealed at the Jordan is the inner life of the Trinity breaking into human history. The baptism is a theophany, a manifestation of God's life in time. The Spirit descends, the Father speaks, the Son stands in humble obedience. The Kingdom is present.

But more than this is revealed. The baptism shows that the Spirit who overshadowed Mary now rests upon Jesus in a new manner—as the public seal of His messianic mission. From this moment forward, Christ's ministry will move with a particular clarity: "Jesus, full of the Holy Spirit, returned from the Jordan and was led by the Spirit into the wilderness." The Spirit does not wait for Jesus to act; the Spirit initiates. The desert is not a detour but a deliberate stage in the Spirit's formation of the Messiah's mission. The temptations that follow are not random assaults but the confrontation between the Spirit-filled Christ and the kingdom of darkness. In resisting each temptation, Jesus demonstrates that His humanity is entirely governed by the Spirit.

This government of the Spirit becomes the hallmark of everything Jesus does. When He returns from the desert, Luke makes the connection unmistakable: "Jesus returned in the power of the Spirit." He enters the synagogue at Nazareth and claims His identity by reading from Isaiah 61: "The Spirit of the Lord is upon me, because He has anointed me." This is not metaphor. It is the deepest truth of His human existence. The humanity of Jesus has been shaped, filled, and perfected by the Spirit from its first moment, and now that reality is proclaimed openly. When He rolls up the scroll and sits, He is not merely claiming prophetic authority; He is revealing the inner source of all He will say and do.

This Spirit-anointing explains the astonishing authority of His teaching. When Jesus interprets the Scriptures, He does so not as a scholar arguing from tradition, but as the One whose humanity is illuminated from within by the Spirit. The crowds marvel at His authority because He speaks from a depth that no rabbi had ever possessed. The Spirit reveals the Father to Him and through Him. His parables, His rebukes, His blessings, His silences—each carries the resonance of divine wisdom communicated through a human voice. He does not merely speak in the Spirit; He speaks the words the Spirit gives.

The miracles of Christ also flow from this anointing. When He casts out demons, He does so "by the Spirit of God," announcing the invasion of the Kingdom. When He heals the sick, it is the Spirit restoring creation's proper order—signs that life is stronger than decay. When He raises the dead, it is the Spirit who breathes into lifeless bodies the first fruits of resurrection. These acts are not displays of raw power; they are revelations of what humanity looks like when fully alive in the Spirit. Christ is the new Adam, and the Spirit's touch upon Him is the first sign that creation is being made new.

Even the compassion of Christ is Spirit-born. The Gospels note again and again that He is "moved with compassion." This movement is not emotional volatility; it is the stirring of the Spirit within His human heart. His tears at Lazarus's tomb, His weeping over Jerusalem, His tenderness toward the sinner, His patience with the disciples—these are the human expressions of the divine love poured into His heart by the Spirit, the love that will one day be poured into ours.

What emerges through all these scenes is the fundamental truth that defines the Messiah: the Spirit is not an accessory to His mission; the Spirit is its source. He acts in the Spirit, He speaks in the Spirit, He suffers in the Spirit, He loves in the Spirit. His miracles reveal the Spirit's power, His preaching reveals the Spirit's wisdom, His compassion reveals the Spirit's tenderness, His obedience reveals the Spirit's strength.

And the hour approaches when this Spirit-led obedience will reach its climax, not in public glory but in surrender.

The obedience of Jesus is often imagined as the triumph of a heroic will, standing firm in the face of unbearable burden. Yet the Gospels reveal something far more profound. Christ's obedience is not the achievement of isolated strength; it is the manifestation of a humanity perfectly attuned to the Spirit. His surrender is not stoicism but communion. The Spirit who overshadowed His conception and guided His ministry now shapes every movement of His final ascent toward the Cross. If the miracles reveal the Spirit's power, the Passion reveals the Spirit's love.

This becomes visible from the moment Jesus turns His face toward Jerusalem. Luke notes this with an almost liturgical solemnity: "He set His face." The resoluteness of that phrase does not spring from human grit. It is the Spirit strengthening the humanity of Christ for the hour He has come to embrace. Every prophet who once carried the Word of God bore a portion of this burden; Christ bears the fullness. The Spirit has descended upon Him not only for proclamation but for sacrifice. The Messiah will not save by avoiding suffering but by entering it with the Spirit's fire burning within His heart.

Gethsemane unveils this mystery in its starkest form. Here the humanity of Christ trembles with holy fear. He enters the garden not as an actor following a script, but as a man stepping into the abyss of human misery, carrying every sin, every grief, every cry of every heart. His prayer—"not my will but Yours be done"—is not a declaration of defeat but the Spirit's deepest victory. In this moment the Spirit holds Him, strengthens Him, steadies Him. The obedience He offers is not the crushing of desire but its purification. He allows the Spirit to draw His human will into perfect alignment with the Father's love, even when that love demands the Cross.

Hebrews reveals the inner truth of this scene: "Through the eternal Spirit He offered Himself." This is one of Scripture's most astonishing lines. Christ's sacrifice is not a solitary act. It is a Trinitarian event. The Son offers Himself to the Father, and the Spirit is the bond, the flame, the inner energy of that offering. Augustine saw in this union the very heart of the Trinity: the Father loves the Son, the Son loves the Father, and the Spirit is that love made person. At Calvary, this eternal love passes through the fragile humanity of Christ. The Spirit who has always bound the Son to the Father now binds the humanity of Jesus to that same eternal exchange.

This sheds light on the agony of the garden. The sweat like drops of blood is not the sign of failing courage but of love pushed to its utter limit, love bearing the whole weight of sin through a human heart. The Spirit sustains Him, not by removing suffering but by filling it with divine meaning. His sorrow becomes intercession. His anguish becomes redemption. His silence becomes prayer. What the world sees as collapse is in truth the Spirit strengthening the Messiah to carry humanity's darkness into the blazing holiness of God.

When Jesus rises from prayer and meets His captors, the Spirit's strength becomes visible in His serenity. He rebukes Peter's violence not out of weakness but out of a courage that does not need the sword. He speaks with clarity before the Sanhedrin because the Spirit gives Him the words. He stands silent before Pilate because the Spirit holds Him in a peace beyond fear. He carries His Cross not as a symbol of defeat but as the visible sign of a will surrendered completely to the Spirit's movement. Every step toward Golgotha is an act of obedience suffused with divine fire.

The words spoken from the Cross carry this same fire. When He forgives His executioners, it is the Spirit praying through His humanity. When He promises paradise to the thief, it is the Spirit revealing mercy stronger than death. When He entrusts His mother to the beloved disciple, it is the Spirit shaping the new family of the redeemed. Even His cry of abandonment—"My God, my God, why have You forsaken me?"—is a cry sustained by the Spirit. It reveals the depth of His solidarity with sinners, entering the very places where the human heart feels most distant from God. The Spirit permits Him to drink this cup so that no human suffering will ever be outside His reach.

The final act of His offering comes in a breath: "Father, into Your hands I commend my spirit." This is not resignation but triumph. It is the Son, in His humanity, handing His life back to the Father through the Spirit who has carried Him from the first moment of His Incarnation. He dies as He has lived—in communion. The Spirit who overshadowed Mary now receives the final surrender of the Son. His death is not the extinguishing of life but the giving of life. His last breath is the very breath that will be breathed back into the Church at Pentecost.

Even in the moments following His death, the Spirit's presence remains. The centurion's confession—"Truly this was the Son of God"—is a revelation granted by grace. The rending of the veil signals that the Spirit will no longer remain behind symbols. The opening of Christ's side, from which blood and water flow, reveals the sacraments the Spirit will animate. The silence of Holy Saturday is the stillness before a new creation. The Spirit waits, not in absence, but in readiness.

Everything in Christ's Passion reveals a profound truth: the Spirit is not merely the One who empowers the Messiah's miracles or inspires His teaching. The Spirit is the One who makes His sacrifice possible. The Cross is not simply the obedience of a heroic man—it is the self-offering of a humanity fully yielded to the Spirit's love. Through this obedience the world is saved, not by force but by a fire that burns in perfect union with the Father's will.

And in the darkness of the tomb, the Spirit prepares the next revelation.

The tomb becomes the hidden workshop of the Spirit. In that sealed chamber, where no human eye can witness and no human hand can assist, the same Spirit who overshadowed Mary and descended at the Jordan now enters the silence of death. The Fathers speak of this moment with hushed awe: the Spirit breathes where breath has ceased. He touches the sacred body of Christ from within, for the humanity of Jesus has never existed apart from the Spirit who formed it. Even in death, the bond between Son and Spirit remains unbroken. The descent into death is not a rupture but a profound continuation of the Spirit's work. Where Christ goes, the Spirit goes, because the love that unites them cannot be severed.

Paul captures this mystery with a phrase that shimmers with power:

"the Spirit of Him who raised Jesus from the dead." Resurrection is not merely reversal; it is re-creation. The body that rises is the same and yet transfigured. The humanity of Christ now bears the marks of death, yet those wounds have become windows of glory. This transformation is the work of the Spirit—He does not merely return life; He elevates it. He brings Christ's humanity into the state for which all humanity was destined: incorruptible, radiant, utterly filled with divine life.

This is why the resurrection appearances are marked by both continuity and strangeness. Jesus walks, speaks, eats, and shows His wounds—yet passes through locked doors, appears in unanticipated places, and vanishes from sight. These are not tricks or illusions; they are signs that His humanity now moves according to the freedom of the Spirit. The body of the risen Christ is the first fully Spirit-glorified human body. The disciples encounter a presence that is familiar yet overwhelming, intimate yet majestic. They meet the One they loved, now shining with the life that the Spirit gives.

In these encounters, the anointing of the Messiah reaches its perfection. Everything the Spirit has done in Christ—forming His humanity, empowering His ministry, sustaining His obedience—now bursts forth in visible glory. The resurrection is not simply the vindication of Jesus; it is the revelation of what a Spirit-filled humanity becomes. The Messiah's anointing is no longer hidden or contested. It is manifest. The risen Christ stands as the ultimate testimony that the Spirit's work is stronger than death, stronger than sin, stronger than the ancient curse that bound the human race.

But even this glory is not the final movement. The Messiah rises not to remain alone in His anointing but to share it. On the evening of the resurrection, Jesus appears to the disciples and breathes on them: "Receive the Holy Spirit." This gesture is deliberate and divine. The breath that formed Adam is now the breath that forms the new humanity. Christ gives the Spirit because His mission is to make others what He is: Spirit-bearing children of the Father. He is the firstborn from the dead, not the only born. His anointing is unique in its fullness, but its purpose is to overflow.

What He has received without measure, He will pour out without reserve. Pentecost is already promised in this breath. The Spirit who has shaped Christ's humanity will soon shape the Church. The fire that filled the Messiah will soon fill His disciples. The anointing that empowered His words, His miracles, His compassion, and His sacrifice will soon empower theirs. Christ's entire mission points toward this moment when the Spirit who rests upon Him becomes the inheritance of His people.

This is why the forty days between resurrection and ascension are marked by teaching. Luke tells us Jesus spoke to them about the Kingdom, but the content of that teaching is inseparable from the Spirit. The risen Christ prepares His disciples not to admire Him from a distance but to receive the same life that animates His glorified humanity. He tells them plainly: "You will be clothed with power from on high." The language is striking. The Spirit is not given as an optional devotional supplement; He is given as clothing, as the garment of the new creation. The disciples will wear what Christ Himself wears—the mantle of divine fire.

The ascension itself reveals the Spirit's next movement. As Christ is lifted into the glory of the Father, He ascends not to depart but to share. His humanity, now fully Spirit-filled, enters the heavenly sanctuary as the first-fruits of the new creation. The Spirit accompanies Him even here, for the unity of Son and Spirit is eternal. The human nature of Jesus is brought into the heart of the Trinity, and in this exaltation the path is opened for all humanity. The Spirit who glorified Christ will glorify those who belong to Him.

And so, Christ sends His disciples back to Jerusalem with a single promise burning in their hearts: "You will receive power when the Holy Spirit has come upon you." The language echoes Isaiah's prophecy of the Messiah Himself. The same Spirit who rested upon the Son will rest upon them. The same Spirit who filled Christ's humanity will fill theirs. The Messiah's anointing becomes the Church's anointing. What Christ received as Son, He gives as Lord.

In this light, the entire mystery of Christ's anointing becomes clear. The Spirit is not a companion to His mission; the Spirit is its inner life. The Spirit is not an intermittent visitor; the Spirit is the atmosphere of His humanity. The Spirit shapes Him, strengthens Him, teaches Him, consoles Him, empowers Him, and raises Him. The Messiah is the Spirit-filled One, the human life fully alive because it is fully surrendered.

And this is the mystery that now stands before the believer. Christ's anointing is not a spectacle to admire but a destiny to receive. The Spirit who rested upon Him is the Spirit who comes at Pentecost. The Spirit who fashioned His obedience will fashion ours. The Spirit who filled His heart with compassion will fill ours. The Spirit who raised Him from the dead will raise us. The Messiah's anointing does not remain His alone; it becomes the pattern and promise of every Christian life.

The chapter thus rests in the quiet splendour of this truth: the Spirit who moved in creation, who spoke through the prophets, who rested upon the Messiah, will soon descend again—this time not upon one man, but upon the whole Church. The fire that filled Christ will become the fire that fills the world.

8

The Spirit Who Illuminates: Jesus Teaching in the Spirit

When Christ speaks, something in the human heart recognises a depth it has never encountered before. The crowds sense it without being able to explain it. Fishermen leave their nets. Scholars fall silent. Hearts burn. Children draw near. Even His opponents feel the weight of His words, though they resist them. The Gospels repeatedly note this strange authority—not loud, not forceful, not theatrical, yet irresistible. "He taught as one having authority, and not as the scribes." Something more than human eloquence is at work. The voice that speaks is the voice of a man fully alive, fully transparent to the Spirit.

Christ's teaching does not rise from intellectual brilliance alone, though His intellect is unsullied by ignorance and sharpened by perfect virtue. It arises from communion. His wisdom is not the product of study but of union. The Spirit who overshadowed His conception and descended upon Him at the Jordan now fills His human mind with the light of divine knowledge. He sees the Father not through concepts but through immediate intimacy. What He knows, He knows by participation. And what He speaks, He speaks from the place where divine truth has entered human speech.

This is why His words have such purity and power. The Spirit is not merely assisting Christ's teaching; the Spirit is its inner energy. The humanity of Jesus is the instrument, the Spirit the musician. Every parable, every rebuke, every blessing, every silence comes from this shared life. The words that fall from His lips are not borrowed wisdom. They are the fruit of a human mind wholly illuminated from within. He teaches as the One who rests eternally in the Father's embrace, and the Spirit communicates that vision into the contours of His human thought.

The prophets had sensed this coming. Isaiah spoke of the Messiah in terms that captured this interior brightness: "The Spirit of the Lord shall rest upon Him—the Spirit of wisdom and understanding, the Spirit of counsel and might, the Spirit of knowledge and the fear of the Lord." These gifts, scattered like sparks among the prophets and saints of the Old Testament, converge like a single flame in the humanity of Jesus. He possesses wisdom because the Spirit breathes wisdom in Him. He understands because the Spirit illumines His understanding. He counsels because the Spirit guides His every choice. He is strong because the Spirit strengthens His human will. His knowledge of the Father is radiant because the Spirit opens that knowledge within His humanity.

When He walks among the people, this radiance becomes visible. Not in spectacle, but in simplicity. He sees the interiority of the human heart with penetrating clarity—not to expose but to heal. He recognises faith where others see only emptiness. He forgives where others condemn. He honours trust where others see naivety. He welcomes the sinner without excusing the sin. The Spirit reveals to Him not merely what people do, but who they are. He reads the heart with the gentleness of one who dwells in the Father's love and the strength of one who has come to restore the heart to that love.

This interior illumination shapes His every encounter. When the rich young man approaches Him with earnest desire, Jesus looks at him "and loved him." That gaze is the Spirit's gaze, seeing beyond the man's question into the longing that shaped it. When the woman caught in adultery stands trembling before Him, He sees in her not only guilt but the possibility of renewal. When Zacchaeus hides in the tree, ashamed and curious, Christ sees the heart seeking salvation before it knows what salvation is. His knowledge is personal because the Spirit reveals persons, not merely actions. His teaching is living because the Spirit's light is alive within Him.

The Beatitudes offer perhaps the clearest manifestation of this illumination. They are not moral slogans or poetic ideals; they are the description of a world seen through the Spirit's eyes. To declare the poor blessed, the meek exalted, the persecuted joyful—this is not the logic of fallen humanity. It is the logic of divine love entering human perception. Christ teaches what He sees, and what He sees is the Kingdom. His human vision is suffused with the Spirit's light, and He invites His disciples into that same vision, not as a distant ideal but as an attainable participation in His own way of seeing.

This is why His teaching awakens both recognition and resistance. Recognition in the humble, who sense the truth resonating in their hearts. Resistance in the proud, who sense that truth dismantles their illusions. Illumination exposes. It reveals the architecture of the heart. It unveils the motives behind actions, the desires behind choices, the fears behind hesitations. Christ's words penetrate because they are spoken in the Spirit, and the Spirit searches all things. When Christ speaks, the Spirit shines through His words like light through stained glass—gentle, colourful, beautiful, but unmistakably divine.

Even His silences are filled with illumination. The Spirit governs not only His speech but His restraint. He refuses to answer certain questions not from ignorance or evasion but because the heart before Him cannot yet bear the truth. He withdraws to pray because the

Spirit draws Him into deeper intimacy with the Father, and from that intimacy His teaching flows. He pauses before healing because the Spirit prepares the moment. He speaks in parables because the Spirit knows that truth must be revealed in a way that provokes desire, not merely satisfies curiosity.

The parables, in particular, reveal the unique character of Christ's illumination. They are not riddles but invitations—windows that open into the Kingdom. They reveal truth by concealing it, turning the heart into a seeker. They offer images capable of growing with the listener, capable of unfolding into deeper meanings as the Spirit prepares the soul. A parable is not understood because the mind is clever but because the heart is receptive. It is grasped only when the Spirit awakens spiritual sight.

This is why Christ ends so many parables with the piercing refrain: "He who has ears to hear, let him hear." He does not mean, "Let the intelligent decipher the puzzle." He means, "Let the Spirit grant you the inner hearing needed to receive the truth." Illumination is not a matter of decoding symbols; it is a matter of receiving light.

And the disciples, watching and listening, begin to sense that they are standing before a wisdom unlike anything they have known—a wisdom gentle enough for children and vast enough for eternity.

The disciples often stand bewildered in the presence of this luminous wisdom. They walk with Christ, hear His parables, witness His miracles, and yet remain strangely incapable of entering the meaning that seems so clear and effortless for Him. They grasp fragments but never the whole. The pieces scatter in their minds like seeds cast on stone. They see but do not perceive; they hear but do not understand. Their confusion is not a sign of stupidity but a sign of humanity still waiting to be filled with the Spirit.

Christ does not mock their slowness. He recognises it as the natural human condition before illumination. To understand divine truth, the soul must be prepared and opened. The heart must be softened, the intellect purified, the will attuned. Illumination is not granted as information but as communion. It is a gift, and the gift cannot be forced. This is why Christ often concludes His teaching not with explanation but with prayer. He entrusts His words to the Spirit, confident that the time will come when they will ignite within the disciples as fire.

This dynamic becomes clearest in the Upper Room. The air is thick with sorrow, fear, and confusion. Christ speaks of His departure, of betrayal, of suffering, of glory, and the disciples sit like children overhearing a conversation in another language. They sense the weight of what He says but cannot penetrate its meaning. Christ addresses this directly: "I have yet many things to say to you, but you cannot bear them now." The limitation does not lie in His teaching but in their capacity. The truth would overwhelm them if given without preparation. Illumination requires the Spirit.

He promises them precisely that: "The Holy Spirit…will teach you all things and bring to your remembrance all that I have said to you." Christ does not imagine that His words will be forgotten. He knows they will be remembered—but without the Spirit they will remain like unopened seeds, dormant and inert. The Spirit is the one who causes the memory to bloom into understanding. The Spirit does not add new doctrine; the Spirit reveals the depths of the doctrine already spoken. What Christ teaches openly, the Spirit teaches inwardly.

In this promise, the entire future of the Church is hidden. Every homily, every theological insight, every saint's commentary, every moment of spiritual enlightenment—these are not advancements beyond Christ but entries into Christ, made possible by the Spirit who illumines from within. Theology is simply the slow unfolding of Christ's words under the breath of the Spirit. Spiritual growth is the gradual yielding of the heart to the light that Christ already revealed.

The fullness has already been spoken; illumination is the grace of hearing it.

This inner teaching of the Spirit is not a private vision detached from the humanity of Christ. The Spirit does not lead the disciple beyond the Gospel but deeper into it. The Spirit does not bypass Christ to reveal hidden secrets; the Spirit opens the disciple's eyes to the secrets hidden *in* Christ. "He will take what is mine," Jesus says, "and declare it to you." This is the logic of illumination: the Spirit leads the believer into Christ's own knowledge of the Father. The disciple comes to see as Christ sees, love as Christ loves, and trust as Christ trusts.

The difference between pre-Pentecost and post-Pentecost discipleship lies entirely here. Before Pentecost, the disciples hear Christ's words with natural ears. After Pentecost, they hear with hearts made luminous by the Spirit. Before Pentecost, they interpret Christ through the lens of their own expectations. After Pentecost, they interpret their expectations through the lens of Christ. The Spirit transforms not the content of Christ's teaching but the capacity of the disciples to receive it.

This change is dramatic. Those who once argued about greatness now preach about self-emptying love. Those who once fled from danger now embrace martyrdom. Those who struggled to understand the parables now teach them with clarity and conviction. Illumination is not superior intelligence; it is the mind transfigured by the Spirit. The fisherman becomes a theologian, the tax collector an evangelist, the doubter a missionary. The Spirit does not erase personality; the Spirit elevates it.

This explains why Christ speaks in ways that both reveal and conceal. His words meet people where they are, but they wait patiently for the Spirit to complete the work. A parable is a seed that refuses to sprout without sunlight. Christ plants; the Spirit shines. Christ forms the question; the Spirit shapes the answer. Christ awakens desire; the Spirit fulfils it. Without this cooperation, the Gospel would be a mere text. With it, the Gospel becomes the living Word.

The illumination Christ offers is not merely intellectual. It involves the whole person. When He teaches, He calls the heart into conversion, the will into freedom, the imagination into wonder. He does not offer abstractions; He offers life. "Learn from Me," He says, not "Study Me." To learn from Him is to enter His relationship with the Father through the Spirit. His teaching is not simply a message but a way of seeing—a way of being.

This becomes especially clear in how He teaches prayer. He gives the Our Father not as a formula but as an invitation to share His own posture before the Father. The Spirit is the breath in this prayer. The Spirit forms the cry of "Abba." Christ teaches the words, but the Spirit teaches the intimacy. Prayer is the most explicit case of illumination: it is the moment where Christ's teaching and the Spirit's indwelling meet within the believer. The words of Christ become the experience of the disciple through the Spirit.

Those who follow Him sense this illumination even before they understand it. They know that their hearts burn when He speaks, though they cannot yet articulate why. They realise that His words resonate like music from a forgotten homeland. They cling to Him because they feel the light within Him, a light they cannot yet contain. Their desire precedes their understanding. Illumination always begins as longing.

And Christ, knowing this, speaks to them with patience. He does not force comprehension. He trusts the Spirit to complete the work. The seed is planted; the light will come.

The Gospels reveal that Christ's wisdom is not simply superior; it is of a different order entirely. He teaches as one who knows the Father from within the very life of the Trinity. The Spirit is the atmosphere of that knowledge, the inner light in which the Son eternally beholds the Father. When Christ speaks, He draws on this inexhaustible well. The disciples sense the strangeness of this authority. It does not resemble the scribes who cite traditions or the philosophers who refine arguments. Christ speaks with the serenity of someone who is at home in truth. The source of this serenity is the Spirit.

This is why His teaching always produces a double effect. For some, it clarifies; for others, it confuses. The same ray illumines and blinds depending on the state of the eye. Christ's words reveal God, yet they also reveal the condition of the hearer. His teaching is like fire: it warms those who welcome it and scorches those who resist it. This dual effect is not intentional cruelty but the natural consequence of divine light encountering the human heart. Light exposes. Light judges. Light heals. The Spirit is this light, moving through the words of Christ.

Consider the Sermon on the Mount. The words are simple enough for a child to memorise, yet deep enough to occupy the meditation of saints for centuries. Christ's teaching does not operate on a single level. It speaks to the surface and to the depths simultaneously. The Spirit accomplishes this. Every sentence becomes a doorway into divine life, but the doorway opens only as widely as the heart allows. Illumination is not imposed; it is invited.

A similar pattern emerges in Christ's parables. They are not riddles meant to frustrate but mysteries meant to awaken hunger. A parable is a compressed world, crafted with the precision of a poet and the vision of a prophet. It hides truth in order to stir desire, because only desire can receive revelation properly. The Spirit uses the parable to draw the soul out of spiritual laziness. Those who merely listen hear a story. Those who yearn for truth open the story like a seed. Christ Himself explains this dynamic: "To you has been given the secret of the Kingdom…but to those outside everything is in parables."

Illumination is grace.

The Spirit is the one who makes the parable bloom into meaning. When the disciples later ask Christ to explain, He does not reveal a secondary teaching. He simply unfolds the logic already hidden within the story. After Pentecost, they no longer need to ask. The Spirit interiorises the parables. He transforms them from words remembered into truths inhabited. The soil of their hearts has changed; it now bears fruit.

This inner illumination becomes unmistakable in the resurrection narratives. Christ appears to the disciples on the road to Emmaus and opens the Scriptures to them. He does not introduce new ideas; He reveals the unity of God's plan, a unity invisible without the Spirit. Their hearts burn while He speaks, yet they still do not fully understand until "He opens their minds" to grasp the Scriptures. The opening of the mind is the work of the Spirit.

The same moment unfolds again in the Upper Room. Christ breathes on them and says, "Receive the Holy Spirit." This breath echoes the breath of Genesis and anticipates the wind of Pentecost. Illumination is inseparable from this breath. Christ's teaching is not complete until the Spirit fills the disciples with the same light that fills Him. Only then do His words acquire their full force within them. Only then does understanding become participation.

The Spirit's work is not limited to insight. Illumination always moves toward transformation. The goal is not to comprehend the truth but to be shaped by it. Christ's teaching is performative: it accomplishes what it reveals. When He says, "Blessed are the meek," He is not describing certain personalities. He is revealing what the Spirit will form in those who cling to Him. When He says, "Love your enemies," He is not proposing an ethical challenge alone. He is summoning the believer into the very generosity of the Father—a generosity only possible in the Spirit.

THE SPIRIT WHO ILLUMINATES: JESUS TEACHING IN THE SPIRIT

The Sermon on the Mount is therefore not an ideal to admire but a promise to receive. Its demands exceed human strength precisely so that the believer will learn to rely on the Spirit. Christ does not teach a morality for the unaided soul; He teaches a way of life that requires the Spirit's indwelling. This is illumination: the capacity to live the truth one sees.

Even Christ's corrections carry this logic. When He rebukes the Pharisees, He does so because their refusal to receive the Spirit makes them unable to see. They cling to the letter of the Law without its breath. The Law is divine, yet without the Spirit it becomes an idol. Christ exposes this not to condemn but to liberate. He restores the Law to its fullness by returning it to the Spirit who inspired it. Illumination restores what legalism disfigures.

At the same time, Christ is patient with those who struggle. He praises the centurion who sees with surprising clarity yet gently guides Thomas who cannot believe without touching. Illumination is not uniform. Some hearts open quickly; others slowly. The Spirit works with the rhythm of each soul. Christ trusts this rhythm. He gives what the disciples can bear. He knows the dawn is coming.

This is why Christ often teaches in silence as much as in speech. He withdraws to pray, spends nights in communion with the Father, remains quiet before accusers, writes on the ground before speaking to the adulterous woman. Silence is the Spirit's first language. Those who watch Him learn that illumination is never rushed. The Spirit moves gently, yet with irresistible strength. Christ's silence forms His disciples as deeply as His words.

Illumination reaches its high point in love. Christ teaches this directly: "If anyone loves Me, he will keep My word, and My Father will love him, and We will come to him and make Our home in him." The home Christ describes is the heart illumined by the Spirit. Understanding is not the condition of love; love is the condition of understanding. The Spirit is the Love who makes this possible.

Christ's teaching is therefore not simply instruction; it is invitation into the life of the Trinity. Illumination is the disciple's entry into that life. The Spirit draws the believer into the vision the Son has of the Father. Nothing less is offered. Nothing less is given.

Illumination takes on its fullest clarity when Christ tells the disciples that His departure is not a loss but a gift. "It is to your advantage that I go away," He says, a sentence that would have sounded absurd to those who had built their entire lives on His physical presence. Yet Christ insists because He sees a deeper truth: the Spirit who dwells in Him will soon dwell in them. His presence will no longer be beside them but within them. The intimacy they know will not diminish; it will deepen.

This is the heartbeat of illumination. It does not reach its maturity while Christ stands before them in visible form. It begins when the Spirit forms Christ within them in invisible power. The Spirit takes everything the Son is—His wisdom, His obedience, His meekness, His strength, His vision of the Father—and imprints it into the fabric of the disciple's being. Illumination is this imprint. It is the dawning awareness that the life of Christ is gradually overtaking one's own.

Christ explains this in rich, almost tender language. "He will guide you into all truth…He will declare to you the things that are to come." Guidance, not pressure. Declaration, not coercion. The Spirit's illumination is not the flashing of heavenly data across the mind. It is the gentle but steadfast formation of the heart into the likeness of Christ. He reveals truth not only by showing it but by shaping the one who sees it. Illumination is recognition: the soul begins to delight in what Christ delights in, to reject what Christ rejects, to hope as Christ hopes.

This is why the illumination of the Spirit always carries a moral weight. Truth is never given to the soul as spectacle. Divine truth is given so that the soul may walk in it. Christ expresses this through the image of light: "The one who walks in darkness does not know where he is going." Illumination is the gift that restores direction. It is the grace by which the believer learns to move through the world with the steady confidence of one who sees by a light that does not come from himself. The Spirit makes this possible.

Here the early Church Fathers speak with remarkable unity. Origen describes the Spirit as the "interpreter of Christ," the one who unlocks the inner meaning of His teachings. Augustine says the Spirit is "the interior Master," teaching from within what Christ teaches from without. Basil calls the Spirit "the place of the saints," because illumination makes the soul spacious enough for God. These are not poetic exaggerations. They name the concrete reality the first Christians experienced: the Spirit made Christ's words come alive.

This experience becomes especially vivid in the Acts of the Apostles. Peter, who once stumbled through Christ's teaching, now interprets the Scriptures with precision and boldness. He proclaims Joel's prophecy with a clarity he never possessed before Pentecost. Stephen speaks with a wisdom the crowds "could not withstand," not because he is clever, but because he is Spirit-filled. Paul, schooled in the Law yet blinded to its fulfillment, receives illumination not from intellectual training but from the Spirit who reveals Christ to him. In each case, the pattern holds: illumination is the fruit of the Spirit.

The apostolic preaching reveals another aspect of illumination: courage. Understanding the truth and proclaiming it require different graces. The apostles do both because the Spirit gives both. Illumination strengthens the mind and fortifies the will. It gives the disciple the calm conviction that truth is not fragile, that truth carries its own authority, that truth does not depend on human eloquence to prevail. This courage flows from the Spirit who makes the soul steadfast.

Yet illumination is not triumphal. It often begins in weakness, confusion, and humility. The disciple must come to the end of his own understanding before he can receive the mind of Christ. The Spirit brings the soul into this poverty gently. He allows the limits of natural thought to become visible. He invites surrender—not surrender of reason, but surrender of pride. Illumination grows in the soil of humility. The soul learns to say, "Speak, Lord, for your servant is listening," and the Spirit answers.

The fruit of this humility is discernment. Christ speaks often of false prophets, false messiahs, false signs, and false wisdom. The Spirit equips the disciple to distinguish what belongs to God from what merely imitates Him. Illumination is therefore not only the reception of truth but the purification of perception. The noisy voices of the age lose their glamour. The soul recognises the difference between the glamour of novelty and the simplicity of divine wisdom. The Spirit trains the heart to prefer what is eternal.

One of the deepest expressions of illumination appears in the Beatitudes. These blessings are not ethical achievements; they are windows into the mind of Christ. The poor in spirit, the meek, those who hunger for righteousness—these are the dispositions formed by the Spirit. The Beatitudes are the lens through which the illuminated disciple sees the world. They transform vision. They reveal that holiness is not an extraordinary rarity but the normal condition of a soul filled with the Spirit.

Illumination culminates in love. Paul names charity as the greatest of the Spirit's gifts because only love unites the knower with the known. Knowledge without love remains external; love brings the truth into the marrow of the soul. This is why John, the disciple who rested on Christ's heart, speaks so simply: "You have no need that anyone should teach you; His anointing teaches you everything." John does not dismiss teachers; he emphasises the source. Illumination is the anointing of the Spirit—a knowledge warmed by love.

When Christ ascends, the disciples finally understand what He meant when He called the Spirit "another Helper." They realise that illumination is companionship. The Spirit walks with them, prays within them, consoles them, corrects them, strengthens them. He does not replace Christ. He brings Christ to life within them. He is the Teacher who never leaves.

Illumination is therefore not a phase but a lifelong reality. The Spirit continues to unveil Christ until the believer sees Him face to face. Every insight, every moment of clarity, every movement of prayer, every experience of Scripture opening from within—these are glimpses of the eternal light that will one day flood the soul without shadow.

The flame that burned in Christ now burns in His disciples. The light by which He walked now becomes the light by which they walk. Illumination is the Spirit's greatest gift in this life: the gift of seeing everything in the light of Christ.

9

The Spirit and the Cross: The Fire of Love

The closer one draws to Calvary, the more the mystery deepens. Everything in the life of Christ has been steeped in the Spirit from the first moment: His conception in Mary's womb, His baptism in the Jordan, His preaching in Galilee, His tenderness toward the poor and the broken. Yet when the Gospels lead us toward His Passion, the Spirit seems to fall silent. The scene darkens. The language becomes sparse. Christ appears alone. But this apparent silence is not absence—it is depth. The Spirit is not withdrawn from Christ; the Spirit descends with Him into the heart of suffering.

Hebrews makes this explicit: Christ "offered Himself *through the eternal Spirit.*" Those words are among the most overlooked in the New Testament, yet they open the inner sanctuary of divine love. The Cross is not the solitary endurance of a heroic man. It is the self-offering of the Son to the Father in the communion of the Spirit. Every movement of Christ's Passion is carried, sustained, and filled by the Spirit who is the Love shared eternally between Father and Son. Calvary is not merely the place of atonement; it is the place where the Trinity is revealed in its deepest act.

Christ hangs on the tree not by human strength but by divine love.

The nails hold His body, but the Spirit holds His will. The anguish of Gethsemane shows the cost of this obedience. Christ's prayer—"not My will, but Yours be done"—is not stoic resignation. It is the human will of Jesus opening itself completely to the Spirit who forms in Him the perfect surrender of the Son. The Church Fathers insist that Christ's agony is real. His fear is real. His shrinking back from suffering is real. Yet His obedience is more real still, because the Spirit strengthens His humanity with the very love that unites Him eternally to the Father.

In this sense, the Passion reveals the Spirit's most hidden work. Throughout Christ's ministry the Spirit acts visibly: descending like a dove, driving Him into the desert, filling Him with wisdom and wonder-working power. At the Cross, the Spirit acts interiorly, sustaining Christ's love at the moment when every human instinct falls into collapse. The Spirit is the fire that keeps the sacrifice burning. The Spirit is the breath that fills Christ's final exhalation. The Spirit is the strength hidden inside weakness.

Augustine's insight becomes luminous here. For him, the Spirit is the *nexus amoris*—the bond of love between Father and Son. If this is true, then the Cross is the supreme revelation of the Spirit's identity. The Son offers Himself to the Father *in* the Spirit because love cannot be offered without love. The giver, the gift, and the giving are united in this moment of outpouring. The Father receives the Son's total surrender, and the Spirit is the surrender. The Spirit carries the Son's obedience into the heart of the Father. Calvary is the Trinity bending toward the world in mercy.

This Trinitarian vision changes the way we approach Christ's suffering. The Cross is not God demanding blood to appease wrath. The Cross is God giving God. The Father gives the Son. The Son gives Himself. The Spirit gives the love by which the Son offers Himself. The sacrifice is not imposed; it is given freely. "No one takes My life from Me," Christ says, "I lay it down of My own accord." His freedom is not self-generated. It is the fruit of the Spirit's fire within Him.

If we approach the Cross with this understanding, the whole scene becomes transformed. The jeers of the crowd do not define Him. The weakness of His limbs does not diminish Him. The apparent abandonment does not separate Him from the Father. The Spirit fills the silence. The Spirit bears the weight. The Spirit makes the human obedience of Christ radiant with divine love. What appears to the world as failure is, in truth, the triumph of the Spirit.

Every detail of the Passion attests to this hidden fire. When Christ consoles the weeping women of Jerusalem, the tenderness is the Spirit's. When He forgives His executioners, the mercy is the Spirit's. When He entrusts Mary and John to one another, the communion is the Spirit's. When He cries out to the Father, the yearning is the Spirit's. The Cross is not only the place where Christ reveals the Father; it is the place where the Spirit reveals Christ.

This is why the Church reads the Passion not as tragedy but as revelation. The divine plan is not that Christ should suffer for its own sake. The divine plan is that the Spirit should reveal divine love in the deepest human darkness. The Spirit is present where love costs the most. The Spirit is present where the human heart breaks open. The Spirit is present where obedience becomes agony. Christ does not descend into suffering alone. The Spirit descends with Him.

This truth reaches its summit in Christ's final act. "Into Your hands I commend My spirit." These are not merely words of resignation. They are the consummation of the offering. Christ returns His human life to the Father in the very breath of the Spirit. The surrender is complete. The gift is total. The Son hands Himself over through the Spirit into the eternal embrace of the Father. The Cross is the place where divine Love flows unbroken, even when the world sees only death.

When viewed through this lens, Calvary becomes the furnace where the Spirit's fire is revealed without disguise. In Christ's humanity, the Spirit burns with perfect intensity: love stronger than death, surrender stronger than fear, obedience stronger than suffering. The Cross is not the extinguishing of the Spirit's flame. It is the moment when the flame rises into its full brilliance.

The Spirit is the fire of the Cross.

The mystery of Christ's obedience becomes even more striking when one considers the depth of His kenosis—His self-emptying. Paul's hymn in Philippians names this descent with breathtaking clarity: though He was "in the form of God," Christ did not cling to equality but emptied Himself, taking the form of a servant, becoming obedient unto death, even death on a Cross. This is not the humiliation of a reluctant victim. It is the deliberate movement of the Son who allows the Spirit to shape His humanity into a perfect offering.

Kenosis is often misunderstood as the stripping away of divinity. In truth, it is the full expression of divine love within human limitation. Christ does not cease to be God; He reveals what it means for God to love. The self-emptying is not the reduction of power but the disclosure of the Spirit's tenderness and strength in human form. The Spirit does not make Christ less divine; the Spirit reveals His divinity in the form of humility. The divine Son, upheld by the Spirit, bends low to redeem humanity from within.

This descent touches every aspect of Christ's experience. In Gethsemane, when His soul is "sorrowful even unto death," He enters the full weight of human vulnerability. His anguish is not feigned. His prayer is not theatrical. The sweat that falls like drops of blood reveals the strain placed on His humanity as He confronts the cup He must drink. Yet even here—especially here—the Spirit is present as the one who strengthens Christ's human will to embrace the Father's plan. The agony is real, but the obedience is more real still, because it flows from divine love poured into His human heart.

The Gospel writers do not diminish this agony; they invite us to enter it. Christ falls to the ground. He pleads for another way. He tastes the loneliness of those who suffer without consolation. The apostles sleep beside Him, yet the Spirit watches with Him. The Spirit upholds Him. The Spirit draws His trembling humanity into that eternal "Yes" the Son speaks to the Father. The obedience that seems impossible becomes possible because the Spirit breathes divine love into every fibre of Christ's fatigue.

In some of the earliest Christian reflections, this moment is described as the place where Christ heals the human will. Maximus the Confessor writes that Christ, in His agony, unites the natural human inclination for life with the divine will for salvation. The Spirit is the artisan of this union. He takes the human fear that recoils from suffering and fills it with divine courage. Christ's prayer—"not My will, but Yours"—is not the crushing of His humanity but the transfiguration of it. The Spirit makes this transfiguration possible.

Christ's suffering does not diminish His authority; it reveals its essence. When He stands before Pilate, silent and dignified, He is not powerless. He is surrendered. There is a difference. Power seeks to dominate; surrender seeks to love. Christ's silence is not defeat but strength—the strength of the Spirit who fills Him with unwavering fidelity. Pilate's authority is external. Christ's authority is interior, rooted in the Spirit who binds Him to the Father. The governor cannot perceive this, but the faithful can. Divine love reveals itself most clearly when it appears weak.

This is why the early Church saw the Cross as the moment when the Spirit displays His greatest work: the transformation of suffering into self-gift. The Cross is not simply endured; it is embraced. Christ does not simply survive; He offers. He does not collapse; He gives. The Spirit turns agony into offering, pain into prayer, death into love. What the world sees as destruction becomes the altar of divine generosity.

The Spirit's work can be seen even in the gestures Christ makes during the Passion. When He forgives His executioners, it is the Spirit's mercy that flows through His words. When He consoles the repentant thief, it is the Spirit's tenderness that embraces a soul in its final hour. When He cries out in dereliction, it is the Spirit who sustains His faith in the Father even when the Father's presence is unfelt. Every breath is charged with the Spirit's fire.

This is particularly evident in His cry, "My God, My God, why have You forsaken Me?" This is not the collapse of divine love but its fullest expression. Christ enters the extremity of human desolation—the abyss where the human heart feels abandoned—and He brings the Spirit with Him. He prays the opening line of Psalm 22, the prayer of a righteous sufferer whose trust endures even in apparent abandonment. The Spirit does not shield Him from this darkness; the Spirit renders His trust unbreakable within it. This cry is not despair; it is faith carried to the threshold of death.

The Fathers saw this cry as the moment when Christ descends into the depths of human experience so that no suffering, no loneliness, no grief remains untouched by God. And because He suffers in the Spirit, the Spirit now fills every place where human sorrow is found. There is no wound Christ has not entered. There is no darkness where the Spirit has not gone. The Spirit who strengthened Christ in His agony now dwells in the hearts of the suffering, whispering the same unbroken cry of trust.

The culmination of this Spirit-filled obedience arrives in Christ's final words: "It is finished." The Greek *tetelestai* is more than a declaration of completion; it is a word of victory. The mission the Father entrusted to the Son is accomplished in perfect love. The obedience the Son embraced in the Spirit has reached its fullness. The divine-human act of self-giving love is complete. What began with the overshadowing of Mary ends with the outpouring of Christ's life. The Spirit who conceived Him now receives His final breath.

This breath is not merely the end of biological life; it is the handing over of His entire existence to the Father. Christ commends His spirit to the One who sent Him. But because He lives and moves and acts in the Spirit, this final act is an offering made through the Spirit. The Cross becomes the moment where the Spirit's fire, burning in the humanity of Christ, rises like incense to the Father.

In this sense, the Passion is not simply a story of endurance. It is the revelation of how the Spirit transforms suffering from within. Christ's humanity, fragile and exhausted, becomes the place where divine love shines most clearly. The Cross is the altar, Christ is the offering, and the Spirit is the flame.

To understand the Cross fully, one must enter the Trinitarian depth from which it arises. The Gospels describe what happens; the Spirit reveals why it happens. At the centre of this "why" is the eternal life of God—Father, Son, and Holy Spirit. The Cross is not an event that interrupts divine life. It is divine life entering human history in its most complete and self-revealing form. Every movement of Christ's Passion flows from that eternal communion.

For Augustine, the Spirit is the Love who stands between the Father and the Son as their shared Gift. He is the bond that unites them, the personal Love exchanged eternally within the Trinity. If this is true, then the Cross—Christ's total self-offering to the Father—is the supreme revelation of the Spirit in time. Christ can offer Himself because He is filled with the Spirit. Christ can love unto death because He is borne by the very Love that binds Him to the Father. When the Son pours Himself out on the Cross, the Spirit is the outpouring.

This means the Passion cannot be reduced to a physical agony or a moral example. The Cross is the temporal expression of an eternal reality: the Son eternally receives all from the Father and eternally returns all to the Father in love. At Calvary, this eternal exchange is translated into flesh and blood, pain and surrender. What Christ lives eternally in joy, He now expresses historically in suffering. The Spirit remains the same in both: the Love who makes the Son's self-gift possible.

This perspective also corrects a common misunderstanding. Many imagine the Father as demanding sacrifice and the Son as appeasing wrath. But the Trinitarian truth is deeper and far more beautiful. The Father does not stand over against the Son; the Father is the One who gives the Son to the world in love. The Son does not beg for mercy; He freely offers Himself in love. The Spirit does not hover as a distant witness; He unites Father and Son in love. Divine justice is not punishment; it is the unbreakable fidelity of divine love healing a broken world.

Seen in this light, every detail of the Cross becomes luminous. Christ's thirst is not merely physical; it is the thirst of the Spirit within Him for the salvation of the world. His silence before His accusers is not weakness; it is the serenity of One who rests in the Spirit's strength. His wounds are not marks of defeat; they are openings through which divine love pours out. The Cross becomes the visible form of invisible Love.

The early Fathers delighted in this vision. Irenaeus spoke of the Son and the Spirit as the "two hands of the Father," shaping salvation together. Cyril of Alexandria insisted that Christ's human obedience is empowered by the Spirit. Gregory Nazianzen described Christ's blood as "the wine of the Spirit." These reflections are not poetic embellishments. They articulate a concrete truth: the Cross is Trinitarian through and through. The Spirit does not arrive at Pentecost as a late addition; He is already the soul of Christ's sacrifice.

This Trinitarian foundation also explains why the Cross has the power to transform human suffering. If Christ suffered only by His own human effort, then His pain would be admirable but not redemptive. But because He suffers in the Spirit, His suffering becomes the channel through which divine love enters the darkest corners of human existence. The Spirit unites the divine to the human in Christ's agony, and this union becomes the wellspring of our healing. Where human suffering is powerless, divine love is omnipotent. The Spirit makes this union actual.

Here the language of fire becomes unavoidable. Scripture uses fire to describe the Spirit again and again, and never more fittingly than at the Cross. Fire purifies; the Spirit purifies. Fire consumes; the Spirit consumes selfishness and fear. Fire gives light; the Spirit illumines even the night of suffering. Fire ascends; the Spirit draws the soul upward to the Father. Calvary is the furnace where the human and divine meet in a single flame—the flame of sacrificial love.

Consider Christ's pierced side. Blood and water flow from it—symbols of Eucharist and Baptism, sacraments of the Spirit's work. The Fathers saw this outpouring as the birth of the Church. But beneath the symbol lies a deeper reality: the Spirit who filled Christ now flows into the world through His wounds. The Cross becomes the fountain of the Spirit, because the Spirit is the Love poured out.

Christ breathes His last—and immediately John tells us He "gave up the spirit." This expression carries two meanings at once: He surrenders His life to the Father, and He releases the Spirit for the world. The death of Christ is the moment when the Spirit who binds Him to the Father becomes available to humanity. The veil of the Temple is torn, not only because judgment has fallen, but because the Spirit now passes freely from the Holy of Holies into the world of sinners.

Nothing about the Cross is chaotic or accidental. Every detail is the choreography of divine love acting through human fragility.

Christ enters the depths of human suffering so that no depth remains untouched by the Spirit. His descent into weakness becomes the place where the Spirit reveals strength. His descent into loneliness becomes the place where the Spirit reveals communion. His descent into death becomes the place where the Spirit reveals life.

And because Christ suffers in the Spirit, He invites all suffering humanity into a new possibility: that pain, when united to Him, can become love. The Spirit does not eliminate suffering; He changes its character. What would crush the soul now becomes prayer. What would embitter the heart now becomes offering. What would isolate a person now becomes intercession. The Spirit takes what is unbearable and makes it fruitful. This transformation is not symbolic. It is real and lived in the marrow of the Christian life.

When the saints speak of suffering as fire, they are not romanticising pain. They are describing the experience of the Spirit's presence in the midst of agony. John of the Cross names this presence a "living flame." Teresa of Ávila speaks of it as the "science of the Cross." Ignatius of Antioch, walking toward martyrdom, calls it "the Spirit's wheat being ground into Christ." Their language is daring because the reality is daring: suffering touched by the Spirit becomes love.

At Calvary, this truth stands unveiled. Christ offers Himself through the eternal Spirit. The Spirit is the fire within the sacrifice. The Father receives the gift. The world is redeemed by the love that flows between them.

The mystery of the Spirit at the Cross does not end with Christ's final breath. It begins for us there. Everything the Spirit accomplishes in the humanity of Jesus—strengthening, purifying, sustaining, transforming—He now desires to accomplish in the humanity of those who belong to Christ. The Cross is not only revelation; it is invitation. It does not merely display divine love; it draws us into it. And the one who accomplishes this drawing is the Spirit.

Paul speaks of this with astonishing clarity: "If we suffer with Him, we shall also be glorified with Him." Suffering *with* Christ is not a poetic idea. It is a concrete participation granted by the Spirit who unites us to Christ's self-offering. Without the Spirit, suffering reduces a person to fear, resentment, or despair. But with the Spirit, suffering becomes a means by which the heart is joined to the love that saved the world. The Cross does not teach us to romanticise pain; it teaches us to receive the Spirit who makes pain redemptive.

Here the union between Christ's Passion and our own becomes intimate. The Spirit who upheld Christ in His agony now dwells within the believer, shaping the same obedience within us. The Spirit does not take suffering away—He fills it with meaning. He does not silence the cry—He transforms it into prayer. He does not remove weakness—He makes weakness the place where divine strength appears. The Spirit who carried Christ through His Passion now carries us through ours.

This is why the saints speak of suffering with such daring reverence. They do not love pain. They love what the Spirit does in pain. In every wound, the Spirit writes the likeness of Christ. In every surrender, the Spirit forms the Son's obedience. In every act of forgiveness, the Spirit pours out the mercy of the Crucified. The believer who suffers in the Spirit does not withdraw inward; he opens outward. His wounds become windows, not walls.

The Spirit transforms suffering first by reordering desire. On our own, pain turns us inward. We become preoccupied with our own survival. But the Spirit, who filled Christ with love even as His body was falling apart, fills the believer with a love that rises above fear. The Spirit teaches the heart to desire God even when God feels distant. He teaches the will to choose love even when love feels impossible. He teaches the soul to surrender even when surrender feels like loss. The Spirit shapes the inner movements of suffering into the movements of Christ.

One of the most mysterious works of the Spirit is this transformation of grief into intercession. When the believer allows the Spirit to unite his pain to Christ's sacrifice, suffering becomes prayer. It becomes a hidden participation in the redemption of the world. The saints insist on this over and over: the Spirit makes the soul's wounds fruitful. Suffering without love is empty. Suffering with love becomes offering. And love is the Spirit.

This is why the Spirit's groaning in Romans 8 is so critical. Paul tells us that the Spirit "intercedes for us with sighs too deep for words." These sighs echo the cry of Christ on the Cross. They are the Spirit praying within us when our own strength collapses. When the believer can no longer articulate hope, the Spirit becomes hope. When the believer cannot form words, the Spirit forms prayer. When the believer feels forsaken, the Spirit unites him to the One who cried, "My God, My God, why have You forsaken Me?" There is no deeper solidarity than this.

The Spirit also transforms suffering by purifying it. In the fires of trial, the Spirit burns away what is not love: pride, self-reliance, bitterness, illusion. Suffering becomes the crucible where the human heart is stripped of falsehood and made transparent. The Spirit does not wound; He reveals. He exposes the hidden attachments that keep us from God. He uncovers the fears that prevent surrender. He purifies our desire until it becomes simple, clean, single: God alone.

This purification is not punitive. It is creative. The Spirit who hovered over the chaotic waters of Genesis now hovers over the chaotic waters of the human heart. What He did for creation, He does again for the soul: He brings order out of chaos, beauty out of formlessness, life out of darkness. The same Spirit who filled Christ's suffering with divine light now fills ours. The Cross becomes the new creation of the human heart.

Participation in Christ's suffering is not merely interior. The Spirit also forms a new way of living in the midst of affliction. Christ forgave from the Cross; the Spirit enables us to forgive. Christ loved His enemies; the Spirit enables us to love those who wound us. Christ entrusted Himself to the Father; the Spirit enables us to surrender. In every virtue exercised under trial, the Spirit reveals the life of Christ within us. This is not stoic endurance. This is the fire of divine love.

This participation does not glorify pain; it glorifies Christ. The Spirit teaches the believer to see pain not as a wall that separates him from God but as a place where God has already gone ahead. Christ has filled suffering with His presence. The Spirit makes that presence real within us. The Cross becomes the meeting place of divine love and human frailty. When we carry our own crosses, we do not walk alone; we walk in the Spirit who walked with Christ.

And here the mystery reaches its final height: the Spirit prepares every Christian for the moment when his own offering will be completed. Death is not the extinguishing of the Spirit's work but its consummation. The Spirit who breathed life into us at birth will be the One who receives our final breath and carries it into the Father's hands. Christ's final act—commending His spirit to the Father—is the pattern of every believer's last act. The Spirit who was the fire of the Cross becomes the fire of our own surrender.

The believer who dies in the Spirit does not fall into emptiness; he falls into Love. The Cross becomes the doorway into the life that never ends. The Spirit who revealed divine love in Christ's suffering now reveals divine love in ours. The world sees death; the Spirit sees offering. The world sees loss; the Spirit sees union. The Spirit completes in us the work He revealed in Christ.

The Cross, then, is the place where the Spirit's fire burns with perfect clarity. It is the furnace of divine love, the altar of self-gift, the meeting of God and humanity in a single act of surrender. Christ offers Himself through the eternal Spirit. And through the eternal Spirit, we learn to offer ourselves in Him.

10

The Spirit of Resurrection: New Creation Begins

Before dawn breaks on the first day of the week, creation holds its breath. The world lies in a stillness deeper than silence, the kind of stillness that follows collapse and precedes rebirth. The Cross stands behind us, stark and unyielding; the tomb lies before us, sealed and cold. To human sight, nothing is happening. To human imagination, all seems finished. Yet in this hidden hour, the Spirit is moving. The same Spirit who hovered over the formless waters of Genesis now moves through the darkness of death. The same Breath who gave life to Adam now breathes into the Second Adam. The world does not yet know it, but new creation has already begun.

Scripture gives only the faintest hints of this moment. It does not describe the instant of Resurrection, because such an instant cannot be described. It is not an event within history alone; it is history touched by eternity. What the evangelists do give us is a single decisive truth: Christ is raised by the Spirit. Paul states it with crystalline clarity: "If the Spirit of Him who raised Jesus from the dead dwells in you, then He who raised Christ from the dead will give life to your mortal bodies also through His Spirit who dwells in you." The Resurrection

THE SPIRIT OF RESURRECTION: NEW CREATION BEGINS

is the work of the Spirit—the divine life who enters the depths of Christ's humanity and draws Him into an incorruptible existence.

This means the Resurrection is not a resuscitation, not the return of biological life as though Christ were simply restored to His former condition. It is the transformation of human nature by the Spirit. The risen Christ is no ghost, no apparition, no metaphor. He is the fullness of humanity flooded with the Spirit's power, humanity at its climax, transfigured yet still bearing the marks of love. The Resurrection reveals what the Spirit can do with human flesh when nothing remains but obedience, surrender, and divine life.

Here Athanasius becomes a trustworthy guide. He teaches that the Word became flesh so that flesh, united to the Word and filled with the Spirit, might become incorruptible. In the Resurrection, this purpose reaches its zenith. Christ's humanity—fragile, vulnerable, mortal—is now permeated by the Spirit in such a way that death can no longer touch it. The Spirit does not simply animate the dead body of Christ; He glorifies it. He saturates every fibre of Christ's humanity with divine light. He reveals the human body as temple, as fire-bearing, as capable of immortality.

This is why the early Church insists that the Resurrection is both a divine act and a human victory. Christ rises not by shedding His humanity but by perfecting it in the Spirit. What Adam lost through disobedience, Christ restores through the fire of divine love. Humanity receives its first taste of the life for which it was created. In the Resurrection we glimpse the world's future, the destiny of every person sealed with the Spirit. We see humanity not as it often appears—broken, weary, decaying—but as it is meant to be: luminous, free, whole.

The Gospels bear witness to this transformed humanity through the strange beauty of the Resurrection appearances. Christ stands before Mary Magdalene, and she does not recognise Him—not because He is less real, but because He is more real. He walks with the disciples to Emmaus, opening the Scriptures, igniting their hearts, yet they only perceive Him in the breaking of bread. He stands among the apostles in a locked room, yet His presence does not depend on walls or distance. He bears wounds, yet these wounds no longer bleed; they shine. Everything about Him is familiar, yet everything is changed. This is humanity filled with the Spirit.

The Fathers loved to linger here. Gregory the Great reflects that Christ appears "in a form to show what He has become"—not abandoning His identity, but revealing its destiny. The risen Christ is not a different person; He is the same Son, now unveiled. His humanity is the first revelation of what the Spirit intends to accomplish in the world: not escape from the body but the glorification of the body; not flight from creation but the renewal of creation.

Creation itself participates in this renewal from the moment Christ steps out of the tomb. John notes that the Resurrection occurs in a garden—a deliberate echo of Eden, as though God intends to plant the world anew. The new Adam rises where the old Adam fell. The garden that once witnessed humanity's exile now witnesses humanity's restoration. The Spirit who breathed over the first creation now breathes into this garden the life of the new creation. The stone rolled away is more than an opening in rock—it is the opening of the age of the Spirit.

The silence of the early morning becomes the birthplace of a joy that will never be taken away. Death has not simply been overturned; it has been transfigured. Christ does not escape death; He passes through it, fills it, conquers it from within. Death becomes the doorway into life because the Spirit has entered death itself. The Spirit does not abandon Christ in the tomb; He raises Him from the tomb, making the grave the place where divine life breaks forth.

This is the moment the entire universe has been waiting for. Paul writes that creation "groans" for the revelation of the children of God. That revelation begins with the Resurrection. The Spirit who raised Christ is the same Spirit who will renew all things. The tomb is the epicentre of a transformation that will extend to the ends of the cosmos. New creation does not begin with the apocalypse; it begins with the empty tomb.

The Resurrection is therefore not simply the vindication of Christ. It is the unveiling of the Spirit. The Spirit reveals Himself as the One who brings life from death, order from chaos, new creation from old. The Spirit reveals Himself as the divine Breath that cannot be constrained by stone, guarded by soldiers, or silenced by death. The Spirit reveals Himself as the future of the world.

And yet the Spirit's work at the Resurrection is not detached from us. The Resurrection is not only Christ's triumph; it is the promise of ours. The Spirit who raised Jesus from the dead now dwells in those who belong to Him. The same life that filled Christ's humanity is planted like seed within our own. The Resurrection is not distant history but the beginning of our destiny. And the Spirit is the guarantee of that destiny.

The Gospels linger over the Resurrection appearances because in them the disciples encounter something they have no category for: a human life so filled with the Spirit that it surpasses every boundary without ceasing to be human. The risen Christ does not glow with an ethereal otherworldliness, yet He is unmistakably changed. He walks upon the earth with the quiet ease of One who is utterly free. He speaks with the familiar warmth of a teacher and friend, yet every word carries the resonance of eternity. His presence is immediate, overwhelming, gentle—like light that warms and disarms at the same time. This is humanity saturated with the Spirit.

His first appearance is not to crowds or rulers but to a single weeping woman. Mary Magdalene, heartbroken and disoriented, stands outside the tomb searching for a body. She sees Him and mistakes Him for the gardener. In a sense, she is not wrong. Christ is the Gardener of the new creation, the One who tends the restored garden and invites all humanity to return. But recognition comes only when He speaks her name. This is essential: the Spirit does not reveal Christ by spectacle but by intimacy. Illumination happens through personal encounter. Mary is not startled by a vision of glory; she is awakened by the tone of a voice she knows. The Spirit reveals the Risen One through love.

On the road to Emmaus, the same pattern unfolds. Two disciples walk away from Jerusalem, weighed down by disappointment, interpreting the events of the Passion through the lens of defeat. Christ walks beside them, but they do not recognise Him. Their eyes are kept from seeing until their hearts are prepared. He opens the Scriptures to them, not as an academic exercise, but as the divine Teacher interpreting His own story. Their hearts burn within them, yet they remain blind until He takes bread, blesses it, and breaks it. Only then do they recognise Him. The Spirit uses the Scriptures and the Eucharistic gesture to reveal the Risen Christ. Illumination is not only understanding; it is communion.

The locked room encounter intensifies this mystery. The disciples are paralysed by fear—fear of death, fear of failure, fear of a future without their Master. Then, without fanfare, Christ stands in their midst. Walls do not hinder Him; distance does not limit Him; fear does not repel Him. His greeting is simple: "Peace be with you." It is the peace of the Spirit—the peace that comes not from escape but from victory. He shows His wounds, not to shame them for abandoning Him, but to show that love has triumphed. The wounds remain, yet they are no longer signs of violence; they are signs of glory. The Spirit does not erase the marks of suffering; He transfigures them.

This transfiguration becomes central in the meeting with Thomas.

THE SPIRIT OF RESURRECTION: NEW CREATION BEGINS

Christ does not rebuke his doubt. He invites it. "Put your finger here…place your hand in My side." The invitation is shocking in its tenderness. Christ draws the doubter into a personal contact with glory. Thomas touches not just flesh but flesh filled with the Spirit—flesh that once suffered, flesh that once bled, flesh that now radiates incorruptible life. His cry, "My Lord and my God," is the clear sign that illumination has taken root. The Spirit who raised Christ now raises Thomas's faith. Doubt gives way to worship because the Spirit reveals the truth of Christ through the very wounds that once scandalised him.

The risen Christ is not distant or abstract. He makes breakfast for His disciples on the shore of the sea. He cooks fish over charcoal. He restores Peter with words that heal rather than punish. Each detail is saturated with the Spirit's gentleness and strength. The Resurrection is not only the defeat of death; it is the revelation of divine tenderness. The Spirit reveals God not merely as power but as presence, not merely as judge but as healer, not merely as creator but as companion.

These appearances are not random episodes; they are manifestations of the new creation. Christ's humanity is now the first instance of what the Spirit intends for the entire world. He is the "firstborn from the dead," the pioneer of a new way of being human. His body is no longer subject to decay. His life is no longer limited by space or time. He is the bridge between the world that is passing away and the world that is coming. The Spirit who raised Him has begun the renewal of all things.

If the Cross was the descent of divine love into death, the Resurrection is the ascent of humanity into divine life. The Spirit's work at the tomb is the turning point of the ages. Death remains, but its character has changed. It is no longer a prison; it is a passage. It is no longer the triumph of darkness; it is the threshold of glory. The believer does not deny the reality of death, but death no longer defines reality. The

Spirit who raised Christ now stands within the grave as Lord.

This new creation is not merely future. It is already unfolding. The disciples themselves become signs of it. Once fearful, they become courageous. Once confused, they become clear. Once hesitant, they become bold. Their transformation is not psychological; it is spiritual. The Spirit who raised Christ begins to raise them—raising their minds, raising their courage, raising their desire for holiness. The Resurrection is not only Christ's event; it is the beginning of our transformation.

The early Church understood this instinctively. The Paschal shout, "Christ is risen!" is not a slogan. It is the proclamation that the Spirit has changed the structure of the world. The light that burst into the garden will one day flood the universe. The life that entered the tomb will one day enter every mortal body that belongs to Christ. The Resurrection is the beginning of a world with death behind it.

The Risen Christ stands as the living proof of what the Spirit will accomplish in all who believe. His transfigured flesh is the template of our future. His victory is the promise of our own. The Spirit who raised Him now dwells within us as the seed of resurrection. New creation has already begun—in Him first, in us next, in the whole cosmos at the end.

The New Testament never treats the Resurrection as an isolated miracle. It treats it as the unveiling of the Spirit's deepest identity: the Giver of Life. The Spirit is not an afterthought to Easter; the Spirit is the interior cause of Easter. "If the Spirit of Him who raised Jesus from the dead dwells in you..." Paul writes, binding together Christ's victory and the believer's destiny in a single breath. The power that rolled away the stone is the same power awakening the heart to faith, the same power strengthening the will to choose God, the same power that will one day raise the body from the dust. Easter is not a moment in time; it is the revelation of who the Spirit is.

THE SPIRIT OF RESURRECTION: NEW CREATION BEGINS

The disciples do not yet understand this, though they experience it. Their world has been overturned three times in rapid succession—first by the crucifixion, then by the absence of the body, and finally by the presence of the risen Lord. They struggle to grasp what they are touching, seeing, hearing. Yet the Spirit is already illuminating their minds, even before Pentecost, giving them the first glimmers of a truth too vast to articulate: the Resurrection is not an event added to history. It is the beginning of a new creation.

The evangelists capture this subtly. Every Resurrection scene carries a quiet echo of Genesis. A garden. Morning light. Breath. Peace. Food blessed and given. A new Adam standing in the place where death once reigned. The Spirit hovers again—this time not over waters but over wounds, not over chaos but over fear. The first creation emerges from darkness into light; the new creation emerges from a tomb into glory. This parallel is deliberate. What the Father spoke into existence through the Word in the beginning, He now renews through the Word made flesh in the power of the Spirit.

Consider the details of the risen Christ's humanity. He bears scars, yet they no longer testify to violence. They radiate meaning. He eats fish, yet He is not dependent on food. He appears and disappears, yet no hint of restlessness clings to Him. His humanity is solid, touchable, familiar—and at the same time glorified, free, luminous. This is not the abandonment of the body but the transfiguration of the body. Matter has become porous to divine life, not consumed by it but fulfilled. The Spirit is not undoing creation; He is completing it.

This completion is revealed most clearly in the way Christ communicates peace. His "Peace be with you" is not a polite greeting; it is the transmission of divine stability. It is the imparting of the Spirit's own serenity. Fear dissolves not because circumstances improve but because the divine life enters into the disciples' frailty. The Spirit does not remove suffering; He transforms the interior landscape so that suffering no longer has the final word. Peace is the fruit of resurrection life.

This transformation appears vividly when Christ breathes on the disciples in John's Gospel. "Receive the Holy Spirit." The act is not symbolic. It is a direct participation in the same divine movement that animated Adam. The breath that entered the first man now enters the Church. The gesture signifies continuity and renewal: the same Creator Spirit who gave life in Genesis now gives life anew through the risen Christ. The disciples are not simply forgiven or encouraged—they are re-created. The new creation begins with breath.

This moment reveals something crucial about the Spirit's role in the Resurrection. The Spirit is not only the One who raises Christ. The Spirit is the One through whom Christ shares that risen life with others. The Resurrection is not self-contained. It flows outward. It expands. It becomes contagious. Christ is not raised for Himself alone; He is raised as the head of a new humanity. The life that fills His body now seeks entry into ours.

This outward movement is why the Resurrection is inseparable from mission. Christ does not simply reveal Himself to His friends to console them. He commissions them. "As the Father has sent me, so I send you." Mission is born not from human enthusiasm but from encounter with the risen Lord. The Spirit who raised Christ is the same Spirit who will soon descend at Pentecost to empower the disciples to witness. The Resurrection illuminates mission in a new light: evangelisation is not persuasion but participation in divine life. The Church does not spread an idea; the Church communicates a life.

This life is resurrection life—life that has passed through suffering, conquered death, and returned with peace. It is life that does not fear the grave because the grave has become a gateway. It is life that bears wounds without despair because those wounds are now places where divine glory has entered. It is life that sees the world not as a closed system but as a creation awaiting transfiguration. Everything the disciples will do after Pentecost—preaching, healing, suffering, forgiving—flows from this new perception of reality.

The Resurrection therefore reshapes the imagination of faith. Before Easter, holiness might be conceived as moral improvement or disciplined obedience. After Easter, holiness is participation in resurrection life. The Spirit is not given merely to help the believer avoid sin. He is given so that the believer may share in Christ's own life—His clarity, His courage, His compassion, His freedom. Christianity becomes less about delay until heaven and more about transformation in the present. The believer becomes a living anticipation of the world to come.

Paul articulates this most powerfully in Romans 8. The Spirit who raised Jesus dwells within believers as the guarantee of future glory. This indwelling is not static; it is dynamic, propelling the entire cosmos toward renewal. Creation itself groans, awaiting the revelation of the children of God. Resurrection life is the first fruits of what the Spirit will accomplish universally. Easter is the seed; the new creation is the harvest.

This means every Christian carries within themselves a double identity: they are still marked by mortality, yet they carry immortality as promise. They are still susceptible to fear, yet they bear the Spirit who conquered fear at the tomb. They still walk in a world wounded by sin, yet they are bearers of the life that will one day heal the world. The Resurrection reveals not only Christ's glory but the believer's future.

The Spirit unveils this future gradually, tenderly. Illumination is not immediate comprehension but progressive vision. The disciples do not suddenly understand everything once Christ rises. Their journey continues. The Spirit will teach them to interpret the Resurrection not merely as a past event but as the key to their present and future.

The risen Christ opens the Scriptures, opens their minds, opens their hearts. The Spirit completes the work by making their hearts burn with understanding. The Resurrection is not only seen; it is interiorly grasped.

The Resurrection is the unveiling of the Spirit's ultimate intention—that humanity should not merely be restored to innocence but elevated to glory. The early Fathers repeatedly speak of this elevation not as an afterthought to salvation but as its very heart. What emerges from the tomb on the third day is the destiny of every human soul touched by the Spirit. The risen Christ is not only the Redeemer; He is the revelation of the fully Spirit-filled human being. In Him, the divine life saturates every fibre of His humanity. Nothing in Him resists God. Nothing in Him remains opaque. He is wholly permeated by the Spirit, like iron placed in fire until the metal glows with the light it receives. The Spirit is the fire; Christ's glorified humanity is the iron.

This radiance becomes the key to understanding why the Resurrection is not simply a divine victory over death. It is the disclosure of a new mode of existence. Before Easter, human life unfolds within the boundaries of frailty, decay, and fear. After Easter, human life is opened toward glorification, participation, and immortality. The Resurrection does not erase the limits of creaturehood. It fills those limits with divine energy. The risen Christ is still human, still tangible, still recognisable—yet transformed. His humanity is no longer locked within the rhythms of this world. It breathes the air of the age to come.

This new mode of life is what the Spirit imparts to the disciples, though they do not yet comprehend the magnitude of what they are receiving. When Christ appears to them behind locked doors, He is not merely proving He is alive. He is demonstrating the nature of resurrection humanity—freely present, unbound by space, yet profoundly personal. The Spirit who raised Him is the same Spirit who enables Him to stand among them, to speak peace into their fear, to reveal glory through gentleness rather than spectacle. Resurrection glory does not overwhelm; it invites. It calls the heart without crushing it. It draws without coercing. This is the way of the Spirit.

This invitation reaches its apex in the encounter between Jesus and Mary Magdalene outside the tomb. When she hears her name, something deeper than hearing awakens. The Spirit opens her heart to recognise the One she loves—not through explanation but through illumination. Her tears do not cease because her questions are answered but because Presence eclipses confusion. Resurrection faith begins not with understanding but with recognition. The Spirit reveals the risen Christ not mainly to the intellect but to the heart. The intellect will follow; the heart must awaken first.

That same illumination unfolds on the road to Emmaus. The disciples speak with Jesus without knowing Him, their minds clouded by grief, their vision narrowed by disappointment. Yet when He breaks the bread, the veil lifts. The Spirit reveals what the eyes alone cannot see. Their hearts burn before their minds understand, and this burning is not emotional excitement. It is the interior flame of the Spirit preparing them for recognition. The Resurrection is understood only through this flame. Without the Spirit, the risen Christ stands unrecognised. With the Spirit, the risen Christ becomes the centre of reality.

The Resurrection therefore becomes the interpretive key to Scripture because the Spirit who reveals the risen Christ is the same Spirit who inspired the Scriptures. When the evangelists describe Jesus opening the disciples' minds, they are describing the action of the Spirit. Illumination is not an enhancement of ordinary understanding; it is an entrance into Christ's own understanding of the Father's plan. The Spirit leads the mind into the logic of divine love—a logic that sees suffering transformed, death defeated, and humanity lifted toward communion. Scripture becomes luminous not because human intelligence has improved but because the Spirit has entered.

This illumination has moral consequences as well. Resurrection faith reshapes the way the believer sees the world. Death no longer defines the horizon. Sin no longer determines identity. Fear no longer dictates decisions. The believer begins to perceive reality through the lens of glory—quietly, steadily, imperfectly, yet truly. Life becomes a pilgrimage toward transfiguration. Every act of love becomes a participation in resurrection life. Every sacrifice becomes a seed planted in the soil of the age to come. Every act of forgiveness becomes a small Easter morning in the heart. The Spirit who raised Jesus is now raising the believer, not in a single moment but through a lifetime.

This interior resurrection carries an unmistakable signature. It produces hope that cannot be extinguished by circumstances. Hope is not optimism; hope is the awareness that the power that raised Christ is at work in the believer's depths. Hope is the quiet conviction that the grave is not the end, the wound is not the final word, and the night is not absolute. Hope is the fruit of the Spirit's presence. The Resurrection plants this hope; the Spirit causes it to grow.

Yet the Resurrection not only transforms individuals; it transforms the cosmos. Paul writes that creation itself groans, waiting for the revelation of the children of God. This groaning is not despair but expectancy. The Resurrection signals that the material world is not destined for annihilation but renewal. Matter itself will share in the glory that fills Christ's risen body. The Spirit does not abandon creation. The Spirit transfigures creation. The world will not simply be repaired. It will be filled with God.

This cosmic horizon reveals why the Resurrection is inseparable from Pentecost. Christ rises in the Spirit so that He may give the Spirit. The life unveiled in Him becomes the life offered to all. The Resurrection is the fountain; Pentecost is the river flowing from it.

The disciples must first behold the risen Christ so that they know what the Spirit will make of them. They must see glory before they can bear witness to it. Pentecost is not the beginning of the story but the expansion of the Resurrection into the Church.

Everything in the Church's sacramental life flows from this union of Resurrection and Spirit. Baptism plunges believers into Christ's death so they may rise in His life. Chrismation seals them with the fire of the Spirit who raised Him. The Eucharist feeds them with the body of the risen Lord, suffused with divine life. Confession restores the resurrection life when it is wounded. Every liturgy is a descent of the Spirit who reveals the crucified and risen Christ. Easter is not an annual memory. It is the interior atmosphere of the Church.

The believer who lives in the Spirit therefore lives in resurrection light even while still walking through the shadows of this world. Mortality remains, but its sting is blunted. Suffering persists, but its meaning shifts. Death waits, but its victory is undone. The Spirit does not remove the realities of this world; the Spirit infuses them with a new horizon. Resurrection life becomes the quiet heartbeat of ordinary days.

What rose from the tomb is the beginning of what will rise in every believer and, one day, in all creation. The Spirit who raised Jesus is leading the world toward a future already revealed in Him. The stone was rolled away not only for Christ to emerge but for humanity to see what it is called to become.

11

Pentecost: The Descent of Fire

The days after the Ascension carry a silence unlike any other in Scripture. Christ has returned to the Father, yet the promise of the Spirit has not yet descended. Heaven is opened, but earth waits. The disciples gather in the upper room not as strategists preparing a mission but as children who have been told to wait for a gift they cannot imagine. They cling to the last command given to them: "Remain in the city until you are clothed with power from on high." They have the memory of Christ, the teachings of Christ, the wounds of Christ, the peace He breathed upon them—but they do not yet have the fire of Christ. They know everything and possess nothing. Their hearts are full, yet their strength is empty. This waiting is not failure; it is preparation. Grace shapes longing before it satisfies it.

The upper room becomes the cradle of the Church precisely because it is the place where human power ends. No miracles occur there. No sermons are preached. No crowds gather. The disciples simply pray. They pray not as masters of theology but as people who know their poverty. They pray not as those who expect a spectacle but as those who trust a promise. Mary is there—not to teach them new doctrine, but to show them how to wait, how to receive, how to let the

Spirit overshadow human weakness with divine strength. The One who once received the Spirit at the Annunciation now waits with the disciples so that they may receive the same Spirit in a new way. Her presence turns the room into Nazareth once more: a small, hidden place where the Spirit prepares to reshape the world.

The stillness of those days is the threshold of Pentecost. The Spirit comes when the heart knows that without Him there is no mission, no holiness, no life. The disciples know this now. They do not know how to preach; they barely understand Christ's mysteries. Their courage falters, their memory wavers, their hope flickers. They only know that He said the Spirit would come—and that without that coming, nothing He commanded could be fulfilled. Their prayer does not rise from confidence but from need. This is the soil in which Pentecost grows. The Spirit is not drawn to strength; He is drawn to surrender.

The descent begins with sound. A rush of wind fills the house, not as a gentle breeze but as a mighty presence that cannot be contained. It is the echo of Genesis, the breath of God moving once more across the face of creation. The same breath that hovered over the waters now hovers over human hearts. What happened at the beginning of the world now happens again at the beginning of the Church. Creation and new creation share the same breath. The disciples do not interpret the sound; they are immersed in it. Wind becomes the first sacrament of Pentecost: invisible, irresistible, shaping what it touches.

Fire follows. Not a distant blaze on a mountain as at Sinai, but divided tongues resting gently upon each person in the room. The fire does not burn; it beautifies. It does not consume; it creates. It does not remain external; it enters. In the Old Covenant, fire marked the presence of God from afar—pillar of flame, blazing summit, smoking temple. In the New Covenant, fire touches flesh. The distance collapses. What Israel could not approach without fear, the disciples now receive with joy. The fire that once carved commandments into stone now shapes hearts into living tablets.

The tongues of fire communicate a mystery older than creation itself. They reveal the Spirit as the love of God made visible. Augustine would later say that the fire of Pentecost is the same fire that binds the Father and the Son in eternal communion. When this fire descends upon the disciples, it is not merely empowerment; it is participation. The Spirit does not give them courage as a separate gift. He draws them into the very love by which the Son loves the Father and the Father loves the Son. The boldness they receive is not psychological transformation. It is the overflow of divine communion entering human speech.

This is why the disciples begin to speak. The Spirit's first action is not to create a new language but to transfigure the old ones. Every tongue becomes capable of proclaiming the wonders of God. Pentecost reverses Babel not by erasing difference but by sanctifying it. Unity comes not through uniformity but through communion. The Spirit does not flatten cultures; He fills them. He does not produce a single holy language; He makes every language a vessel for divine praise. The nations gather, not because they share vocabulary, but because they share wonder. The Spirit speaks in every heart the same truth: God has drawn near.

This nearness, this descent, this fire—this is the beginning of union. There is no Christianity apart from Pentecost. There is no Church apart from Pentecost. There is no holiness, no mission, no sacrament, no revelation apart from Pentecost. The Spirit is not an accessory to the Christian life; the Spirit is its source. The disciples who cowered now stand. The hearts that trembled now burn. The voices that whispered now proclaim. Not because they have changed themselves, but because Someone has entered them.

The crowd understands the miracle imperfectly, yet even confusion becomes a doorway. Some marvel; others mock. But the fire remains unthreatened by misunderstanding. Peter stands—not as a man who finally understands everything, but as a man overshadowed by the Spirit. His words are not polished rhetoric; they are the overflow of the fire within. He does not argue the Resurrection; he bears witness to it. He does not explain Pentecost; he embodies it. His voice carries authority not because of eloquence but because the Spirit speaks Christ through him.

The Church is born not through planning but through ignition. What begins in the upper room does not stay in the upper room. Fire spreads. That is its nature.

Pentecost does not wash over the disciples as a wave of spiritual emotion. It enters them with deliberate tenderness, touching each heart in a way that reveals the personality of the Spirit. Fire descends, yet the fire is gentle. It rests, but does not crush. It burns, but does not wound. What appears dramatic from the outside is, from within, an act of exquisite intimacy. The Spirit never overwhelms; He indwells. His power is the power of communion, not domination. The fire that rests upon the disciples is the same fire that rests eternally upon the Son. What the Father pours out upon Christ, Christ now pours out upon the Church. The Spirit who glorifies the Son now glorifies Christ in those who belong to Him.

This is why Peter's voice becomes transparent. The courage he now possesses is not bravado but clarity. The Spirit does not inflate the ego; He frees it from self. When Peter speaks, the words do not draw attention to the speaker but to the One he proclaims. His mind is illumined, not in the sense that he suddenly becomes an expert in Scripture, but in the sense that Scripture has been ignited from within. The words of Joel, once familiar, now burn with a meaning he could never have seen without the Spirit. The past is no longer a collection of ancient scrolls; it is the living testimony to the fire now descending. Peter does not interpret the prophets so much as let the Spirit unveil them.

The crowd listening to Peter experiences something unprecedented: truth carried not by argument but by fire. Many have memorised the words of the prophets. Many have heard rabbis speak of the covenants. Many have debated the signs of the Messiah. But none have heard divine truth spoken with the warmth of divine love. The Spirit does not merely furnish Peter with a message; He transforms Peter into a living witness. The listener detects the difference instinctively. Words born of human insight reach the mind. Words born of the Spirit reach the heart. This is why three thousand souls respond. They are not persuaded. They are pierced.

Pentecost therefore becomes the first revelation of the Church's true nature. The Church is not built by agreement, by shared memory, or by collective enthusiasm. The Church is built by the Spirit who descends. What gathers the disciples into one body is not their affection for Christ, nor their shared suffering, nor their common past. What gathers them into one body is the fire of God. The Spirit who hovered over Christ now hovers over them. The communion between Father and Son now becomes the communion between Christ and His people. What unites them is not organisation but indwelling. The Church is born from above.

This means Pentecost is not a moment at the end of Christ's mission. It is the moment Christ's mission becomes ours. The Spirit who empowered Christ's preaching now empowers theirs. The Spirit who moved Christ to compassion now moves them to charity. The Spirit who strengthened Christ in His Passion now strengthens them for witness. What Jesus lived in His earthly life, the Church now lives in her sacramental life. The Spirit does not change His nature; He extends His work. Pentecost is the continuation of the Incarnation in the world, the ongoing presence of Christ through those who bear His Spirit.

PENTECOST: THE DESCENT OF FIRE

The early Fathers saw this clearly. They spoke of Pentecost as the moment the Church becomes the "extension of the Incarnation" across time. But they also saw it as the moment humanity becomes capable of God. The Spirit does not simply assist human weakness. He elevates human nature. He makes the believer capable of divine things—capable of loving with divine charity, forgiving with divine tenderness, enduring with divine strength, praying with divine intimacy. Pentecost therefore reveals the truth of Christ's promise: "You will do the works that I do, and greater works than these." The promise is not hyperbole. It is pneumatology.

The sacramental life of the Church flows directly from this mystery. Baptism becomes the personal Pentecost of the believer. It is the moment the Spirit enters not with tongues of fire but with the same power. Chrismation seals the new creation with the fragrance of the Spirit who rests upon Christ. The Eucharist feeds the soul with the Body of the One who lives entirely in the Spirit. Every Sunday becomes a little Pentecost, every Liturgy an upper room where fire descends, not visibly but truly. The Church does not recall Pentecost; she relives it.

Pentecost also marks the moment the Spirit becomes the new law. Not a law written on tablets of stone, but a law engraved upon the heart. The disciples do not begin obeying Christ because they fear punishment or seek reward. They obey because the Spirit has reordered their desires. Love becomes their instinct, not their achievement. Augustine expressed this transformation with a single line: "Love, and do what you will." The Spirit makes this line possible. The Spirit writes love into the soul as its new principle of action.

This interior writing of the law turns the believer into a living temple. In the Old Covenant, the temple was the singular dwelling place of God. In the New, God takes up residence in human hearts. The fire that once hovered above the Ark now hovers above the apostles. The presence that once filled the Holy of Holies now fills human bodies. Pentecost does not abolish the temple; it multiplies it. Every Christian becomes a sanctuary of fire. The Spirit does not visit occasionally; He abides. His presence is not seasonal; it is permanent.

Yet Pentecost is not given for contemplation alone. The fire that fills the disciples compels them outward. Mission is born not from zeal but from indwelling. The Spirit does not send them into the world as preachers of ideas but as bearers of a presence. They do not go to deliver information; they go to extend communion. The nations gathered in Jerusalem receive the first spark of a fire meant to cross continents and centuries. The Spirit who fills the upper room begins moving through the arteries of humanity until the world itself becomes the arena of divine revelation.

Pentecost is therefore the turning point of all existence because it marks the moment God takes up residence in humanity, not symbolically but really. Everything Christ accomplished in His earthly life—His obedience, His compassion, His wisdom, His sacrifice, His glory—now begins to unfold in His Body, the Church. What began in Mary's womb now begins in the world. What took flesh in Nazareth now takes life in every believer. Pentecost is the Incarnation extended, the Resurrection shared, the Ascension opened. It is the beginning of union.

Pentecost reveals the Spirit not only as fire that descends, but as fire that gathers. Humanity, fractured since Babel, finds in this moment its first true restoration. Where language once became a battleground of confusion, it now becomes the medium of communion. The Spirit does not reverse the diversity of tongues—He sanctifies it. Divine love does not erase difference; it makes difference capable of unity. What was once a sign of scattering becomes a sign of belonging. Each nation hears the Gospel not in a borrowed religious dialect but in its own mother tongue, as though God had stepped across every cultural threshold to call each heart personally. The Spirit does not require humanity to climb upward toward comprehension; He descends to meet every person where they stand.

This is the first glimmer of a truth the Church will grow into across centuries: the Spirit is the architect of catholicity. Catholicity is not institutional size or geographic spread. It is the miracle that the one Gospel can take root in every culture without belonging exclusively to any of them. Pentecost is the genesis of this miracle. Fire rests on Galileans, but its light belongs to the nations. In one moment, the Spirit shows the Church her destiny: to become one Body with many faces, many voices, many cultures—and one heart burning with the same divine flame.

Yet this gathering is not merely horizontal; it is vertical. The Spirit gathers humanity not only to one another but to the risen Christ. The unity He creates is not sociological but sacramental. It arises not from shared ideals but from shared indwelling. The believers who stand shoulder to shoulder in the streets of Jerusalem are united not because they have become alike but because they are inhabited by the same Presence. Unity is not the fruit of their cooperation; it is the gift of their communion. It is the Spirit who makes the Church one, because it is the Spirit who makes the Church alive.

This new unity spills immediately into a new way of living. The Acts of the Apostles describes a community marked by devotion, generosity, simplicity, and joy. These characteristics do not arise from communal enthusiasm but from the Spirit's presence. The early Christians are not idealists building a utopian society. They are people whose hearts have been reordered by divine fire. Possessions lose their tyranny because love has become stronger than fear. Prayer becomes their breath because God is no longer distant. Joy becomes their natural atmosphere because death has lost its finality. Every detail of this life points to one truth: the Spirit has not merely touched them.

He has entered them.

This interior transformation gives rise to the Church's boldness. The apostles do not force themselves into courage; they are compelled by the Spirit who dwells within them. Peter and John stand before the Sanhedrin with a freedom that astonishes their accusers. The council sees uneducated men, yet perceives an authority they cannot explain. The authority is not their own. It is the authority of the Spirit speaking Christ through them. The nerve of the early Church is not stubbornness but surrender. They are bold because they are not alone. Fear dissolves not through effort but through indwelling.

Every miracle that follows in Acts testifies to this new reality. A crippled man walks not because Peter possesses power but because Christ acts through the Spirit. An Ethiopian official finds faith not because Philip is persuasive but because the Spirit orchestrates the encounter. Communities form in unexpected places because the Spirit guides the missionaries in ways they themselves barely comprehend. The expansion of the Church is not the success of a movement. It is the movement of God.

This divine movement reveals another truth at the heart of Pentecost: the Spirit who descends is the Spirit who sends. The fire given in the upper room is not meant to be contained. Fire spreads by its nature, and the Spirit advances through the hearts He ignites. Mission is not a programme. It is the overflow of communion. The apostles do not decide to evangelise. They burn, and therefore they go. Their words carry weight not because they have mastered technique but because they have surrendered to the Spirit's inner prompting. The Spirit is both the message and the power that carries it.

Out of this missionary fire grows the discernment of charisms. Pentecost unveils the Church not as a crowd of identical believers but as a living Body with many gifts. Each gift arises from the same Spirit but expresses a different dimension of Christ. Teaching, prophecy, service, healing, hospitality, wisdom—these are not natural talents polished for religious use. They are extensions of Christ's own humanity communicated through the Spirit. Every charism is a small epiphany of Jesus in the world, a unique way the Spirit makes the Lord present. The diversity of charisms is not a problem to be managed but a harmony to be revealed. The Spirit never fragments; He composes.

This harmony becomes most visible when the Church prays. In the breaking of bread, in the psalms, in the laying on of hands, the Spirit draws human voices into a single act of worship. The early Christians do not gather to perform a ritual. They gather because the fire within them seeks expression. The Liturgy is not an event they attend. It is the divine life rising in them toward the Father. Pentecost turns prayer into participation. When the Church lifts her voice, it is Christ who prays in her, through the Spirit.

This same Spirit reshapes the inner world of every believer. Pentecost ushers in a new form of interior life—a life marked by an awareness of God's nearness. The disciples no longer pray to a distant throne; they pray from a heart now inhabited by God. Their thoughts begin to bend toward charity, their desires toward purity, their fears toward trust. None of this happens overnight, nor does it erase the human struggle. But the axis of the soul shifts. The Spirit becomes the quiet centre around which everything else begins to turn. The believer discovers a new intuition, a new freedom, a new tenderness toward God. What was once effort becomes response. What was once discipline becomes delight.

Pentecost is therefore not simply the birth of the Church but the birth of the new human being. A humanity capable of God. A humanity in whom God dwells. A humanity called not merely to obedience but to communion. The fire that appeared above the apostles is the same fire that now smoulders in every baptised soul. It is the warmth behind every act of forgiveness, the light behind every moment of clarity, the strength behind every sacrifice freely embraced. Pentecost does not change the world from without. It changes the world from within.

The fire of Pentecost not only gathers and sends; it endures. The Spirit does not descend and then withdraw. His coming inaugurates a new era of divine nearness, a new mode of God's presence within the world. The Incarnation reveals God with us. Pentecost reveals God within us. The two mysteries are inseparable, but they unfold differently. The Incarnation takes place in one body; Pentecost takes place in many. The Word becomes flesh in Christ; the Spirit becomes breath in the Church. The same divine life that filled Jesus of Nazareth now fills those who bear His name.

This enduring presence shapes how the early Christians understand the whole of salvation. They do not look back to Pentecost as a miraculous moment that belongs to the past. They look around and within. They recognise the Spirit's action in their courage under persecution, in their unity amid diversity, in their joy under hardship, in their charity that defies logic. They see in their own lives the continuation of the same fire that descended in Jerusalem. Memory becomes experience. Pentecost becomes the air they breathe.

This becomes especially clear in the Church's understanding of sacrament. The sacraments are not rituals that merely commemorate Christ's work. They are the vessels through which the Spirit applies that work. Baptism washes away sin because the Spirit descends into the waters. Chrismation seals the believer with the Spirit who rested upon Christ. The Eucharist becomes Christ's Body because the Spirit overshadows the bread and wine just as He overshadowed Mary. Confession restores the sinner because the Spirit of mercy indwells the absolution. Marriage becomes a bond of divine love because the Spirit binds bride and groom in the charity that flows from Trinity. Holy Orders consecrate a man not by human selection but by the

Spirit's anointing. The Anointing of the Sick communicates healing not as a wish but as a touch of the same Spirit who raised Jesus from the dead.

Every sacrament is, in essence, a Pentecost—fire taking shape in matter to draw a soul into union with God. The sacraments are not magical. They are relational. The Spirit works through them because He desires to inhabit the whole fabric of human life. Nothing is too mundane, too physical, or too wounded to become a place of His descent. God enters through water, oil, bread, hands, breath, words—not because He must, but because He wills to dignify creation with His presence. Pentecost sanctifies the world from within.

This indwelling presence also transforms suffering. The early Christians do not interpret persecution as a sign of abandonment but as evidence of communion. The same Spirit who strengthened Christ in Gethsemane strengthens them in their trials. The same fire that descended in the upper room now burns in their fidelity. When Stephen stands before the council, Scripture says he is "filled with the Holy Spirit." His martyrdom is not the extinguishing of a flame but its consummation. His final vision of Christ standing at the right hand of the Father is not granted to console him. It is granted to reveal what Pentecost has made possible: a human being able to see divine glory even as stones fall upon him. The Spirit does not spare him suffering. The Spirit transforms suffering into witness.

This transformation extends even to death. For the believer, death is no longer a descent into darkness but an ascent into the fullness of the Spirit's life. Pentecost does not remove mortality; it infuses mortality with hope. The Spirit who raised Christ will raise all who belong to Him. Death becomes a threshold, not a terminus. The Spirit becomes the pledge—the arrabōn—of the resurrection to come. The fire given in the upper room is the same fire that will one day kindle every tomb with light. Pentecost bends history toward transfiguration.

Yet even this does not capture the whole mystery. For Pentecost is also the beginning of mission that stretches across centuries and continents. The Church that emerges from the upper room is not a local fellowship but the seed of a universal communion. The Spirit pushes outward, always outward—toward Samaria, toward Antioch, toward Greece, toward Rome, toward the ends of the earth. Missionaries go not because they are enthusiastic but because they are compelled. The Spirit becomes the wind in their sails, the fire in their words, the tenderness in their charity. Their failure does not extinguish the Spirit; their weakness does not limit Him. The Spirit chooses instruments, but the mission is His.

This missionary movement reveals a final truth: Pentecost is the unveiling of God's desire to dwell with humanity forever. From the beginning, God sought union. In the garden, this union was offered; in Israel, it was promised; in Christ, it was revealed; in Pentecost, it begins to be realised. God does not simply save humanity from sin. He draws humanity into His own life. Pentecost is the descent of divine love into human hearts so that human hearts may ascend into divine love. It is the marriage of heaven and earth. It is the moment humanity becomes the dwelling place of God.

And this indwelling does not fade. The Spirit remains. He remains when the believer prays and when the believer cannot pray. He remains when faith is bright and when faith trembles. He remains in the sacraments, in Scripture, in the Liturgy, in the communion of saints, in the small obedience's of daily life. The Spirit remains because Pentecost is not an episode. It is the state of the Church. It is the atmosphere of Christian existence. It is the beginning of union.

The fire that descended upon the apostles has never been extinguished. It burns in the hidden fidelity of monks, in the quiet charity of mothers, in the bold preaching of evangelists, in the tears of penitents, in the perseverance of the suffering, in the joy of saints. It burns wherever a heart turns toward God. It burns wherever the Eucharist is celebrated. It burns whenever a sinner returns home. It burns even in darkness, because the darkness cannot overcome it.

Pentecost is the moment God crosses the threshold into humanity with finality. The Spirit who rested upon Christ now rests upon His Body. The fire of divine love enters the world not to scorch but to sanctify, not to terrify but to transfigure. The God who once descended upon a mountain now descends upon human hearts. And from those hearts He spreads, until the whole world becomes the dwelling place of His glory.

12

From Illumination to Indwelling

The story so far has traced the Spirit's approach—from the vastness of creation to the chambers of the human heart. Every movement that preceded has been a descent. The Spirit has come toward the world, toward Israel, toward Christ's humanity, toward the interior of the believer. His way is always the same: He enters before He transforms, and He transforms by dwelling. Purification clears a space; illumination fills that space with light. Both stages are facets of one divine gesture—the gesture of God drawing near.

From the first page of Genesis, creation is taught to recognise the Spirit through His manner of moving. He does not erupt like a storm. He hovers. He broods. He enfolds. He brings cosmos out of chaos not by force but by presence. The Light of the First Day is not kindled by violence; it is summoned by the Spirit's nearness. Where He rests, order arises. Where He breathes, life awakens. Where He broods, beauty appears as if responding to a subtle invitation. The pattern is unmistakable: the Spirit does not begin by speaking; He begins by drawing close.

Humanity's story bears the same imprint. The breath placed in Adam's lungs was not simply animation but communion—an interior place where God could dwell. The tragedy of sin is not the loss of nature but the obscuring of capacity. The image remained but dimmed, the likeness fractured but not erased. Purification begins in that dimness, not as moral strain but as divine compassion. The Spirit's first act is to return to the place where the likeness was lost, to hover again over the darkened waters of the heart, coaxing it back toward the light for which it was created.

Israel's story unfolds this same pattern on a grand scale. The Spirit who hovered over the waters now descends upon judges, kings, prophets, and priests—each an icon of the future anointing. The cloud and the fire that overshadow the Temple echo the brooding at creation's dawn. The prophets speak with a clarity not their own, carried by the Spirit who begins to sketch the contours of a new humanity. Israel learns, slowly and painfully, that holiness cannot be achieved by effort alone. Law reveals the path, but only the Spirit can give the heart strength to walk it.

The promises sharpen as the story advances. A new heart. A new spirit. A law written not on stone but within the flesh of the soul. A cleansing not wrought by ritual effort but by divine fire. These promises are not moral upgrades; they are prophecies of a new creation. The same Spirit who shaped galaxies will shape souls. The same Breath who gave life to Adam will breathe again. The same Fire who led Israel will burn within the heart. Purification reveals its true nature: it is God preparing a sanctuary, clearing space for His own indwelling.

This preparation reaches its climax in Christ. Everything the Spirit once did from outside He now accomplishes within a human nature personally united to Him. The overshadowing of Mary is creation revisited; the baptism in the Jordan is anointing renewed; the preaching of the Kingdom is illumination embodied; the Passion is love aflame; the Resurrection is new creation unveiled; Pentecost is the descent of the Fire who rested upon the Messiah now resting upon His Body. Illumination is nothing less than participation in Christ's own vision of the Father, a sharing in His light, His understanding, His obedience, His compassion.

Through all of this, the Spirit has been teaching humanity one truth: God does not wish merely to cleanse or to instruct; He wishes to dwell. The Spirit purifies the heart so that it may see God. The Spirit illumines the mind so that it may know God. Yet both purification and illumination serve a deeper purpose—they prepare the soul to become the home of God Himself.

Union is the miracle for which every earlier movement exists.

Everything the Spirit hovered over now becomes the place He inhabits. The deep becomes a dwelling. The heart becomes a temple. The Church becomes a Body. Humanity becomes capable of bearing the fire of divine life without being consumed. This is the mystery toward which creation has been groaning since the beginning: not simply forgiveness, not mere enlightenment, but indwelling—the Spirit living within the creature He shaped from dust.

The soul that has passed through purification and illumination crosses a threshold. It ceases to seek God as though He were distant and begins to discover Him at the centre of its own existence. Prayer changes. Scripture opens. Sacraments unveil their hidden splendour. Virtue becomes less a task and more a flowering. The interior world shifts from fragmentation to harmony—not by human technique but by divine habitation. The believer senses, perhaps for the first time, that holiness is not distant; it is present. God is not merely above; God is within.

The Fathers describe this moment as the soul becoming "spacious." Sin narrows the heart into a cramped interior, filled with noise and shadows. Purification clears it. Illumination brightens it. Indwelling enlarges it until it becomes capable of receiving the fullness of divine life. The Spirit makes the heart wide enough to contain joy, strong enough to bear love, and deep enough to echo eternity.

This spaciousness is not an escape from the world but the capacity to inhabit it with divine vision. The illumined soul begins to see as Christ sees, love as Christ loves, judge as Christ judges, forgive as Christ forgives. Not metaphorically. Mystically. Actually. The Spirit forms Christ within the believer, and the believer becomes transparent to God.

The entire history of salvation has been a preparation for this: the moment God lives in humanity as within His chosen home.

When the soul begins to recognise the Spirit dwelling within, it does not feel like possession but like freedom. The interior life is no longer a battlefield between scattered desires but a single movement toward God. The heart that once strained after fragmented goods now gravitates toward the One Good with a clarity that surprises even itself. It is not that effort disappears, but that effort becomes cooperation rather than resistance. The soul discovers that obedience is not servitude but resonance—its desires aligning with divine desire the way strings of an instrument vibrate when the proper note is sounded nearby.

Indwelling is the place where divine charity becomes the logic of the soul. The love with which Christ loved His Father begins to take root in the believer, not as imitation but as participation. What Christ lived on earth—His tenderness, His firmness, His purity, His mercy, His reverence, His single-hearted devotion—becomes the pattern impressed upon the soul by the Spirit. The believer tastes what Jesus Himself knew: that the Father is never far, that His will is not oppressive, and that His presence can become the air one breathes.

This changes the whole landscape of the spiritual life. Prayer ceases to be an attempt to reach God and becomes a dwelling in God. Scripture ceases to be a text to decipher and becomes a voice that resounds within. Sacraments cease to be rituals and become encounters. Virtue ceases to be a discipline imposed from without and becomes the blossoming of Christ's life from within. The Christian does not rise by climbing; the Christian rises by indwelling. The Spirit does in the soul what He did in the body of Christ—He fills, He sanctifies, He glorifies.

Everything that once felt external now becomes interior. The commandments no longer appear as distant ideals but as the natural movements of a heart steeped in divine desire. The soul that once fought against sin with clenched teeth now simply sees the ugliness of sin and turns away because it has tasted something more beautiful. The soul that once feared suffering now sees it in the light of the Cross, not as absurdity but as a moment to love. This is not stoicism; it is transformation. The Spirit aligns the inner world with the rhythms of the Son.

This interior transformation, however, is not a private experience. Indwelling creates communion. The Spirit never forms isolated mystics; He forms a Body. The God who dwells within the soul also knits souls together in unity, so that communion with God and communion with others become inseparable. The believer discovers that to love God within is also to love the brethren without. The more deeply the Spirit takes root, the more the soul becomes attentive, compassionate, patient, forgiving. Divine love cannot remain locked inside the heart; the Spirit presses outward, forming relationships, reconciling divisions, healing wounds.

This outward expansion of love is not an add-on to indwelling; it is its fruit. A heart that carries God cannot remain small. A person who houses divine life cannot remain self-contained. The Spirit who indwells is the Spirit who unites, and He carries each believer into the mystery of the Church—a communion not of shared interests but of shared life. The Body of Christ is not an institution that happens to possess God; it is a people in whom God dwells. Every Christian becomes a living stone because the Spirit makes the Church God's living temple.

Indwelling also deepens the mystery of suffering. The soul no longer views suffering as abandonment but as participation. The Spirit who accomplished the sacrifice of Christ now allows the believer to join that sacrifice in love. Suffering becomes the place where divine life is most revealed, not because pain is good, but because the Spirit turns pain into love. The wounds of life become openings through which grace flows. The soul does not glorify suffering; it glorifies God in suffering. This is the paradox of union—the believer carries the Cross not as weight but as communion.

The gradual work of the Spirit in the soul reveals a truth that purification and illumination only hinted at: humanity was not merely designed to receive God's gifts but to receive God Himself. The image was not merely the capacity for reason or freedom; it was the capacity for indwelling. The likeness was not merely moral resemblance; it was participation in divine life. Everything that Adam lost, Christ restores—and more. The Spirit does not lead the soul back to Eden but forward to deification. Union is not the recovery of a past glory but the unveiling of a greater glory.

The ascent of the soul reaches a new horizon here. What began with the Spirit hovering over the waters now ends with the Spirit resting within the heart. What began with creation now culminates in communion. The soul that was once formless and void has become a sanctuary. The heart that once knew only shadows now becomes luminous. The person who once sought God as distant now knows Him as interior. The Spirit does not simply reveal God to the soul; He reveals God within the soul.

And yet union is not the end of the journey. It is the atmosphere in which the rest of Christian life unfolds. Indwelling prepares the believer for works of love, for discernment, for sacramental encounters, for sanctification of mind and memory, for transformation of passions, for steady growth into the likeness of Christ. The life of union is not stillness alone; it is fruitfulness. The Spirit's presence is fire, and fire cannot remain idle. The soul that carries God becomes a vessel of His energy—healing, teaching, discerning, loving, forgiving, creating, reconciling.

The God who dwells within the believer is the same God who dwells within the Church. The Spirit shapes not only individuals but communities, not only hearts but sacraments, not only prayer but mission. Indwelling is the beginning of the Spirit's outpouring into every dimension of Christian existence. What He has purified and illumined, He now vivifies. What He has cleansed and enlightened, He now fills with divine energy.

Every thread of the story leads to this truth: the Spirit does not touch the human heart from afar. He enters it. He lives in it. He transfigures it from within, so that the believer may become what Christ is by nature—one who lives in the Father's love.

Purification prepares the heart.

Illumination opens the mind.

Indwelling completes the embrace.

The next movement unfolds from this embrace, as the Spirit interiorly forms the Church, ignites the sacraments, opens Scripture, shapes prayer, heals the wounds of the heart, and leads the soul into the full splendour of divine life.

This is the world in which the soul now stands—the world of union, the world of indwelling, the world of the Spirit who makes His home in humanity.

III

The Spirit Who Indwells (Union)

13

The Spirit Who Makes the Church: Body, Temple, Bride

The mystery of union does not reach its fulfilment when the individual soul discovers God within. It reaches its fulfilment when that indwelling becomes communion — when the Spirit who dwells in one draws that one into the life of many. Nothing in the spiritual life is more counter-intuitive to the modern imagination. Modern spirituality prizes interior authenticity but mistrusts shared life. It loves the idea of God in the heart but bristles at the idea of God forming a people. Yet the Spirit never indwells merely to console. He indwells to gather. He does not build sanctuaries of solitude; He builds a living communion through which the Son continues His presence in the world.

Pentecost reveals this unmistakably. The Spirit descends not upon a lone seeker but upon a gathered assembly. The flame rests on each, yet the sound from heaven enfolds all. The Spirit individualises by giving each person a distinct tongue of fire, yet unites by giving all one voice that proclaims the mighty works of God. Here the Spirit discloses His nature: He creates persons and communion at once. He restores the uniqueness sin fractures and restores the unity sin dissolves. The

Church's birth is not an organisational event but a theophany — the moment the Spirit binds many into one life in Christ.

From this moment onward, the Church does not grow by strategy or structure but by the Spirit extending Christ's life into new persons. When the Acts of the Apostles says, "The Lord added to their number day by day," the full truth underneath is that *the Spirit knit new members into the Body*. Evangelisation is the Spirit drawing new hearts into the current of divine life. Communion is not the achievement of human cooperation; it is the work of the Spirit who shapes a humanity capable of love.

To understand the Church as communion, we must see how the Spirit works. The Spirit does not unite by erasing distinction. He unites by making distinction luminous. The flame at Pentecost does not turn the disciples into identical embers. Each flame remains uniquely itself, yet all burn with one fire. The Spirit draws people into unity by intensifying their personhood, not diluting it. Love does not require sameness; it requires relation. Relation requires difference. The Spirit is the bond of love because He is the One who holds difference together without dissolving it. This is why the Church is never a collective mass but a communion of persons — each one known, called, and sanctified by the Spirit.

The first Christians perceived this instinctively. They understood that what bound them was not shared ethnicity, language, temperament, or background, but the Spirit who had taken up His dwelling in them. They did not gather because they liked one another. They gathered because each recognised the same divine fire in the other. The Church is the place where the Spirit recognises Himself in human hearts and unites those hearts with a strength no human bond can match. Friendship, sympathy, and cooperation may sustain associations, but only the Spirit creates communion.

This communion is not optional to the Christian life. It is the form the Christian life takes once the Spirit indwells. The Spirit does not simply whisper "Abba" in the heart; He whispers "our." He does not simply draw the soul to Christ; He draws the soul into the Body that belongs to Christ. To be joined to Christ is to be joined to those He has claimed as His own. The Spirit never creates intimacy that isolates, only intimacy that shares. Union with God and union with God's people are two movements of the same love.

This truth unfolds across the whole of Scripture. Whenever God draws near, He gathers a people. The Spirit descends upon the judges to liberate Israel, upon the kings to shepherd them, upon the prophets to recall them, upon the remnant to sustain hope, upon the apostles to establish the Church, upon the saints to build her up. The Spirit always forms communion because God's purpose is not merely to sanctify individuals but to restore humanity to its original vocation: a communion of persons bound together in divine love.

Three images in Scripture reveal this communion in its deepest dimension: Body, Temple, and Bride. These are not metaphors but mysteries. They describe what the Spirit accomplishes in those whom He indwells.

When Paul speaks of the Body of Christ, he does not mean a symbolic unity. He means that the Spirit binds the members of the Church into a real participation in Christ's humanity. The Spirit makes Christians part of Christ's risen Body not by analogy but by incorporation. The divine life that circulates in the Son flows through all who belong to Him because the Spirit is the life of that Body.

When Paul calls the Church the Temple of the Spirit, he draws upon the whole sweep of salvation history — the cloud of glory resting upon the Tent of Meeting, the fire descending upon Solomon's Temple, the yearning of the exiles for God's presence to return. In the Church, that presence descends again, no longer upon stone but upon flesh. The Spirit consecrates the people of God so that they become the place where God dwells.

When Scripture speaks of the Bride, it unveils the most intimate truth of all: the Spirit forms a people capable of loving Christ with the very love that flows eternally between Father and Son. The Church is not merely instructed by Christ but united to Him in covenantal fidelity. The Spirit prepares the Bride's heart, adorns her with holiness, and fills her with longing for the Bridegroom who gives Himself without reserve.

These images will unfold in the movements to come, but one vision must already be clear: union is communion. The Spirit who indwells the soul now stretches the soul into a shared life, enlarging it to contain others, beautifying it to love others, strengthening it to carry others. The very presence that makes Christ known within now makes Christ visible among. The Church is the place where the Spirit's hidden fire becomes a living flame in the world.

The Spirit's work in forming communion becomes clearest when we look at the earliest Christian experience. From the moment the apostles step into the streets of Jerusalem after Pentecost, something unmistakable radiates from them — not brilliance of speech, not political influence, not social strategy, but a presence. Luke describes this with a simplicity that conceals its power: "Great grace was upon them all." The Church's beginning is nothing less than the Spirit Himself shining through human lives. The believers do not merely gather; they *glow*. What binds them is not agreement but grace, not enthusiasm but indwelling.

This is why the earliest Christian community places such emphasis on "the fellowship." Fellowship is not a warm atmosphere or a friendly disposition; it is the lived form of the Spirit's union. They devote themselves to it because it is not something they have built — it is something they have received. The Spirit makes them participants in one another's lives in a way unknown to the ancient world. They hold their possessions loosely because the Spirit has already dissolved fear. They break bread in their homes because the Spirit has inscribed hospitality upon their hearts. They pray together because the Spirit draws their voices into one breath. Everything that looks like virtue is, in truth, the movement of the Spirit shaping a new humanity.

The Spirit's communion proves itself strongest in what the world would call weakness. When persecution arises, the believers do not scatter as individuals; they become even more deeply one. The Spirit does not merely console them; He knits them together. Their unity becomes the witness. Their courage becomes the proclamation. Their endurance becomes the sign that something greater than human will binds them. The early Church survives not because it organises itself well but because the Spirit dwells within it as life, strength, and fire.

To say the Spirit makes the Church, then, is not theological poetry. It is simple realism. Without the Spirit, the Church becomes nothing more than a human association held together by habit, doctrine, or nostalgia. With the Spirit, the Church becomes the earthly visibility of Christ's risen Body. The difference is not subtle. In the first case, unity is fragile, dependent on consensus. In the second, unity is indestructible because it is grounded in the Spirit who cannot be divided.

This leads to a decisive truth: the Church is not the result of human believers gathering around Christ, but the result of the Spirit gathering believers into Christ. The direction of movement matters. We do not create communion by our belonging; we discover communion because the Spirit has woven us into it. We do not join a club; we are taken up into a mystery. The Church is not the sum of Christian hearts; it is the life of Christ extended, through the Spirit, into human form.

Here the image of the Body reaches its full depth. A limb does not join a body by attachment; it arises from the body as an expression of its life. Each Christian becomes a member of Christ's Body not by contribution but by participation. The Spirit gives each member a function, not as a task to perform but as a mode of Christ's own life expressing itself uniquely. The gift is not an assignment but an infusion. Every charism is the Spirit revealing Christ through a particular human personality. Teaching, prophecy, service, mercy, wisdom — these are not spiritual talents; they are the movements of Christ's Spirit in His members.

The Spirit's indwelling therefore makes the Church not a structure but a living organism. Structures are necessary, but they exist to serve life. Life does not exist to serve structure. Whenever the Church forgets this, she becomes rigid, anxious, defensive — because the Spirit has been eclipsed. Whenever she remembers it, she becomes bold, open, radiant — because the Spirit breathes freely again. The health of the Church is measured not by efficiency but by consent to the Spirit. When the Spirit moves, the Church becomes herself.

If the Body reveals the Church's organic unity, the image of the Temple reveals her sanctity. Paul's declaration — "You are the temple of the Holy Spirit" — is not addressed to individuals but to the gathered community. The Spirit dwells in the midst of God's people the way His glory once dwelt in the Holy of Holies. The early Christians grasp this with awe. To enter the assembly is to enter the place where heaven touches earth. Not because of architecture, but because of presence. The Spirit fills the Church the way fire filled the bush before Moses: the community burns with divine life yet is not consumed.

This presence shapes everything. Worship becomes an encounter rather than a performance. Teaching becomes revelation rather than opinion. Discipline becomes healing rather than punishment. Authority becomes service rather than domination. Everything takes its form from the Spirit who works in hiddenness yet manifests in transformation. Holiness is not a moral achievement; it is the atmosphere created when the Spirit dwells among His people.

The Temple image also teaches reverence for one another. If the community is the dwelling of the Spirit, then every member is sacred space. The weakest, the wounded, the overlooked — in them the Spirit rests with special tenderness. The Fathers insist that to harm another believer is not merely to injure a person but to desecrate a sanctuary. The Spirit does not divide His presence into portions; He gives Himself whole to each. The least in the Church can therefore say with truth: the Spirit who overshadowed Mary overshadows me.

Finally, the image of the Bride discloses the deepest dimension of union. The Spirit prepares a people capable of loving Christ with a love that corresponds to His own. This is not a poetic flourish; it is the heart of divine revelation. The Bride is adorned not by her effort but by the Spirit clothing her with holiness, fidelity, and desire. The Spirit gives her the capacity to return Christ's love as gift, not merely as gratitude. Union reaches its summit when love becomes reciprocal — when the Spirit forms in the Church the same love with which Christ gives Himself.

All three images — Body, Temple, Bride — converge in one truth: the Spirit makes the Church by making her share in Christ's own life. The Spirit is not an addition to the Church but her very principle of existence. She lives because He lives in her. She loves because He loves in her. She endures because He carries her.

The Spirit's work in forming the Church becomes visible not only in the community's unity, holiness, and love, but also in its astonishing diversity. The Spirit does not build a monolith. He builds a symphony. Each member receives not merely a place in the Body but a particular grace, a unique way in which Christ desires to manifest His life. Paul speaks of "varieties of gifts, but the same Spirit," and he speaks so not to catalogue functions but to reveal a mystery: the Spirit's generosity expresses itself through difference. He delights in diversity because diversity is the canvas upon which communion becomes beautiful.

This is why the New Testament never imagines a Church in which everyone does the same thing. The Spirit refuses uniformity because uniformity cannot express the fullness of Christ. The Son contains every perfection in Himself; the Church reveals those perfections by distributing them across countless lives. Wisdom appears in one, mercy in another, courage in another, compassion in another, contemplation in another. Taken together, these lives paint an icon of Christ far more radiant than any single life could bear. The Spirit does not flatten individuality; He heightens it until individuality becomes vocation.

Vocation, in this sense, is not primarily about state of life or ministry. It is the unveiling of the way Christ desires to live His life uniquely within a person. The Spirit reveals not only who God is, but who the person is in God. When a Christian begins to sense a particular attraction to prayer, or service, or teaching, or evangelisation, or healing, or silence, what moves beneath that attraction is not preference but presence. The Spirit is shaping the soul for a particular resonance within the Body. A charism is not something one does; it is something Christ does through the Spirit in a particular member.

This becomes especially clear when we look at the lives of the saints. Francis of Assisi is not simply a man who chose poverty; he is a man in whom the Spirit revealed Christ's poverty. Catherine of Siena is not simply a woman who spoke boldly; she is a woman in whom the Spirit revealed Christ's truth. Anthony the Great is not simply a monk who embraced solitude; he is a soul in whom the Spirit revealed Christ's single-hearted communion with the Father. Every saint is a place where the Spirit manifests a facet of Christ's beauty for the sake of the whole Church. Sanctity is never self-contained; it is always ecclesial. Even the hermit is a gift to the community he never sees.

The Spirit's orchestration of these vocations reveals something even deeper: charisms exist for love. They exist so that the Body may be built up. They are not badges of honour or measures of dignity. They are instruments. A charism without charity becomes noise. A charism animated by charity becomes a window through which the Church glimpses Christ. The Spirit distributes gifts freely, but He orders them toward the bond of love. The measure of a gift is not its power but its capacity to serve.

This is why jealousy, comparison, and rivalry suffocate spiritual life. They arise when the eyes turn away from the Spirit and fix instead on the self. In such moments the person forgets that every grace is given, that no one possesses anything except what the Spirit entrusts for the sake of others. The early Church understood this deeply. Their unity was not a sentimental feeling but a recognition: each person bore something from God that the others needed. The hand needed the eye; the eye needed the foot; the foot needed the heart. No part could boast; all belonged to one another because all belonged to the Spirit.

The Spirit's creation of communion does not happen only in moments of glory. It happens in conflict as well. When disagreements arise — as they inevitably did even in the apostolic age — the Church does not resolve them by mere debate. She seeks the Spirit. This is why the Council of Jerusalem concludes its decree with the astonishing phrase: "It has seemed good to the Holy Spirit and to us." The Church discerns not by power but by surrender. True authority is exercised when leaders listen for the movement of the Spirit more intently than they listen to the noise of competing desires. The unity that emerges is not compromise but revelation — the Spirit showing the Church how to remain faithful to Christ.

This discernment continues through the centuries. In every age, the Spirit raises up teachers, mystics, martyrs, pastors, and reformers to guide the Church through new challenges. When corruption appears, the Spirit inspires prophets who recall the Church to holiness. When confusion arises, the Spirit enlightens theologians who clarify the faith. When persecution comes, the Spirit strengthens martyrs who witness to Christ with their lives. When renewal is needed, the Spirit awakens saints whose hidden fidelity rekindles the fire in the whole Body. History is not the Church's story of survival; it is the Spirit's story of fidelity.

This fidelity, however, is never abstract. It is experienced in the concrete forms of community life: shared worship, mutual forgiveness, bearing one another's burdens, correcting one another with gentleness, rejoicing together, mourning together. The Spirit creates communion not by idealising life but by sanctifying its ordinary rhythms. The Christian who prays for another, forgives another, consoles another, or serves another participates in the Spirit's own movements. The Spirit's presence is not proven by ecstasy but by charity. A community where love endures suffering, misunderstanding, and imperfection reveals a greater miracle than any external sign: the miracle of the Spirit dwelling where human strength fails.

Within this life of communion, the deepest mystery shines through: the Spirit makes the Church able to love Christ with a love that corresponds to His own. Human affection is not enough to form the Bride. Only the Spirit can shape the heart to desire Christ with the same longing Christ has for His people. The Spirit awakens in the Church the cry, "Come, Lord Jesus," the cry that echoes the eternal longing between Father and Son. In this cry the Church discovers her identity. She is the Bride, and her love is not self-generated but Spirit-breathed.

All of this leads to a single truth: the Church is not simply the place where the Spirit acts — the Church is what the Spirit forms.

Everything that makes the Church holy, one, catholic, and apostolic arises from His presence. Without Him, there is no Body, no Temple, no Bride. With Him, the human community becomes the dwelling of God, the continuation of Christ's presence, and the seed of the new creation.

The life the Spirit forms in the Church does not remain enclosed within her walls. Communion is expansive by nature. Love pressed into the heart longs to overflow, and the Spirit is this longing. From the beginning, Christ commissions His disciples not by giving them a strategy but by promising them the Spirit: "You will receive power when the Holy Spirit has come upon you, and you will be my witnesses." The Spirit does not merely sanctify the Church; He thrusts her outward. Union becomes mission. Contemplation becomes witness. The inner fire becomes a light for the world.

This outward movement is not activism. It is the radiance of an indwelling Presence. What the apostles carry into the world is not their enthusiasm, eloquence, or courage; it is the Spirit who lives within them. Their preaching is carried by the Spirit; their miracles are signs of the Spirit; their sufferings reveal the Spirit's endurance. When the world encounters the apostles, it encounters the Spirit's continuation of Christ's life in human form. Evangelisation is not the Church speaking about Christ; it is the Spirit speaking Christ through the Church.

This is why Christian mission has always been marked by paradox. The Church grows through the weak, not the strong; through the simple, not the clever; through those who depend on the Spirit, not on their own resources. The apostles carry no earthly power, yet the Spirit turns the world upside down through them. Martyrs possess no weapons, yet their testimony breaks empires. Missionaries bear no guarantees of success, yet nations receive faith through their hidden fidelity. The Spirit magnifies what the world ignores. He chooses ordinary instruments so that His work may be recognised as His, not theirs.

As the Spirit sends the Church outward, He also draws her inward — deeper into communion, deeper into holiness, deeper into the mystery of Christ. The rhythm of the Church's life is not linear but circular, like breath. The Spirit draws the community together in worship, fills her with divine life, and then sends her out again into the world — only to gather her once more. This is why the Fathers describe the Spirit as the "circulation of divine love" within the Body of Christ. He is the pulse of the Church's existence, the breath in her lungs, the strength in her limbs.

Within this circulation, the Spirit continues His hidden yet potent work of sanctification. Holiness is not a private pursuit; it is the gift the Spirit gives for the sake of all. When He makes one person humble, others find their pride dissolving. When He makes one person merciful, others find forgiveness possible. When He makes one person courageous, others discover their fear lifted. The holiness of one becomes the blessing of many because the Spirit knits the lives of believers so intimately that grace cannot remain isolated. In the Body, holiness circulates.

This is why the Church venerates the saints. Their holiness is not an accomplishment that earns admiration; it is the Spirit's victory made visible. A saint reveals what the Church is called to be. Each saint shows a particular splendour of the Spirit — Francis burning with poverty, Thérèse burning with trust, Anthony burning with solitude, Catherine burning with truth, Maximilian Kolbe burning with sacrificial love. Sanctity is not uniform; it is the kaleidoscopic beauty of Christ refracted through countless lives because the Spirit delights in revealing Christ endlessly.

Yet the Spirit's work in forming the Church is not always luminous. It is also purifying. The Spirit exposes corruption not to shame the Church but to heal her. He reveals sin not to condemn but to restore. Wherever darkness festers in Christian communities — pride, injustice, exploitation, manipulation — the Spirit agitates, stirs consciences, raises prophets, and compels repentance. The Spirit fights for the Church's holiness even when the Church resists Him. His love does not tolerate what wounds the Body. His fidelity does not allow the Bride to betray her identity. The Spirit is the consuming fire that both warms and burns.

Alongside purifying darkness, the Spirit preserves unity. Unity is not the absence of conflict; it is the refusal to allow conflict to sever communion. The Spirit sustains unity not by suppressing disagreements but by preventing disagreements from becoming divisions. This is why the Church throughout history has endured crises that should have shattered her — theological disputes, cultural upheavals, internal failures — yet remains unbroken. The Spirit binds the Church more deeply than any force can tear her apart. Human frailty, even scandal, cannot nullify divine indwelling.

The Spirit also guards the Church's memory. Tradition is not nostalgia; it is the Spirit preserving Christ's voice across generations. The same Spirit who overshadowed the apostles illumines the Fathers, guides the councils, inspires the liturgy, and sustains the faithful in every age. The Church remembers because the Spirit remembers. The Church teaches because the Spirit teaches. The Church endures because the Spirit endures. Continuity is not the achievement of human institutions but the promise of the Spirit who refuses to abandon what He has made His dwelling.

Finally, the Spirit stirs within the Church a longing that no earthly fulfilment can satisfy. This is the longing expressed at the end of Scripture itself: "The Spirit and the Bride say, 'Come.'" It is the cry of the Church yearning for the Bridegroom, and it is the Spirit crying within her. Union on earth is real but incomplete. The Spirit indwells as pledge, as guarantee, as first-fruits — the foretaste of a glory yet to come. The Church lives between presence and promise, possessing Christ yet longing for His face. This longing is not frustration; it is love stretching toward fulfilment.

All these movements — unity, diversity, holiness, mission, purification, memory, longing — converge in a single truth: the Spirit is the soul of the Church. He is the life within her Body, the fire within her Temple, the love within her Bridehood. The Church exists because He breathes. She suffers because He purifies. She shines because He indwells. She endures because He remains.

Union, then, is not a mystical height attained by a few. It is the ordinary, glorious state of those who live in the Spirit. It is the life of the Church. It is the life the Spirit gives.

14

The Fire of the Sacraments

The sacraments are often described as channels of grace, but such language—though true—can veil the living reality at their heart. They are not static conduits. They are moments of divine activity. They are the places where the Holy Spirit descends with fire, touches matter with His breath, and reshapes human life from within. The Spirit does not observe the sacraments; He performs them. He does not assist the sacraments; He accomplishes them. What the sacraments communicate is not a "thing" called grace but the Spirit Himself, the very Gift of God given in Christ. Every sacrament is an epiclesis before it is anything else: a calling down of the Spirit, a yielding to His creative presence, an overshadowing like that which once fell upon the Virgin. The Spirit who made God present in her womb now makes Christ present in His Church, and He does so through fire.

The clearest place to begin is the Divine Liturgy, because it reveals the logic of all the sacraments. When the priest extends his hands over the gifts and invokes the Spirit—"Send down Your Holy Spirit upon us and upon these gifts here offered, and make this bread the precious Body of Your Christ…"—the Church stands at the moment where heaven bends into earth. Nothing in the liturgy is transformed until the Spirit descends. Nothing becomes holy until He moves. Bread remains bread; wine remains wine; the assembly remains merely human—until the Spirit overshadows. This is the Church's oldest and deepest conviction: the Spirit effects the mysteries. The priest asks; the Spirit acts. The priest stretches out his hands; the Spirit stretches out divine life. The priest invokes fire; the Spirit answers with Himself.

This descent is not metaphorical. The Fathers insist upon it with a clarity modern Christians sometimes neglect. St. Basil calls the Spirit "the perfecting power," the One who completes every divine work. Nicholas Cabasilas speaks of the Spirit as "the soul of the mysteries," without whom the sacraments are empty gestures. St. Cyril of Jerusalem tells the newly baptised that the oil placed upon them is no mere symbol but the very presence of the Spirit—"you have become Christ-bearers"—because the Spirit Himself entered them through the anointing. The sacramental life of the Church is nothing less than the ongoing Pentecost of God in the world. What happened once in the upper room now happens every time the Spirit descends upon water, oil, bread, wine, hands, bodies, wounds, and hearts.

The epiclesis reveals the pattern: the Spirit descends upon matter in order to raise it beyond itself. This is how God has always worked. He hovered over the waters at creation, not to admire them but to turn chaos into cosmos. He overshadowed the Virgin to bring forth the humanity of Christ. He descended at Pentecost to form the Church into the Body of the Son. In each instance the Spirit does not replace nature; He fulfils it. He enters matter not to destroy it but to transfigure it. The sacraments are the continuation of this same descent—God touching creation with His own life so that creation may become the place where God dwells.

This becomes astonishingly clear in Baptism, the sacrament where the Spirit's creative power is most explicitly revealed. Baptism is not simply the washing away of sin; it is the Spirit's re-creation of the human person. The waters are His workshop. When the priest invokes the Spirit over the font, the waters become the womb in which the Spirit forms a new being. "Unless you are born of water and the Spirit," Christ says, "you cannot enter the kingdom." The emphasis is not on water; it is on the Spirit. Water is the material into which the Spirit breathes. In the ancient Church, the newly baptised emerged from the font and were immediately called "illuminated," because the Spirit had entered them like fire entering gold, making them radiant from within. Baptism is the descent of the Spirit into the depths of human identity. The person who rises from the water does not simply have divine life—he is indwelt by the Spirit who gives divine life.

But the Spirit does not merely create new life; He seals it, strengthens it, and equips it for battle. This is the mystery of Chrismation, the anointing with holy oil. The early Christians saw this as nothing less than personal Pentecost. The oil is not merely consecrated; it is Spirit-filled. When the priest anoints the forehead, the eyes, the nostrils, the mouth, the chest, the shoulders, the feet, he is not drawing symbols upon the body but invoking the Spirit to dwell in the senses, the desires, the mind, the heart, the strength of the person. St. Cyril of Jerusalem describes chrism as "the seal of the Spirit," the imprint of divine life upon the soul, guarding, empowering, and filling the believer with the fragrance of Christ. Chrismation is the Spirit clothing the new Christian with fire so that the life given in baptism may grow, mature, and bear fruit.

Already the pattern has emerged. The Spirit descends. The Spirit transforms. The Spirit indwells. Baptism and Chrismation are not ceremonial beginnings; they are the Spirit's first acts of union. He takes the believer into His own life and begins shaping the heart into a place capable of divine presence. Sin is forgiven, but more profoundly, a new capacity is born—a capacity for holiness, prayer, discernment, virtue, communion. What God commands He now empowers. What God promises He now begins to fulfill. The Spirit becomes the interior teacher, the inner light, the breath animating the new creation in the heart.

Yet no sacrament reveals the Spirit's fire more clearly than the Eucharist. For here the Spirit does nothing less than bring forth again the Body and Blood of Christ. The Church does not imagine this transformation as a mechanical process; she attributes it directly to the Spirit's descent. The priest calls for fire, and fire descends. Bread becomes the Body of the crucified and risen Lord. Wine becomes His Blood. But the Spirit's work does not end at the altar. His descent does not stop with matter. He transforms those who receive. The Eucharist is the sacrament in which the Spirit's fire enters the believer, purifying, illuminating, sanctifying, and uniting the soul to Christ's life. Maximus the Confessor calls the Eucharist the "sacrament of deification" because the Spirit uses it to draw the believer into the very energy of God. Communion is not a devotion; it is an infusion. It is the Spirit setting the heart ablaze.

If the Eucharist is the moment when the Spirit transforms bread and wine into Christ's Body and Blood, then Communion is the moment when the Spirit extends that transformation into the believer. The Fathers speak with remarkable boldness about this mystery. St. Cyril of Alexandria writes that through the Spirit, Christ "mingles Himself with our bodies," not in the crude sense of physical fusion, but in the profound sense of life entering life. The Spirit carries the humanity of Christ into the depths of the communicant, igniting what is dead, strengthening what is weak, healing what is wounded. The Eucharist is the furnace of divine love because the Spirit is its fire. We receive not a symbol but the life that the Spirit has made present. We receive not a memory but a Person—the Son—through the Person who reveals Him—the Spirit.

This descent of the Spirit into the heart is not always accompanied by sensible warmth. Sometimes it is hidden, silent, interior. But hidden fire is still fire. The Spirit works through the Eucharist the way He works through the burning bush: the divine flame burns without consuming, purifies without destroying. The believer who approaches Communion with humility, repentance, and longing discovers a transformation that unfolds slowly but surely. Fear becomes trust. Anger becomes compassion. Lust becomes chastity. Pride becomes reverence. The Spirit reshapes the soul not by external force but by interior light. The Eucharist is not merely an encounter with Christ; it is the Spirit's ongoing work of configuring the believer to Christ.

Yet the Eucharist reveals only one side of the Spirit's fire. The other side is mercy. The God who descends to purify and transform also descends to forgive and restore. This is the mystery of Confession, perhaps the most misunderstood sacrament in the Christian imagination. Many imagine Confession as a legal process or a psychological release, but the Fathers saw it otherwise: it is the sacrament of the Spirit's healing fire. When Christ breathed on the apostles after the Resurrection and said, "Receive the Holy Spirit," He handed to them not an administrative function but the Spirit's own power to cleanse the heart. The breath of Christ is the breath of the Spirit; the authority to forgive sins is the Spirit's authority operating through human hands.

In Confession, the Spirit does not merely wipe away guilt; He restores communion. He mends what sin has fractured. He enters the wounds the person cannot reach. St. Symeon the New Theologian speaks of repentance as the place where the Spirit "descends into the heart like a flame," burning away self-deception and illuminating the truth with tenderness. This is why true contrition is simultaneously painful and sweet: painful because the Spirit reveals the truth, sweet because He reveals it with mercy. The Spirit condemns sin but never the sinner. His fire exposes only to heal. Confession is the sacrament where the Spirit unbinds the heart from its ancient chains and breathes new life into what shame once suffocated.

If Baptism gives new life and Chrismation seals it, if the Eucharist divinises and Confession restores, then the other sacraments reveal further dimensions of the Spirit's transformative love. Consider the sacrament of Marriage. Too often it is imagined as a social structure, a romantic union, or a religious formality. But in the Church's deepest vision, Marriage is a descent of the Spirit upon two persons so that their love may become more than natural affection. When the priest invokes the Spirit upon the couple, he is not blessing a sentiment; he is calling down fire. The Spirit unites the spouses not by erasing their difference but by making their difference fruitful. He is the bond who makes two one without dissolving either. Their fidelity becomes participation in the fidelity of Christ and His Bride. Their mutual self-gift becomes participation in the self-gift of the Trinity. Their love becomes a place where the Spirit dwells and reveals God.

The Spirit's role in Marriage becomes clear when we recognise that human love, left to itself, cannot sustain lifelong fidelity, self-sacrifice, or communion. The Spirit does not merely strengthen natural love; He transforms it. He turns affection into covenant, desire into gift, companionship into icon. The fruitfulness of Marriage—whether physical or spiritual—is the Spirit breathing life into their union, the same Spirit who hovered over the waters and overshadowed the Virgin. Marriage is not simply a witness to divine love; it is an arena where the Spirit magnifies that love until it becomes a sign of Christ's union with the Church.

As Marriage reveals the Spirit's fire in human love, Holy Orders reveals His fire in sacred service. When the bishop lays hands upon the one to be ordained, the Church knows that something far more profound than institutional appointment is taking place. The Spirit descends to mark, strengthen, and conform the ordained to Christ the High Priest. The grace of Holy Orders does not come from human lineage; it comes from divine breath. The Spirit consecrates the bishop so that he becomes the guardian of unity, the priest so that he becomes the vessel of mercy and sacrifice, the deacon so that he becomes the icon of Christ's service. Holy Orders is the Spirit forming Christ in His ministers for the sake of His Body. No one can absolve sins, consecrate the Eucharist, anoint the sick, or teach with authority unless the Spirit speaks, sanctifies, heals, and reveals through them. The priest's hands are empty unless the Spirit fills them.

Finally, the Anointing of the Sick reveals the Spirit's tenderness with startling clarity. In this sacrament, the Spirit does not come with thunder or flame but with quiet strength. He descends upon the suffering not to remove all pain but to enter it. He strengthens the weak, consoles the fearful, heals the wounded, prepares the dying for the embrace of God. The anointing oil is the touch of the Spirit upon human frailty. The Spirit is the Consoler not in poetic sentiment but in sacramental reality. He enters the place where strength ends so that love may continue. He descends into the shadow of death so that death itself becomes a threshold of hope. In this sacrament the Spirit shows that divine love does not flee from suffering; it accompanies, transforms, and glorifies it.

The sacraments reveal a pattern so consistent, so unified, that it becomes impossible to misunderstand the Spirit's intention: He desires to touch every dimension of human existence. Nothing is too humble, too physical, too earthly for Him. He reaches into water, oil, bread, wine, hands, bodies, wounds, and hearts. He refuses to save the soul without also sanctifying the senses, the flesh, the history, the relationships, and the destiny of the person. What the Incarnation is in Christ—the union of God and creation—the sacraments are in the Church: the Spirit continuing the Incarnation through created things so that Christ may continue His work in us. The Spirit does not bypass matter; He transfigures it. He does not escape the human condition; He enters it.

This becomes particularly vivid when we consider how each sacrament touches a specific need of the human person. Baptism touches birth; Chrismation touches identity; the Eucharist touches hunger; Confession touches guilt; Marriage touches love; Holy Orders touches service; Anointing of the Sick touches suffering and death. There is no experience of human life the Spirit does not enter, consecrate, or redeem. The sacraments are not arbitrary sevenfold moments scattered across the Christian journey. They are the Spirit's sevenfold descent into the human condition. They are the ways the Spirit ensures that nothing in our earthly existence remains untouched by divine fire.

The Spirit's willingness to reach into matter reveals something even deeper about His nature: He is the one who makes God intimate. The Father sends the Son; the Son reveals the Father; but it is the Spirit who brings God into the depths of the believer. Without the Spirit, the Son remains external, the Cross remains historical, the Resurrection remains distant, Pentecost remains a memory. With the Spirit, Christ becomes contemporary, the Cross becomes personal, the Resurrection becomes interior, Pentecost becomes ongoing. The sacraments are the Spirit's assurance that the mysteries of salvation do not remain in the past but become present. They are the Spirit's way of bringing eternity into time.

Nowhere is this more striking than in the Eucharistic epiclesis. When the priest invokes the Spirit to descend upon the gifts, he is standing at the threshold of creation and re-creation. Bread and wine—symbols of human labour and human dependence—become, under the Spirit's descent, the very presence of Christ. The Church has never hesitated to attribute this transformation entirely to the

Spirit. St. John of Damascus writes with crystalline conviction: "The bread and wine are changed by the invocation of the Holy Spirit." And yet the Spirit does not change the gifts for the gifts' sake. He changes them for ours. The transformation of bread and wine is ordered to the transformation of the believer. The Spirit does not sanctify matter without sanctifying the one who receives it. The altar fire spills over into the heart.

This is why participation in the Eucharist is the summit of the Christian life. Not because of ritual beauty, though the liturgy's beauty reflects divine glory; not because of communal unity, though unity is real and profound; but because the Spirit touches the believer with the same power that overshadowed the Virgin, the same power that raised Christ, the same power that descended at Pentecost. In Communion, the Spirit makes the believer a place where Christ dwells. The sacramental act is simple; its mystery is immeasurable. The Spirit unites the believer to the Son, and through the Son to the Father, drawing the person into the very circulation of divine life.

Confession reveals the Spirit's intimacy in another way. If the Eucharist is the Spirit's fire of union, Confession is His fire of restoration. No sin is too old or too deep for the Spirit to enter. He does not approach the heart with accusation but with truth. He does not expose to shame but to heal. In this sacrament, the Spirit becomes the divine physician, entering the hidden recesses where wounds fester and memories ache. The person who confesses does not simply recount faults; he opens the heart so the Spirit may breathe into it. Forgiveness is not a verdict pronounced from above; it is the Spirit cleansing from within. The absolution spoken by the priest is the echo of the Spirit's interior whisper: "Be made whole."

In Marriage, the Spirit reveals His power to consecrate love itself. Human affection, beautiful as it is, cannot bear the weight of lifelong communion. It falters, weakens, changes. The Spirit does not replace human love; He deepens it. He turns affection into vow, attraction into fidelity, companionship into covenant. He dwells within the spouses so their love becomes a participation in the divine love that binds Father, Son, and Spirit. This is why Christian marriage, in its deepest truth, is not defined by mutual compatibility but by shared indwelling. The Spirit becomes the unity of their unity, the strength of their promise, the endurance of their sacrifice. Marriage is not sustained by emotion; it is sustained by the Spirit who seals the bond.

Holy Orders reveals yet another dimension of the Spirit's transformative descent. The priest is not simply a leader, teacher, or minister; he is a vessel the Spirit fashions for sacred service. When hands are laid upon the one being ordained, the Spirit descends not to elevate personality but to configure the man to Christ. The authority given is the Spirit's authority; the power to sanctify is the Spirit's power. No priest absolves by his own strength; no priest consecrates by his own holiness; no priest preaches by his own insight. Everything is the Spirit's work. The priest becomes a living instrument, a man through whom the Spirit makes Christ present to His people. The Church's sacraments meet the faithful through the hands the Spirit has consecrated.

Anointing of the Sick manifests the Spirit's tenderness in a way nothing else does. When the oil touches the forehead and the hands, it is the Spirit touching the fear of death, the burden of illness, the vulnerability of suffering. He strengthens the heart so it does not lose hope. He consoles the soul so it does not fall into despair. He prepares the dying not for darkness but for glory. This sacrament reveals the Spirit as the One who accompanies us at every threshold of life, even the final one. The Spirit does not abandon us to death; He guides us through it.

What emerges from all of this is a vision too large and too luminous to reduce to mere doctrine: the sacraments are the Spirit's way of weaving divine life into the fabric of human existence. There is no sacrament without Him. There is no grace apart from Him. He is the heart of the mystery, the One who makes the invisible visible, the One who makes the divine tangible, the One who brings Christ into the world again and again. The sacraments are not seven separate events; they are seven entrances of the Spirit into the world, seven movements of the same fire, seven works of the same Love.

The Spirit does not visit the sacraments as an observer, nor does He act in them reluctantly or rarely. They are His chosen instruments. Through them He brings creation toward its final destiny. Baptism is not simply the beginning of faith; it is the Spirit planting the seed of divine life in a soul that could never germinate by its own strength. Chrismation is not simply the affirmation of belief; it is the Spirit empowering the person to bear Christ into the world. The Eucharist is not simply a memorial; it is the Spirit feeding the Christian with the very life He gave to Christ's humanity. Confession is not simply a moral reset; it is the Spirit healing the fracture between the person and God. Marriage is not simply a covenantal promise; it is the Spirit forging a communion stronger than death. Holy Orders is not simply a designation of roles; it is the Spirit consecrating a man for divine action. Anointing is not simply comfort; it is the Spirit strengthening the final ascent to God.

The sacraments reveal not only what the Spirit does but who the Spirit is. His actions disclose His identity. He is the Creator who breathes life into the waters of Baptism. He is the Anointer who seals believers with the fragrance of Christ. He is the Fire who descends upon the bread and wine. He is the Light who restores the penitent. He is the Bond of Love who unites spouses. He is the Power who consecrates the ordained. He is the Consoler who touches the sick and dying. Each sacrament reveals a different facet of His glory. Each sacrament is a window into His heart.

This is why the sacraments must never be viewed as private devotions or pious customs. They are encounters with God. They are the Spirit's chosen means for drawing humanity into the life of the Trinity. Through them the soul learns to breathe with divine lungs, to see with divine light, to love with divine strength. The sacraments are not accessories to the Christian life. They are the Christian life. Everything else flows from them because everything else flows from the Spirit who acts through them.

And yet the Spirit's fire in the sacraments is not automatic. It seeks cooperation. The sacraments communicate divine life, but the heart must receive it. The Spirit transforms, but the person must open. The Spirit burns, but the soul must allow the flame to catch. This cooperation is itself a gift; even the desire to respond is stirred by His presence. When the believer approaches the sacraments with humility, repentance, and longing, the Spirit works with a power that shapes the entire life. Baptism becomes a wellspring of purity. Chrismation becomes a fountain of strength. The Eucharist becomes the centre of existence. Confession becomes the doorway of peace. Marriage becomes a school of holiness. Holy Orders becomes the path of self-giving. Anointing becomes the threshold of glory.

The sacraments therefore reveal the Spirit's pedagogy: He teaches by touch. He forms by contact. He instructs by indwelling. The outward sign is not a distraction but a sacramental form of revelation. Water teaches rebirth. Oil teaches anointing. Bread teaches communion. Laying on of hands teaches consecration. Confession teaches mercy. Marital vows teach fidelity. Anointing teaches hope. In each gesture, the Spirit speaks without words. He teaches not in abstractions but in actions. He shapes the soul not by information but by transformation.

Because the sacraments are the Spirit's work, they are also the Church's lifeblood. Without the sacraments, the Church becomes an organisation. With the sacraments, the Church becomes the Body in which the Spirit dwells. Everything the Church is—holy, one, catholic, apostolic—flows from the sacraments because everything the Church is flows from the Spirit. The sacraments are not mere rites the Church performs; they are moments when the Church herself is formed. The Spirit builds the Church through the sacraments, and the Church bears witness to the Spirit through them.

This sacramental vision also reshapes our understanding of holiness. Holiness is not primarily moral achievement; it is sacramental transformation. The saints become radiant not by human effort but by consenting to the Spirit's work. Their holiness is the result of a lifetime of sacramental fire entering their hearts. They are men and women who allowed the Spirit to work freely through Baptism, Chrismation, the Eucharist, Confession, Marriage, Holy Orders, or Anointing. Their lives prove that the sacraments are not rituals but encounters with divine energy.

The constant theme is descent. The Spirit descends upon matter, upon hearts, upon communities, upon lives. But the descent always has a purpose: to raise. He descends to lift, to elevate, to glorify. Through the sacraments, He draws humanity into Christ's Body, Christ's death, Christ's Resurrection, Christ's glory. The sacraments are the journey of the soul into God. Every flame begins with a descent and rises into ascent.

By the end of this mystery, one truth shines above all others: union becomes tangible because the Spirit touches matter and turns it to fire. Christianity is not a religion of ideas or sentiments. It is a religion of divine contact. God reaches into the world, and the Spirit is His hand. God breathes into creation, and the Spirit is His breath. God pours His love, and the Spirit is the Gift.

Through the sacraments, that Gift is given again and again, shaping believers into a people who share the very life of God.

15

The Spirit in Scripture: Inspiration and Illumination

The story of Scripture begins the same way the story of creation begins: with breath. Before there is word, there is wind; before there is revelation, there is the Spirit moving in silence. Nothing in the Bible exists apart from that movement. Long before ink touches parchment or prophets open their mouths, the Spirit bends low over the human heart, preparing it to bear a message greater than itself. This is the first miracle of the Bible: God does not merely speak to humanity; He speaks through humanity. The divine Word takes on human voice, human grammar, human memory, human imagination, without ceasing to be divine. The Book is born of breath.

When Paul writes that "all Scripture is God-breathed," he is not offering a metaphor. He is naming the most intimate act of God toward His creatures. The breath that brought Adam to life becomes the breath that brings the biblical word to life. The same Spirit who hovered over the waters now hovers over the minds of shepherds, kings, poets, exiles, fishermen, evangelists. Inspiration does not erase their personalities; it elevates them. Moses does not sound like David, and David does not sound like Isaiah, and Isaiah does not sound like

THE SPIRIT IN SCRIPTURE: INSPIRATION AND ILLUMINATION

John. Yet beneath all these voices is the One Voice that unites them. The Fathers describe Scripture as "the body of the Word." As the Word took flesh in the womb of Mary, so the Word takes letters in the pens of the prophets and apostles. Both mysteries reveal the same truth: God delights to dwell in what is human.

This indwelling is not mechanical. The Spirit does not treat the authors as instruments to be played, but as hearts to be ignited. He does not dictate; He breathes. Inspiration is not the coercion of a mind but the illumination of it. The prophet becomes capable of seeing with God's eyes, grieving with God's grief, rejoicing with God's joy. The words that arise on the page are wholly human and wholly divine, not because the prophet disappears, but because the Spirit has entered so deeply into him that the human voice becomes the vessel of a divine utterance. Every book of the Bible is a burning bush: it blazes with God, but it is not consumed; it speaks with God, yet it preserves the human shape of the one who bears it.

The Old Testament reveals this in fragment and fire. "The word of the Lord came upon…" is the refrain of a people who have learned that the Spirit is not an idea but an encounter. Elijah feels the Spirit in the whisper; Ezekiel in the whirlwind; Isaiah in the coal that touches his lips; Jeremiah in the fire shut up in his bones. None of them speak on their own. None of them claim originality. Each one stands as witness to a presence that chooses, moves, and compels. The Spirit does not simply inform them; He inhabits them. Their words endure because they are not merely ancient insight but divine breath crystallised into speech.

Yet inspiration is only half the miracle. A God-breathed word requires a God-breathed reading. Without the same Spirit who speaks, the Scriptures remain closed. The disciples walk with the risen Christ on the road to Emmaus, yet they fail to recognise Him until He "opens their minds to understand the Scriptures." This moment is more than an exegetical lesson; it is the revelation of how all Scripture must be read. The Spirit who inspired is the Spirit who unveils. Illumination is the second breathing of God upon the word. It is the breath that awakens the text within the soul.

Illumination does not grant new revelations; it grants new sight. It does not add sentences to the Bible; it opens the heart to perceive what has always been there. Augustine calls the Spirit the "inner teacher," because the deepest truths of Scripture cannot be accessed by analysis or intellect alone. The mind may observe the surface of the text, but only the Spirit reveals its depth. The words of Christ sound simple enough to the natural ear, yet they remain opaque until the Spirit lets the disciple hear them from within Christ's own knowledge of the Father. Illumination is participation. The Spirit draws the reader into the life of Christ so that Scripture becomes familiar not because it is studied, but because it is lived from the inside.

This is why the Fathers warn that Scripture without the Spirit becomes dangerous. The letter without the breath becomes law without life, command without communion, information without transformation. The Spirit is the difference between reading about God and encountering God. Without Him, the Bible becomes an archaeological dig—interesting, instructive, but ultimately inert. With Him, the Bible becomes a burning lamp carried into the hidden chambers of the heart. The Spirit does not merely reveal meanings; He reveals the One who speaks through them.

Every page of Scripture is shaped by this double action of the Spirit. The same fire that descended on the prophets descends on the reader. The same breath that carried Ezekiel's visions carries Christ's voice to the present moment. Scripture is not a collection of ancient writings; it is a living conversation between God and His people, sustained by the Spirit who binds the generations together. The Church does not merely remember what the Spirit once said; the Church hears what the Spirit still says.

More is happening here than interpretation; it is communion. The Spirit does not lead the reader outside the text but deeper into it, into the heart of Christ where every verse finds its fulfilment. The words written in history become the words spoken now, because the Spirit collapses the distance between the then and the now. The Bible becomes a place of encounter—God speaking, the soul listening, and between them a breath that crosses ages and enters the deepest places of the human person.

When read in this light, Scripture becomes a sacrament of presence. The ink becomes a veil; the words become windows; the narrative becomes a path through which the Spirit draws the soul into divine life. Reading in the Spirit is not an intellectual exercise; it is a form of prayer. It is the meeting of two freedoms: God who gives Himself through the word, and the soul who yields itself to the One who speaks.

The same Spirit who once overshadowed the authors now overshadows the reader. The Book that began in breath continues in breath. The word that once took flesh now takes root. The Spirit who inspired now illumines. The breath that wrote now burns.

The Fathers loved to say that Scripture has a face. Not a metaphorical face, but the true face of Christ hidden within every page, waiting for the Spirit to unveil Him. This conviction shaped the way they approached the entire biblical narrative. They did not read the Old Testament as a collection of ancient texts, nor the New Testament as a set of doctrinal clarifications. They read all of Scripture as one single voice—Christ speaking through many forms, at many times, in many ways, but always speaking. Only the Spirit can reveal this unity, because only the Spirit knows the Son from within. To read the Bible in the Spirit is to allow the Spirit to share His knowledge of Christ with us.

This is why the Scriptures cohere with such astonishing depth. Shadows in the Old become substance in the New; promises whispered in Genesis break open at Calvary; images half-seen in the prophets blaze with clarity in the Gospels. None of this is accidental. The Spirit who inspired the beginnings is the same Spirit who brings them to completion. The entire canon is His architecture. Genesis is not simply the first book; it is the foundation stone upon which the entire edifice rests. Exodus becomes the grammar of salvation. The prophets become windows into the heart of God. The psalms become the vocabulary of the soul. The Gospels become the unveiling of the Word made flesh. The epistles become the interpretation of His life for the life of the Church. The Apocalypse reveals the final flowering of everything the Spirit began in the first breath over the waters. And the Spirit holds it all together.

To read Scripture without perceiving this unity is to read it against its nature. The Bible is not a spiritual encyclopedia. It is the living story of God's self-gift, and the Spirit is the storyteller. The Spirit does not merely preserve the text; He preserves the meaning. He is the memory of the Church—divine, faithful, and unbroken. Christ promises His disciples that the Spirit will "bring to remembrance all that I have said to you," and that promise extends beyond the upper room. The Spirit ensures that the Church does not lose her memory, because without memory she cannot recognise her Lord.

This memory is not nostalgia. It is participation. The Spirit does not take the reader backwards; He draws the reader into the eternal now of God's Word. When the psalmist cries, "Today, if you hear His voice," the word *today* is not poetic sentiment; it is theological precision. The Spirit makes every day the day of encounter, every moment the moment of revelation. Scripture becomes the place where eternity enters time and invites the soul to stand in its light. The Spirit alone can grant this immediacy.

THE SPIRIT IN SCRIPTURE: INSPIRATION AND ILLUMINATION

In this light, typology becomes more than interpretive technique—it becomes the natural language of the Spirit. The Fathers saw types everywhere because the Spirit revealed Christ everywhere. Noah's ark becomes the Church; the flood becomes baptism; the exodus becomes salvation; the manna becomes Eucharist; the temple becomes Christ's body; the suffering servant becomes the crucified Lord; the promised land becomes the kingdom; the Davidic throne becomes the messianic throne; the Passover lamb becomes the Lamb slain from the foundation of the world. Typology is not imposed upon the text. Typology is unveiled by the Spirit, who authored the patterns in the first place.

To read typologically is to see Scripture with the eyes of faith—eyes the Spirit grants. It is to recognise that the same God who acts in history acts with consistency, fidelity, and purpose. What He begins, He completes. What He foreshadows, He fulfils. The Spirit weaves the centuries into a single tapestry of revelation, and Christ shines through the weave like light through fabric. This is why the Church proclaims Christ from every page: not because she forces Him into the text, but because the Spirit reveals Him within the text.

Prophecy, too, becomes luminous only in the Spirit. Without Him, prophecy is puzzling poetry, mystical fragments. With Him, prophecy becomes direct encounter with the God who speaks across ages. Isaiah's cry, "The Spirit of the Lord is upon me," finds its fulfilment not by human deduction but by divine unveiling. Jesus reads the ancient scroll in Nazareth and declares, "Today this Scripture is fulfilled in your hearing." The Spirit reveals the identity of the speaker, the identity of the passage, and the identity of the moment. Scripture becomes an event, not merely a record.

Even the structure of Scripture itself bears the mark of the Spirit's breath. The fourfold Gospel arises not from literary preference but from divine intention; the harmony of their witness is the work of the Spirit who sanctifies diversity without erasing distinction. Luke writes with historical detail; John writes with mystical depth; Matthew writes with covenantal precision; Mark writes with relentless urgency. Yet all four speak the same Christ because all four write in the same Spirit. Their differences are not contradictions; they are harmonics. The Spirit ensures that each voice contributes to the fullness of Christ's revelation.

The early Church understood this instinctively. The canon did not fall from heaven fully assembled, nor did it emerge from academic analysis. It emerged from the Spirit-filled discernment of a living community. The canon is not merely a collection of inspired books; it is the inspired collection of those books. The same Spirit who breathed the words breathed the recognition of those words. By guiding the Church into all truth, He ensured that the Scriptures would be received, treasured, proclaimed, safeguarded, and interpreted within the life of the Body of Christ. The Bible is not the Church's possession; it is the Church's inheritance, given by the Spirit and entrusted to the Spirit's care.

Reading Scripture apart from this communion is not simply unwise; it is unnatural. A branch cannot understand the life of the tree if it tears itself away from the trunk. The Spirit speaks in the communion He Himself forms. This is why the Fathers insist that Scripture must be read in the Church—because the Spirit who inspired the text is the Spirit who indwells the Church. He is the bond between revelation and reception. To step outside the communion is to muffle His voice.

When the Spirit illumines the reader, a new world opens. The Scriptures cease to be words about God and become the place where God draws near. They become sacramental—outward signs that open into inward realities. The reader begins to sense that every line carries more weight, more warmth, more depth than ink alone could contain. The soul feels addressed. The heart recognises its Author. The Spirit provides not only insight but intimacy. This intimacy is the beginning of union through the word.

When this intimacy deepens, Scripture becomes something far more than a text to be analysed. It becomes a living chamber where the Spirit and the soul meet. The Fathers often likened Scripture to a burning bush—ordinary in appearance, extraordinary in reality. The bush is a shrub like any other; the fire is divine. The text is human language; the illumination is divine presence. What Moses experienced in Midian is what every believer is invited to experience whenever the Scriptures are opened: a human medium set aflame by God without being consumed. The Spirit makes this possible. Without His fire, the pages remain dry. With His fire, they blaze.

This blazing takes many forms. Sometimes it comes as clarity—the sudden recognition that a passage long familiar has finally revealed its depth. At other times it comes as consolation—a warmth that settles over the heart and assures the reader that God sees, understands, draws near. Occasionally it comes as conviction—the piercing awareness that the Word is correcting, healing, or redirecting the inner life. But always, whatever its form, the illumination is personal. The Spirit does not scatter abstract ideas; He speaks into the contours of an individual soul. He knows the fears that must be calmed, the wounds that must be healed, the sins that must be confronted, the desires that must be awakened. Scripture in His hands becomes not general instruction, but divine address.

This divine address is what transforms reading into prayer. The Fathers never separated the two. To read Scripture was to pray; to pray was to listen to Scripture. The Spirit made both movements one. When the believer reads, the Spirit speaks; when the believer speaks, the Spirit interprets the cry of the heart. Thus lectio divina emerged not as a method, but as the natural posture of a soul taught by the Spirit. Reading became listening. Listening became beholding.

Beholding became union. The text became a ladder of ascent—each rung shaped by the breath of God.

Even silence becomes interpretive in the Spirit. There are moments when the Word stirs something too deep for quick understanding, when the heart senses meaning but cannot articulate it. The Spirit dwells in that silence. He ripens what He plants. He allows the truth to sink down like seed into soil. The Fathers speak of this as "rumination"—not intellectual murmuring but spiritual digestion, the slow incorporation of the Word into the very structure of the soul. The Spirit does not hurry this process; He honours its depth. Truth given quickly is often truth lost quickly. Truth allowed to steep becomes truth that sanctifies.

This sanctification is the ultimate aim of illumination. The Spirit does not reveal Scripture merely to expand knowledge; He reveals Scripture to expand holiness. He illumines so that the believer might live differently, desire differently, see differently. The light He grants is the light of Christ's own mind. When Paul speaks of having "the mind of Christ," he is not suggesting that Christians develop a sophisticated theology. He is describing the fruit of illumination—the Spirit sharing the interior vision of the Son with those who belong to Him. To read Scripture in the Spirit is to enter the Son's way of perceiving the Father.

This is why Scripture has authority—not an authority of external command but of internal transformation. It speaks with weight because it carries the breath of God. It shapes conscience because it echoes the Father's voice. It unveils sin not to shame but to liberate. It guides action because it aligns the believer with the rhythms of divine life. The Spirit ensures that Scripture remains living, piercing, active—never a museum relic, always a present summons.

This authority is gentle yet unyielding. The Spirit does not coerce; He convinces. He does not crush; He kindles. He does not overwhelm; He invites. His illumination honours freedom even as it calls freedom to its highest expression. The believer gradually discovers that obedience to the Word is not oppression but expansion—liberation from the smallness of self into the spaciousness of divine life. Scripture illumined by the Spirit becomes the pathway into this spaciousness.

Over time, the soul begins to recognise patterns not only within Scripture but within itself. The Spirit creates harmony between the Word and the reader. A verse read months earlier suddenly returns unbidden, answering a question the heart never fully articulated. A parable illuminates a hidden motivation. A psalm awakens contrition. A prophecy stirs hope. A command reveals a path. These movements are not coincidences; they are orchestration. The Spirit arranges the interior life with the same care with which He arranged the canon.

This orchestration extends beyond the individual. The Spirit illumines Scripture within the communion of the Church, making the Word fruitful not only for solitary meditation but for the life of the entire Body. The liturgy becomes the primary stage for this illumination. When the Scriptures are proclaimed in the assembly, the Spirit speaks to a people, not merely to persons. He shapes a community into Christ's image. He interprets the Word for the needs of the moment. The same passage heard every year becomes new because the Spirit applies it anew to the wounds and desires of the Church.

The Fathers saw this communal illumination as essential. Scripture cannot be reduced to private interpretation, because the Spirit who illumines is the Spirit who unites. A divided reading is a distorted reading. To read in communion is to read in the atmosphere the Spirit Himself has created. Within that communion, the Word becomes inexhaustible. Each generation brings new questions, and the Spirit grants new depths. Tradition becomes not repetition but unfolding.

Scripture remains the same, yet the Church continues to grow into its meaning.

This growth leads the reader deeper into the mystery of the Word's unity. The Spirit does not illuminate isolated verses; He illuminates the whole. He leads the soul from seed to tree, from shadow to substance, from figure to fulfilment. Gradually, the believer learns to move with divine logic. Genesis finds its answer in John. The psalms find their voice in the crucified Christ. The exodus finds its completion in the paschal mystery. Everything converges. Everything points toward Christ, and everything radiates from Him.

The Spirit performs this convergence quietly, faithfully, unfailingly. He is the true theologian of the Church, the soul of her understanding, the breath of her interpretation. Without Him, Scripture remains a closed door. With Him, Scripture becomes a window into eternity.

As this unity becomes clearer, the soul begins to sense the profound humility of the Spirit's work. He does not draw attention to Himself, though He is the very life within the Word. He hides so that Christ may be seen, yet it is His light that makes Christ visible. He veils His own glory so that the glory of the Son may fill the horizon, yet it is His radiance that gives the soul eyes to see. The Fathers often called Him the "divine Artist," for He paints Christ upon the canvas of Scripture and simultaneously paints that same Christ upon the canvas of the heart. Two works, one movement: revelation and transformation united in a single fire.

The more the soul yields to this artistry, the more Scripture becomes a place of communion rather than merely information. The Word ceases to be a series of lessons and becomes a living presence. Christ emerges not as a figure remembered but as a voice encountered. The Spirit shapes this encounter with extraordinary tenderness. He does not overwhelm the soul with brilliance; He invites it to grow steadily into the light. Passages once obscure begin to open like flowers. Stories once familiar begin to reveal layers previously unseen. Patterns begin to align. The whole landscape of Scripture becomes coherent, not because the mind has mastered it, but because the Spirit has harmonised it.

This harmony changes the way the believer moves through life. Scripture illumined by the Spirit becomes a lens through which reality is understood. The world is no longer merely material; it is sacramental. Events are no longer random; they are providential threads woven by a divine hand. People are no longer obstacles or irritations; they are bearers of mystery. Suffering is no longer senseless; it becomes a place where the Word speaks with deeper resonance. Hope is no longer an idea; it becomes the atmosphere in which the soul breathes. The Spirit grants this new vision not as an escape from reality, but as a deeper reception of it.

At the same time, the Spirit begins to purify the ways the Word is approached. Scripture is easily misused—weaponised for arguments, mined for proof-texts, reduced to moral instruction, or cut into fragments to support private preferences. The Spirit dismantles these distortions. He restores Scripture to its true purpose: communion, revelation, transformation. When a believer approaches the Word with pride, the Spirit resists; when they approach with humility, the Spirit descends. When they demand answers, the Word remains closed; when they seek God, the Word unfolds. The Spirit teaches that Scripture is not mastered but received, not conquered but surrendered to.

This surrender is what allows the soul to be shaped by the great currents of biblical revelation. Over time, the Spirit teaches the believer to inhabit the story of Scripture rather than merely read it. Creation, covenant, exodus, exile, restoration, Incarnation, Cross, resurrection, Pentecost—these are no longer events at a distance; they become the inner geography of the soul. The Spirit draws the believer into Christ's own journey. The more deeply one reads, the more one finds that the Word is reading them. The Spirit uses Scripture as a mirror to unveil the heart, as a lamp to guide the steps, as a fire to purify desire, as a seal to mark the soul with divine likeness.

This sealing is not metaphorical. The Spirit imprints the Word upon the believer in ways that endure beyond memory. A single verse may return years later at the precise moment it is needed. A parable may interpret a season of life. A lament may become the vocabulary of grief. A promise may become the anchor of hope. The Spirit ensures that Scripture is not merely known but lived. He turns the Word into a rhythm, a pulse, a breath. The believer discovers that the Word is not behind them as instruction but ahead of them as destiny.

The destiny is Christ. Every illumination the Spirit grants ultimately orients the soul toward Him. Christ is the meaning of the entire text; Christ is the fulfilment of every figure; Christ is the key that unlocks every mystery. The Spirit's illumination is a participation in Christ's own vision of the Father, and this participation draws the soul into union. Scripture becomes the training ground for contemplation—the place where the Spirit teaches the heart to gaze as the Son gazes and to love as the Son loves. The more deeply the believer enters the Word, the more deeply they enter the life of the Trinity.

This Trinitarian dimension is the hidden depth of illumination. When the Spirit reveals Christ, He simultaneously reveals the Father. The Son is the Word, but the Spirit is the One who makes the Word audible; the Father is the source, but the Spirit is the One who leads the soul into the Father's heart. Illumination is therefore not a private religious experience. It is a participation in divine communion. The Scriptures become the doorway into the eternal conversation between Father, Son, and Spirit, and the believer is drawn into that exchange as listener, worshipper, beloved.

At the end of this journey, the soul recognises that the Spirit has been the true interpreter all along. He inspired the sacred authors; He guided the formation of the canon; He preserved the Word within the Church; He opens the text to the believer; He opens the believer to the text. He is the living thread that connects Moses to Paul, Isaiah to John, the prophets to the apostles, the early Church to the present moment. Without Him, Scripture is a closed book. With Him, Scripture becomes the meeting place of heaven and earth.

The Spirit is the breath within the Word and the breath within the soul. He is the light that reveals and the fire that transforms. He is the silence between the lines and the music beneath the meaning. To read Scripture in the Spirit is to encounter God. To live Scripture in the Spirit is to become His dwelling.

Thus the movement from inspiration to illumination reaches its fulfillment: the Word is given, the Word is opened, the Word becomes life.

16

The Spirit in Prayer: The Breath Within Us

Prayer begins where speech ends. It does not rise from human effort but from divine nearness. Scripture reveals this with a startling simplicity: *"We do not know how to pray as we ought, but the Spirit Himself intercedes for us"* (Romans 8:26). Every authentic prayer is already the Spirit moving in the depths, drawing the heart upward, shaping desire, forming words—or silence—into an offering. No one begins prayer alone. No one sustains prayer alone. No one reaches God except by the God who has already reached into them.

This is why the great mystery of Christian prayer is not that humanity speaks to God, but that God speaks within humanity. The Spirit is not an aid to prayer; the Spirit is the condition of prayer. Prayer is not an activity we perform but a life we enter, a life breathed into us. The Fathers say the Spirit is to the soul what breath is to the body. Just as breathing is the first sign of life and its rhythm remains constant until death, so the Spirit is the continuous breath of the soul. As long as He moves, prayer remains possible. When He is resisted, prayer begins to suffocate.

Christ reveals this truth in His own life. His prayer is not the struggle of a distant heart reaching toward an absent Father. His prayer rises from His union with the Father in the Spirit. Every moment of His earthly life is infused with that interior communion. He prays before dawn not to awaken intimacy but to express the intimacy that never ceases. When the disciples beg Him, *"Teach us to pray,"* they are asking to enter that communion. They do not ask for a technique. They ask for a share in His own relationship with the Father. His answer—*"Abba...Our Father..."*—is not primarily instruction. It is revelation. They are shown the inner life that the Spirit will soon plant within them.

Prayer, then, is not first a discipline of the mind but a participation in the Son's own address to the Father. It is the Spirit who draws believers into that address. The Spirit teaches not by information but by assimilation—by breathing Christ's filial confidence into the heart until the believer can speak to God not as a distant ruler but as the Father who knows and loves. No one can say *"Jesus is Lord"* without the Spirit; likewise, no one can say "Abba" without Him. The cry of adoption is the Spirit's own voice echoing in the soul. Prayer becomes the experience of being carried.

This carrying is subtle. Prayer often feels like the soul approaching God, yet the deeper truth moves in the opposite direction: God is approaching the soul. The Spirit descends, stirs, awakens, enlightens, urges. Augustine describes the Spirit as the "inner guest" who teaches the heart how to desire. Gregory of Nyssa says the Spirit bends the soul toward God the way heat bends wax. The Spirit does not push; He softens. He does not force; He frees. Prayer arises when the softened heart turns toward the One it can finally love.

This interior bending explains why genuine prayer often begins in restlessness. Restlessness is the Spirit interrupting false peace—dislodging the soul from distractions that cannot satisfy, unsettling complacency, making space for longing. Longing is the first true movement of prayer. Desire becomes the door the Spirit opens. When the soul feels an ache it cannot name, this is already prayer beginning. The Spirit has breathed.

Yet prayer does not always feel like longing. Sometimes it descends as silence. Not absence, but depth. Silence is the Spirit's most tender gift, for it draws the soul beyond words into awareness of God's presence. Silence is not emptiness; it is fullness without noise. The Fathers call it "the prayer of the heart," the place where the Spirit's breath is heard not as sound but as stillness. This is why the spiritual life grows more silent the closer it draws to God. Words become insufficient. Images fade. Concepts fall away. Only presence remains. The Spirit prays in that presence without needing to be noticed.

At other times prayer takes the form of tears. Tears are not emotional indulgence; they are purification made liquid. The Desert Fathers distinguish tears of sorrow, tears of repentance, tears of awe, tears of gratitude, tears that flow simply because the soul feels God near. Every form of tears is the Spirit loosening what is knotted within. Tears water the arid soil of the heart. They soften what has hardened. They cleanse the gaze so that God may be seen more clearly. The Church has always considered tears a charism because they reveal the Spirit touching depth.

But prayer is not always gentle. Sometimes the Spirit presses the soul into a struggle. Prayer becomes labour. The mind wanders. The heart feels cold. The will resists. The hour stretches. The soul feels alone. These are not signs of failure but signs of formation. The Spirit does not remove difficulty; He uses difficulty to purify intention. When prayer no longer feels sweet, the soul learns to seek God Himself rather than the comfort of devotion. This is the moment when prayer becomes an act of love rather than an act of consolation. Dryness tests the heart; perseverance refines it. The Spirit accompanies unseen, strengthening the will even when the emotions protest.

In this way, the Spirit teaches the soul to pray without the soul noticing the lesson. He trains desire by trial, attention by silence, surrender by helplessness, and trust by delay. He makes prayer both ascent and descent—our ascent toward God and God's descent toward us meeting in one mysterious exchange. Prayer becomes synergy: divine breath and human openness cooperating.

Yet the Spirit not only prays *within* the soul; He also prays *through* the Church. The Church's liturgy is the place where the Spirit gathers individual hearts into one communal voice. When believers chant psalms, the Spirit unites their voices with the prayer of the Son. When they bow, stand, kneel, listen, respond, the Spirit shapes the body of Christ into a single offering. Prayer in the Spirit is never solitary even when alone. One prays in the communion the Spirit sustains. This is why prayer binds the Church more deeply than structures or policies ever could. The same Spirit breathes through every believer, uniting a diversity of hearts in a single movement toward the Father.

The Spirit, then, is both the interior teacher and the communal conductor. He forms hearts and forms the Church. He brings words and brings silence. He awakens longing and gives peace. He stirs tears and strengthens endurance. He prays within and prays between. Prayer is His breath, His fire, His tenderness at work in the human soul.

The deepest mystery of prayer is the union of two freedoms: God's and ours. The Spirit never overwhelms the human person. He does not commandeer desire or bypass consent. He invites, persuades, inclines, draws. This is why prayer often begins as a choice before it becomes a delight. The Spirit respects the dignity He fashioned— He will not violate the image He intends to fill. So He waits, and the waiting is not distance but reverence. When the soul turns even slightly toward Him, He moves with astonishing swiftness. Augustine captures the mystery perfectly: "You were with me, and I was not with You." The Spirit's nearness precedes our awareness; His work anticipates our response. But the moment the will inclines, the moment desire stirs, the moment attention shifts toward God, the Spirit meets that movement and magnifies it.

This magnification lies at the heart of Christian prayer. A single act of attention becomes a channel of grace. A single act of surrender becomes a descent of peace. A single whispered plea becomes an intercession carried by the Spirit into the very life of the Trinity. Prayer is never measured by eloquence or duration but by openness. An instant of true openness contains more truth than hours of distracted recitation. Yet recitation matters, too, because fidelity shapes the heart even when the heart is numb. The Spirit works through habits, not only heights. The soul becomes available through constancy.

This constancy is why the Church gives the faithful routines of prayer—not to burden but to steady. Morning prayer, evening prayer, prayer before meals, the Jesus Prayer, lectio divina: these are not human inventions meant to manufacture devotion. They are ancient pathways carved by the Spirit Himself through generations of saints. When a believer steps into these rhythms, the Spirit meets them in familiar terrain. The words become vessels; the gestures become doors. The person who prays enters a stream that has been flowing since Pentecost. Prayer becomes participation, not invention.

Lectio divina reveals this pattern with special clarity. The practice is simple: reading slowly, listening inwardly, responding freely, resting gently. Yet the depth of the practice cannot be explained by a technique. The Spirit is the true interpreter. When Scripture is read without Him, it remains text. When it is read with Him, it becomes voice. Words that once seemed inert suddenly speak personally. A verse burns. A phrase consoles. A sentence convicts. A command becomes invitation. The Spirit illuminates not by adding new meanings but by making the heart able to receive the meaning that has always been there. The Word descends into the soul with a weight it did not previously carry because the Spirit has softened the soil to receive the seed.

Icons perform a similar work, though through the eyes rather than the ears. An icon does not impress by aesthetics alone; it forms prayer by perception. The Spirit uses sacred images to anchor attention, lift the mind, and reorient the heart. The believer gazes, and the Spirit uses that gaze to awaken remembrance, longing, reverence. The icon becomes a window, not because of its art but because of the Spirit's presence working through it. Eastern tradition teaches that an icon is not merely looked at; it is prayed with. The Spirit forms a silent dialogue between the one who gazes and the One whose image is revealed.

Even the simplest gesture of prayer—the sign of the cross—becomes, in the Spirit, an entire theology expressed through touch. A hand on the forehead becomes a plea for illumination. A hand on the heart becomes a plea for purification. Shoulders marked become reminders that the yoke of Christ is borne not by human strength but by divine help. The Spirit infuses these gestures with meaning the body remembers even when the mind wanders. Prayer is physical because the Spirit sanctifies the body as His temple.

Yet for all these helps, the most profound work of the Spirit in prayer unfolds beneath perception. Paul speaks of the Spirit "groaning" within believers with "sighs too deep for words." The groaning is not distress but depth—the depth of divine desire interceding through human fragility. This groaning is the Spirit longing in us for the Father with the same longing that exists eternally between Father and Son. When prayer feels inarticulate or confused, when the heart has no words, the Spirit prays through that poverty. The weakness becomes a vessel for divine strength. Silence becomes filled with divine speech.

This is why prayer can be honest, even painfully honest. The Spirit is the Spirit of truth; He permits no illusions. In His presence the masks fall. The soul confesses not only sins but wounds, fears, hopes, desires it barely understands. All this is prayer because all this is placed in the Spirit's hands. Nothing hidden can be healed; the Spirit invites the entire heart into the light so it may be known, forgiven, and transformed. The transparency the Spirit creates is freedom. The soul learns it can stand before God without pretence.

Nevertheless, intimacy with God brings its own purifications. The Spirit draws the soul toward deeper honesty, deeper surrender, deeper desire. For this reason, prayer sometimes feels like the stripping away of false supports. Consolations fade. Familiar insights no longer satisfy. The mind cannot pray as before. This is not regression but invitation. The Spirit is leading the soul out of reliance on emotion and into reliance on love. Love is stronger because it clings without sensation. Prayer becomes simpler, purer, more interior. Less is said, yet more is given. Less is felt, yet more is believed.

In this simplification the believer discovers a paradox: prayer becomes easier and harder at the same time—easier because God is nearer, harder because the soul senses the depth to which God desires to draw it. The Spirit teaches humility through this tension. The soul learns it cannot ascend by willpower. It must accept to be carried. True prayer grows not through multiplication of practices but through surrender. The Spirit forms this surrender like a potter shaping clay—slowly, patiently, through pressure and rest, through touch and removal, until the vessel is ready to hold divine fire.

Prayer, then, is the ongoing miracle of the Spirit making space for God within a human life. It is less a journey the soul makes toward God than a journey God makes into the soul. The Spirit is both guide and destination, both companion and path. Prayer is His movement, and the one who prays becomes transparent to that movement. The Spirit becomes the breath within the breath, the silence within the silence, the longing beneath the longing.

The soul learns this transparency slowly, but once it begins, prayer ceases to be confined to moments and becomes a disposition. The Spirit reshapes attention so that even ordinary tasks become permeable to grace. Not everything becomes explicit prayer, but everything becomes prayer-capable. A conversation, a moment of waiting, a sudden memory, the sight of light across a room—any of these can become an opening through which the Spirit draws the heart upward. The believer discovers that the Spirit is always present, always speaking, always moving; it is the heart that must learn the art of listening. This listening is not strain but availability. The spirit-filled soul becomes porous to God.

At the centre of this transformation stands the "Abba" cry. Paul places it at the heart of Christian identity: "You have received the Spirit of adoption, by whom we cry, 'Abba! Father!'" The cry is not merely a word but an event—a divine act unfolding inside the human person. The Spirit speaks the Father's name within us, drawing our hearts into the Son's own relationship with Him. When a believer prays "Father," the Spirit is not assisting; He is enabling. The intimacy that exists eternally between Father and Son becomes audible within a human chest. Prayer becomes filiation. The human person becomes a child in truth, not metaphor. This filial confidence is the foundation of Christian prayer, and it is the Spirit who grants it.

Confidence, however, is not arrogance. The Spirit teaches boldness that bows. The greatest saints tremble with reverence even as they speak freely to God. The more the Spirit fills the heart, the more the heart recognises the majesty and tenderness of the One addressed. This double knowledge—God's holiness and God's nearness—creates a posture of awe. Awe is not fear but wonder. It is the recognition that love has stooped low. Prayer becomes praise not because praise is commanded but because it becomes inevitable. The Spirit reveals beauty, and the heart responds.

As this praise deepens, the Spirit begins to draw the soul toward a prayer beyond words. Not the refusal of language, but its fulfillment. Words become too small for what the heart receives. Silence becomes not emptiness but fullness. The Fathers describe this as *hesychia*—inner stillness, the quiet that arises when the soul rests in God's presence. This stillness is not passive. It is alive with the Spirit's action. He stabilises thought, calms anxiety, steadies desire, gathers the scattered pieces of the heart. Silence becomes the meeting place between God and creature. The one who prays discovers that God is not found in the noise of striving but in the quiet of surrender.

Contemplation emerges from this stillness. Contemplation is not an achievement; it is a gift. The Spirit grants the soul a taste of God's own life—not a vision, not an image, but a knowing suffused with love. The soul senses God not as an idea but as a presence. The presence is gentle, yet unmistakable. It does not shatter; it enlarges. The Spirit grants this not to elevate the believer above others but to anchor the soul more deeply in humility. Those who taste divine love become more compassionate, more patient, more ready to serve. Contemplation strengthens responsibility, not pride.

In contemplation the Spirit teaches another truth: prayer is not escape from life but fuel for life. The one who prays deeply becomes more capable of charity, not less. The Spirit who draws the soul into silence also sends the soul back into the world with new strength. He unites interiority and mission. Christ often withdrew to pray, and just as often returned to heal, teach, forgive, and restore. The Spirit reproduces this rhythm within the believer. Prayer and action cease to be rivals. Prayer becomes the sap; action becomes the fruit.

This rhythm also reveals why perseverance matters. Prayer matures only through time. Moments of aridity are not failures but invitations. The Spirit leads souls through seasons—springlike warmth, summer intensity, autumn pruning, winter stillness. Each season offers its own grace. Winter teaches faith. Autumn teaches detachment. Summer teaches endurance. Spring teaches joy. The Spirit governs these seasons with the precision of a divine gardener, cultivating virtues through changes the soul does not always understand. To persevere means trusting His timing. What seems like absence is often deeper presence, veiled for the sake of growth.

In these seasons the Spirit begins to shape the believer according to Christ's own pattern of prayer. Christ prayed in solitude and in community, prayed before choosing the apostles, prayed before miracles, prayed before the Passion, prayed from the Cross, prayed in resurrection glory. His entire life was communion with the Father. The Spirit draws the believer into this same communion. The soul learns to speak with Christ, to listen with Christ, to desire with Christ. The Spirit forms Christ's dispositions within the heart—His reverence for the Father, His trust, His compassion, His surrender, His obedience. Prayer becomes participation in the Son's eternal dialogue with the Father.

This participation brings a final transformation: the believer becomes a place of intercession. The Spirit intercedes in the soul, and through the soul, for the sake of the world. Intercession is not merely remembering others in prayer. It is allowing the Spirit to extend Christ's love through one's own heart. The believer carries the burdens of others not as weight but as offering. The Spirit turns compassion into prayer and prayer into healing. The Christian becomes a conduit of divine mercy.

In this way prayer becomes communion—not only with God but with the entire Body of Christ. Every prayer touches every other prayer. The Spirit unites the Church in a single act of worship, a single plea, a single song. The saints, living and departed, join the believer, and the believer joins them. Prayer becomes catholic in the deepest sense: full, whole, universal. The individual voice blends with the vast chorus of the redeemed. The Spirit gathers it all.

The soul that prays becomes a living sanctuary. The Spirit dwells, breathes, intercedes, illumines, consoles, and transforms. Prayer becomes the place where God and human life meet. Not occasionally, but constantly. Not distantly, but intimately. The Spirit becomes the breath within the breath.

When the Spirit has brought the soul into this deepening communion, prayer no longer feels like an activity inserted into life; it feels like the atmosphere in which life unfolds. The believer begins to recognise that prayer is not fundamentally something one *does* but something one *receives*. Every genuine movement of the heart toward God is the Spirit already at work. Every desire for holiness, every act of turning back after sin, every moment of gratitude, every sudden impulse to praise—all of these are the Spirit breathing within the soul. The Spirit does not wait to act until prayer has begun; His action is what begins prayer.

This truth frees the soul from a thousand anxieties. Prayer need not be perfect to be real. It need not be free of distraction to be pleasing. The Spirit takes the scattered words, the wandering thoughts, the small offerings of an imperfect heart and weaves them into something beautiful. Augustine compared the Spirit's work in prayer to a musician tuning strings that are slightly off pitch. The musician does not discard the instrument; he adjusts it gently until it sings. The soul becomes that instrument. Prayer becomes the song. The Spirit becomes the musician.

As the Spirit teaches the soul to pray, He also teaches the soul to listen. Listening in prayer is not a technique but a posture of love. It is the willingness to receive whatever God gives, even if what He gives is silence. Silence in prayer is not failure. Silence is the Spirit's language when words would only distract. The silence He grants can be tender or searching, warm or purifying. Sometimes it is the silence before revelation, sometimes the silence after it. Sometimes it is an invitation to deeper surrender. Sometimes it is the sign that God is nearer than the heart can bear. In all cases, silence is presence shaped into stillness.

Listening also reveals another reality: prayer becomes transformative because the Spirit prays *in* the believer more than the believer prays *to* God. Paul's words in Romans 8 are not poetic exaggeration. The Spirit truly "intercedes for us with groanings too deep for words." These groanings are not disappointment or frustration; they are love. They are the Spirit's compassion swelling within the believer when words fail. They are the movements of divine charity expanding the narrowness of the human heart. The soul that experiences these groanings learns reverence for the mystery within itself. God is nearer than self-awareness, deeper than thought, more intimate than one's own breath.

The Spirit's action in prayer does not always feel sweet. Sometimes He confronts. Sometimes He convicts. Sometimes He exposes motives the heart would rather hide. Yet even this is mercy. The Spirit wounds only to heal. His light never humiliates; it liberates. When the Spirit reveals sin, He does so with the gentleness of a Father lifting a fallen child and brushing the dust from his face. He reveals truth in a way that awakens hope, not despair. Conviction becomes invitation. Confession becomes freedom. The heart learns that repentance is not an interruption of prayer but the deepening of it.

As this truth takes root, the believer begins to pray with increasing simplicity. Not childishness, but childlikeness. Complicated petitions become fewer. Desperate arguments fade. The soul learns to rest in God as Father, Christ as Brother, the Spirit as breath. The prayer of a mature Christian is often nothing more than a word—"Come," "Help," "Thank You," "Father," "Jesus." These small words carry immense weight because the Spirit fills them. The smallest flame can illuminate a dark house.

In this simplicity the Spirit teaches a final lesson: prayer is not merely for consolation, but for conformity. The goal of prayer is not to feel God but to become like Him. The Spirit uses prayer to shape the soul after the pattern of Christ's own heart. The believer becomes more patient, less anxious, more courageous, less resentful. Compassion grows. Humility deepens. Love becomes steady. These changes often occur quietly, unnoticed until others see them reflected in daily life. The Spirit does not sculpt noisily; He shapes the soul as lightly as dawn shapes a horizon.

The deepest fruit of this shaping is *unity*. The Spirit unites the believer not only to God but to all who belong to God. True prayer is always ecclesial. The one who prays is never alone. The Spirit draws the soul into the great river of intercession flowing through the Body of Christ. Even when the believer kneels alone in a quiet room, the Spirit unites that prayer with the liturgy of the saints, the cries of the poor, the petitions of the suffering, the praise of the angels. The Christian becomes a point where heaven and earth meet, where divine love enters the world through a willing heart.

As the soul yields more fully to this communion, prayer expands beyond the boundaries of personal need. The Spirit moves the heart to pray for enemies, for the forgotten, for the lost, for the Church, for the world. These prayers arise not from moral obligation but from the Spirit's compassion beating within the believer. The Christian becomes a bearer of divine mercy. Prayer becomes mission, even before a word is spoken or an action is taken.

In the end the Spirit accomplishes something wondrous: He makes prayer the soul's native language. What began in weakness becomes strength. What began in struggle becomes ease. What began in duty becomes delight. The believer discovers that the Spirit has been praying within them long before they knew how to pray. Every moment becomes an invitation; every breath becomes a reminder; every movement of the heart becomes an echo of divine life.

Prayer becomes participation in the eternal love exchanged between Father, Son, and Spirit. It becomes the place where heaven opens within the human person. It becomes union. The breath the believer draws is no longer merely their own. It is the breath of God breathed into them from the beginning—now awakened, now active, now alive.

With this, the journey of union moves forward. For when the Spirit has taught the soul to pray, He is ready to reveal the final horizon of divine life: the transfiguration of the human person into holiness, virtue, and glory.

17

The Spirit Who Divinises: Virtue, Holiness, Glory

Humanity was never meant to live on the surface of its own existence. Beneath the fragile movements of daily life runs a deeper current—a divine summons woven into the very structure of our being. Scripture calls it glory. The Fathers call it likeness. The New Testament calls it participation in the divine nature. All these words point to a single truth: the human person was created not merely to obey God, admire God, or serve God, but to *share* in God's own life. And the One who accomplishes this staggering elevation is the Holy Spirit.

Divinisation—*theosis*—is not an idea the Church added late. It is the seed planted in Genesis when God breathes His own life into Adam. A creature raised from dust receives more than animation; he receives capacity. The Fathers stress that humanity is *capax Dei*—capable of God. That capacity is not fulfilled by thought or worship alone. Capacity means destiny. Humanity was shaped with a hollow centre only God can fill, and that filling is the Spirit's work.

This is why sin is described not merely as disobedience but as corruption, decay, rupture. Sin does not simply offend God; it damages the vessel meant to receive Him. The Spirit's mission, then, is not only to cleanse the vessel but to enlarge it—to make the human person capable of bearing divine fire without being consumed. Salvation in its fullest sense is not rescue from punishment; it is transformation into glory. The Spirit is not a moral influence or a religious encouragement. He is the divine life dwelling in the human soul, elevating it toward a horizon beyond its natural limits.

This elevation is written directly into Scripture. "He has granted to us His precious and very great promises," Peter declares, "so that through them you may *become partakers of the divine nature*." The words are too bold to soften, too clear to reinterpret. The apostolic vision of salvation is participation, not proximity. The Spirit does not place the believer near God; the Spirit places the believer *in God*. Paul's language shimmers with the same truth. "You are not in the flesh," he writes, "you are in the Spirit, if the Spirit of God dwells in you." To be "in the Spirit" is not a mystical experience reserved for a few. It is the state of every baptized believer, whether one feels it or not. The Spirit's indwelling is not the result of spiritual maturity; it is the cause of it.

Yet Scripture goes further still. The Spirit does not merely dwell within; He shapes. He conforms. He forms Christ in the believer until the believer begins to bear the contours of Christ's own humanity. "All of us," Paul says, "beholding the glory of the Lord, are being transformed into the same image from glory to glory, *for this comes from the Lord who is the Spirit*." The Spirit is the artisan of divine likeness. What He accomplishes in the soul is nothing less than a continuation of the Incarnation. Christ took our humanity so that His humanity—glorified, Spirit-filled—could be given back to us.

This is why the Christian life cannot be reduced to ethics. Ethics matter, but ethics are not the horizon. The horizon is transformation—metamorphosis. Holiness is not primarily moral improvement; it is ontological elevation. The Spirit does not polish the surface of the soul; He pours divine life into its depths. When the Spirit dwells within a person, the divine energies—the real, uncreated operations of God—begin to flow through the human faculties. This is the insight of Gregory Palamas, who defended the truth that God's grace is not a created gift but God's own life communicated. The energies are not symbols. They are God acting. And the One who communicates these energies is the Spirit.

To encounter the Spirit, therefore, is to encounter uncreated light—not the light of perception but the light that made perception possible. This is why Palamas insists that the vision of God is possible not because the intellect becomes powerful enough but because the Spirit illumines the intellect with divine radiance. The Spirit does not give new information; He gives new eyes. He does not merely supply strength; He infuses divine strength. He does not offer encouragement; He pours charity—*agapē*—into the soul, and that charity is God's own love, not a human imitation of it. Augustine, standing on different ground, saw the same truth: charity is the Spirit Himself dwelling in us.

This divine charity becomes the principle of a new life. Natural virtues—prudence, justice, temperance, fortitude—shape the soul according to human excellence. But the infused virtues, as Aquinas teaches, elevate these faculties beyond their natural horizons. Infused prudence is not simply wise decision-making; it is participation in Christ's own discernment. Infused justice is not fairness; it is mercy shaped by the Spirit. Infused fortitude is not grit; it is the strength of the crucified Christ beating in the human heart. Infused temperance is not self-control for the sake of self-mastery; it is desire reordered toward eternal joy.

These virtues do not arise from human effort. They are gifts of the Spirit, rooted in the divine life communicated to the soul. Just as a branch bears fruit because the life of the vine pulses within it, so the believer bears virtue because the Spirit breathes within. This is why Christian holiness cannot be accomplished through self-management. One cannot organise oneself into divinity. One can only receive. Participation, not performance, is the logic of the Christian life.

But the Spirit does not bypass the human faculties; He transforms them. The mind becomes capable of contemplating truth not as an object but as communion. The will becomes capable of choosing the good not merely because it is commanded but because it is loved. Desire itself becomes capable of hungering for God. These movements are not psychological shifts; they are signs of a new creation. The Spirit does not ask the human person to suppress the passions; He takes hold of them and transfigures them. Anger becomes zeal for righteousness. Desire becomes the longing for holiness. Sorrow becomes compassion. Fear becomes reverence. Even the most unruly passions can become servants of love when the Spirit heals their distortions and restores their original purpose.

This healing is crucial to understand. The Spirit does not aim at stoic apathy; He aims at divine beauty. The goal is not emotional sterility but emotional harmony. The passions were created good. They become destructive only when detached from God. The Spirit does not silence them; He tunes them. A soul ruled by the Spirit is a soul whose faculties move in harmony, like instruments in an orchestra responding to a single conductor. The Spirit is that conductor. He brings order where there was chaos, unity where there was fragmentation, beauty where there was distortion. The soul becomes, in the words of the Fathers, a "living icon of Christ"—not by imitation alone but by participation.

As the Spirit heals and elevates the human faculties, something remarkable begins to occur: virtue becomes luminous. It is no longer simply the steady practice of good habits; it becomes a radiance, a quiet shining, a brightness of soul that others can perceive even if they cannot name its source. Scripture calls this radiance the "fruit of the Spirit." It is not accidental that Paul describes this fruit not in terms of achievement but in terms of beauty—love, joy, peace, patience, kindness, goodness, faithfulness, gentleness, self-control. These are not virtues the believer constructs; they are the manifestations of divine life. When a tree bears fruit, it is not demonstrating skill; it is expressing life. So too with the Spirit's fruit. It is the external signature of an internal participation.

Each fruit reveals something of God's own character. Love is the sign that the Spirit Himself dwells in the heart, because love is His very essence as the eternal bond between Father and Son. Joy is the overflowing gladness of divine life breaking into time. Peace is the stillness of God's own rest imparted to the restless human spirit. Patience is the shining forth of God's endurance. Kindness is the tenderness of God touching the world through human gestures. Goodness is divine generosity made visible. Faithfulness is God's constancy expressed in human commitment. Gentleness is the humility of Christ becoming a human posture. Self-control is the mastery of desire by the Spirit who orders all things toward love.

The fruits of the Spirit are therefore not moral benchmarks but eschatological signs—the foretaste of glory. They are the qualities the human person will possess in fullness when transformed entirely by divine light, and they appear now as seeds of the coming resurrection. Paul describes the Spirit as the "arrabōn"—the down payment—of our future inheritance. This means that every moment of genuine love, every act of patience, every surge of deep, inexplicable peace is itself a small eruption of the Kingdom. Holiness begins in time what glory will complete in eternity. The Spirit makes the soul porous to heaven.

Yet this transformation does not occur in isolation. The Spirit, who is communion in the Trinity, creates communion in those He inhabits. Holiness is never solitary. The saint is not a spiritual athlete training alone; the saint is a person whose life has become transparent enough for others to glimpse God through them. The community around such a person experiences consolation, conviction, encouragement, challenge. The Spirit uses the holy to draw others toward holiness. Divine beauty is always diffusive. When the Spirit fills a soul, that soul becomes a point of diffusion through which the world is warmed.

This diffusive power of holiness reveals another dimension of theosis: it changes not only the person but also the quality of their presence. When Moses descended from Sinai, his face shone with reflected glory. The same is true of the saints. They shine. Not metaphorically, but spiritually. Their presence carries weight. Something in them is alive with a light that does not belong to human nature alone. Saints are not interesting because they are disciplined; they are compelling because they are transformed. They have become vessels of divine energy, bearers of uncreated light. They draw the heart upward without speaking a word.

This upward pull is the sign of true holiness. Holiness does not attract toward itself; it attracts toward God. The Spirit divinises not to produce religious celebrities but to reproduce the humanity of Christ in countless ways across countless lives. Each saint reveals something unique—an angle of divine beauty no one else can show. Holiness is the diversity of Christ's radiance refracted through different personalities, histories, and gifts. In this diversity the unity of the Spirit is revealed. He does not produce clones; He produces icons.

The deepest dimension of this divinising work unfolds in the transformation of desire. Human desire is not eradicated by the Spirit; it is expanded. Divine life does not shrink the human heart; it enlarges it until the heart can desire with divine freedom. Augustine's words—"Love and do what you will"—become literal truth for the soul formed by the Spirit. When the Spirit fills desire, the will becomes ordered not by duty but by delight. Virtue ceases to feel like constraint and begins to feel like liberation. The person discovers that sin was the real confinement and holiness is the real spaciousness.

This freedom is not the absence of limits; it is the ability to embrace the good wholeheartedly. The Spirit does not free the believer from the demands of love; He frees the believer to fulfil them. Divine liberty is the capacity to choose what God chooses because the heart has been reshaped by divine affection. This is why Aquinas insists that charity is the form of all the virtues. Without charity, virtue becomes mere performance. With charity, virtue becomes participation in God's life.

Participation also reshapes the believer's perception of the world. The Spirit gives an infused knowledge—a kind of contemplative vision—allowing the believer to recognise divine presence in the ordinary. The world is no longer flat but sacramental. Events are no longer random but threaded with grace. Suffering no longer appears meaningless but becomes a place where divine strength manifests. Joy is no longer fragile but becomes a glimpse of eternal gladness. The Spirit does not provide an escape from the world; He reveals its true depth. Deification is as much a transformation of vision as it is a transformation of being.

This contemplative vision, however, is not reserved for the mystics alone. Every believer touched by the Spirit begins to see differently. Ordinary kindnesses become revelations of God's tenderness. The beauty of creation becomes a mirror of divine wisdom. Scripture becomes luminous. Prayer becomes natural. Even the struggles of daily life acquire new meaning. The Spirit does not erase the human condition; He saturates it with God.

When this saturation begins to deepen, the believer discovers something astonishing: holiness feels less like effort and more like surrender. The Spirit does the heavy lifting. The believer consents. The Spirit inflames love. The believer responds. The Spirit pours divine life. The believer receives. This is the paradox at the heart of divinisation: the more the Spirit acts, the more human the person becomes. Grace does not crush nature; it completes it. The Spirit does not replace the human faculties; He perfects them, elevating them into the very life of God. This is the dignity of the human person—to become by grace what Christ is by nature. Theosis is not a dream. It is the Spirit's intention for every soul.

The more the Spirit fills the soul, the more clearly one sees that deification is not an abstract doctrine but a lived reality. It unfolds quietly, often unnoticed at first, like dawn spreading across a dark horizon. The early signs appear not in dramatic ecstasies but in the gentle reordering of the interior life. A person finds themselves able to forgive more quickly than before. A desire for prayer grows, not because of obligation but attraction. Resentments that once clung stubbornly now begin to loosen. Joy that had felt impossible flickers back to life. These are not self-improvements; they are symptoms of divine life at work. The Spirit has begun to divinise the heart.

This transformation deepens as the Spirit heals the passions. The passions—those movements of the soul that, after the fall, became unruly—were created by God for good. Anger was meant to defend what is holy. Desire was meant to move the soul toward communion. Sorrow was meant to awaken compassion. Fear was meant to guard against danger. The fall disordered these movements, turning them inward, bending them toward self-protection or self-indulgence. But the Spirit does not despise the passions He once breathed into the human soul. He restores them. He purifies without destroying, heals without diminishing, reclaims without erasing.

This is the meaning of apatheia in the Eastern tradition—a word often misunderstood. It does not mean emotional numbness. It means the passions have been brought under the governance of love. Evagrius describes apatheia as "the peaceful state of the soul in which it becomes easily moved toward God." When anger, desire, sorrow, and fear become instruments of charity, the soul has begun to share in divine harmony. Aquinas expresses the same truth in another key: virtue perfects the passions by directing them toward what is truly good, and the infused virtues—given by the Spirit—direct them toward the good that surpasses human nature. The Spirit does not silence the passions; He orchestrates them.

As this orchestration unfolds, a new kind of strength enters the believer. It is not the brittle strength of self-discipline but the resilient strength of divine life taking root. The person finds a capacity to endure trials with a peace that does not make psychological sense. They discover courage in moments that once triggered fear. They speak truth with a gentleness that surprises even themselves. They begin to love in a way that is unforced, steady, and free from calculation. This is the Spirit imprinting the character of Christ on the soul. Divinisation is not merely a future hope; it is a present power.

Yet even these changes, beautiful as they are, are only the beginning. The Spirit's deepest work occurs in the innermost chamber of the soul—in the transformation of desire. When desire becomes ordered toward God, holiness becomes not a demand but a delight. What once felt like sacrifice becomes freedom. What once felt like burden becomes rest. The believer discovers that sin never truly satisfied; it only distracted. The Spirit reveals this through experience, not argument. He enlarges the heart until it aches for God. Augustine's cry, "You have made us for Yourself, and our heart is restless until it rests in You," becomes the living condition of the soul.

Desire transfigured in this way becomes a flame—a hunger that does not consume but lifts. Gregory of Nyssa described the soul's ascent as an eternal stretching toward God, a movement propelled not by lack but by love. The Spirit ignites this movement. He places within the heart a longing that pulls the person forward even when the intellect does not understand it. Theosis is not merely a theological concept but a gravitational pull: the Spirit draws the believer into the life of God with the same quiet force that draws fire upward.

In this ascent, the believer begins to taste the first sweetness of glory. Glory is not external brightness but the radiance of divine life in the soul. Moses reflected it on his face; the saints reflect it in their presence. Glory is the atmosphere of God's being, and the Spirit makes that atmosphere breathable for human nature. When the Spirit dwells deeply in the soul, glory begins to shine through the cracks of daily life. A word becomes luminous. A gesture becomes sacramental. A moment of silence becomes full. This is not imagination; it is participation. Glory is God's life touching human life in a way the senses cannot fully articulate but the heart recognises as real.

This recognition is itself a gift of the Spirit. No one can see glory unless the Spirit gives the eyes to see. The spiritual senses—long forgotten after the fall—awaken gradually. The soul learns to perceive God's movements within itself. It becomes alert to the stirrings of charity, the whisper of conscience, the quiet pressure of mercy, the subtle warmth that rises in prayer. These are not psychological impressions; they are the beginnings of spiritual sight. The Spirit teaches the believer to discern divine presence as surely as the body discerns sunlight. The soul becomes porous to God.

As divine life fills the soul, another transformation occurs: humility becomes effortless. Humility is not self-belittlement; it is the recognition that all goodness is received. The soul touched by the Spirit knows that everything beautiful within it is a gift. Pride dissolves not by force but by wonder. Gratitude becomes the atmosphere of the heart. This is one of the clearest signs of divinisation: the more divine a person becomes, the more human they appear—gentle, approachable, unassuming, radiant. Holiness does not inflate; it bows.

This bowing opens the final dimension of theosis: communion. The Spirit who divinises does not elevate individuals into isolated peaks of spiritual achievement. He draws them into the communion of the Body of Christ. The holier the soul becomes, the more deeply it loves. Holiness is not private perfection; it is shared life. The Spirit binds the saints not only to God but to one another, weaving their transformed lives into a tapestry of divine beauty. Each person reflects Christ uniquely; together they reflect Him more fully.

This communion is not sentimental; it is ontological. The Spirit is the bond of unity in the Trinity, and He becomes the bond of unity in the Church. Those who share the Spirit share life. This is why the saints recognise one another instinctively. They breathe the same air. They burn with the same fire. They move toward the same glory. The Spirit makes their lives interpenetrate without confusion, echoing the Trinitarian pattern that gave rise to creation itself.

Divinisation, then, is not merely an upward ascent toward God; it is an outward expansion toward others. The soul filled with divine life becomes spacious enough to hold the joys and sorrows of many. The Spirit enlarges the heart until it becomes a place where others can rest, heal, and be strengthened. The saint is a shelter, because the Spirit within them is shelter. The saint is warmth, because the Spirit within them is fire. The saint is living water, because the Spirit within them is the river of life.

As this communion deepens, the believer begins to understand that theosis does not end with the inner life; it extends into the body itself. The Spirit who dwells within is not content to sanctify thoughts and desires alone. He intends to glorify the entire human being. Paul's words in Romans 8 shimmer with this promise: "If the Spirit of Him who raised Jesus from the dead dwells in you, then He who raised Christ will give life to your mortal bodies also through His Spirit who dwells in you." The spiritual life is not an escape from the body; it is the preparation of the body for resurrection. Divinisation is incarnational to its core.

The Spirit does not disdain the material world; He fills it. The body becomes a temple not in a metaphorical sense but in a sacramental one. The spiritual transformations that occur in the soul begin to radiate outward into gestures, habits, postures, relationships. The transfiguring work of the Spirit becomes visible in the way one speaks, the way one listens, the way one walks into a room. Divine life reshapes human presence. The marks of the old humanity—restlessness, grasping, rivalry, bitterness—begin to fall away. In their place emerges a presence marked by peace, mercy, integrity, and strength. This is the beginning of glory in the body, a quiet echo of what resurrection will complete.

Resurrection is the consummation of theosis. The Spirit who hovered over the waters at creation will hover again over humanity in the final renewal of all things. What He began in the soul, He will finish in the flesh. The uncreated light that now dwells invisibly within the believer will one day break forth visibly, as it did in Christ's transfiguration. The glorified body is not a different body but the same body suffused with divine life. The Spirit does not discard creation; He transfigures it. He does not undo nature; He perfects it. He does not annihilate individuality; He sanctifies it into radiance.

This promise frees the believer from fear. The world may wound, age may weaken, suffering may scar, but none of these can prevent the Spirit from bringing the human person to glory. The Spirit is stronger than decay. He is stronger than sin. He is stronger than death. The whole Christian journey is the unfolding of this strength in the fragile contours of human life. Divinisation is not a fantasy of escape; it is God's final word over creation. The last breath of history will be the Breath of God filling all things with life.

In the present, this truth reshapes how holiness is understood. Holiness is not a spiritual résumé. It is not the accumulation of religious accomplishments or the performance of moral competence.

Holiness is surrender to the Spirit who alone can make the human person what they were created to be. The work of transformation belongs to Him. The work of consent belongs to us. Consent is not passive; it is an act of trust, a posture of receptivity, a willingness to let the Spirit touch what sin has disordered and heal what suffering has broken.

This trust is learned gradually. The believer discovers that the Spirit does not rush transformation; He ripens it. Holiness grows like fruit—slowly, silently, according to its season. The Spirit shapes through ordinary faithfulness, through small obedience's, through quiet acts of charity, through hidden moments of repentance. Glory does not erupt all at once; it permeates. The Spirit weaves divine life into the fabric of daily existence until the soul becomes, almost without noticing it, a dwelling place of God.

A dwelling place is not static. It is a space shaped by the One who inhabits it. The Spirit arranges the interior of the soul the way light arranges a room: gently, gradually, but decisively. Shadows recede. Corners brighten. Shapes become clearer. What once felt cramped becomes spacious. The soul becomes a home for God and a refuge for others. This is why the saints seem so at ease in God's presence. They have been furnished by the Spirit. Their hearts are arranged according to divine preferences.

In this furnishing, humility becomes the crown. Nothing reveals divinisation more clearly than a humble heart. Pride is the refusal to receive; humility is the delight in receiving. The Spirit delights to fill such hearts. The saints are not great because they achieved much, but because they allowed much to be done in them. God could pour Himself into them without resistance. The vessels of their souls, once small and cracked, became wide and whole. The Spirit did not find perfection; He created it.

Theosis culminates in love—love that is no longer limited by fear or calculation, love that gives without counting, suffers without despairing, forgives without hesitation. This is the love that comes from the Spirit, the love that reflects the eternal exchange of the Trinity. When such love appears in a human life, even in small glimpses, divinity has become visible. Holiness is simply love perfected by the Spirit.

Everything the Spirit accomplishes in this life is a prelude. The full symphony will sound only in the Kingdom, when God is all in all and the light of the Spirit fills creation without shadow. But the prelude matters. The Spirit divinises now so that glory will not be foreign later. He prepares the soul to bear eternal joy without breaking. He expands the heart to contain a happiness beyond human measure. He teaches the believer to breathe the air of heaven even while still walking the earth.

Union with God, then, is not reserved for the next world; it begins in this one. The Spirit is already at work making the believer a participant in divine life, a bearer of uncreated light, a vessel of glory. Divinisation is not the privilege of the few; it is the destiny of all who yield to the Spirit's fire. Holiness is not an achievement; it is a participation. Glory is not a reward; it is a gift. And the Spirit who began this work will bring it to completion, until every human life surrendered to Him becomes, in the end, a living flame.

18

The Spirit Who Heals: Wounds, Passions, Conscience

The journey of union cannot proceed unless the heart is healed. This is not because God withholds Himself until we reach some level of spiritual adequacy, but because the human heart cannot bear divine life while fractured. A cracked vessel cannot hold water; a divided heart cannot hold God. The tragedy of the fall is not only guilt but fragmentation—reason pulled one way, desire another; memory chained to pain; conscience clouded; imagination inflamed; the passions untethered and often hostile to the very things the soul longs for. The human person becomes internally dispersed, scattered like dust in the wind. Holiness demands wholeness, and wholeness is the work of the Spirit.

The Spirit heals, not by standing outside the soul offering advice, but by descending into its broken places. The Spirit never approaches the wounded human heart with clinical detachment. He approaches it with the tenderness of the Father toward the prodigal, the compassion of Christ toward the leper, the gentleness of the dove that rested on Jesus in the Jordan. His entire movement is the movement of divine love bending low to lift what humanity could never repair. Healing is not a side-effect of the Spirit's presence. Healing *is* the Spirit's presence. Wherever He dwells, wounds begin to lose their power, fear begins to melt, shame begins to loosen, and the interior world begins to feel breathable again.

The first movement of this healing is simple but profound: the Spirit does not recoil from our wounds. He is not embarrassed by emotional disorder, not repulsed by moral failure, not intimidated by trauma or fear or despair. The Spirit goes where no human comforter can go. He enters the hidden chambers of memory, the unspoken places where pain has been locked away for years. These are the rooms we would rather avoid—the rooms we fear will drown us if we open them. The Spirit opens them gently. He does not force memory to the surface; He illuminates it. Light heals differently from force. Light reveals truth without violence. Light allows a person to see their life not through the lens of fear, but through the eyes of God.

Memory is one of the deepest places the fall has wounded. Augustine, wandering through the labyrinth of his own memory, understood that the self is stored there, wounded and unhealed. Memory preserves not only events but meanings. A wound is not only what happened; it is the interpretation that attached itself to the event—"I am alone," "I am unworthy," "I am unloved," "I must protect myself," "I must never trust again." These meanings take root like thorns, shaping decisions, reactions, relationships, prayer. A person may believe the creed with their mind, but their memory believes another gospel entirely—one written by pain rather than truth.

The Spirit heals memory by rewriting meaning. Jesus promised, "The Spirit will teach you all things and bring to your remembrance everything I have said." This "bringing to remembrance" is not a mental trigger; it is healing. The Spirit places Christ's truth beside every painful memory until the memory begins to breathe in a new atmosphere. The self no longer stands alone before the wound; Christ stands there too. A painful memory touched by the Spirit does not disappear. It becomes translucent. The bitterness drains away. The shame loosens. The fear dissolves into something simpler, quieter, more human. The Spirit does not erase the past; He redeems it.

But the Spirit's healing does not remain in memory alone. The passions—the interior movements that once served love but now often serve self-preservation—are next to be touched. Human emotions were created to be instruments of love. Anger was meant to defend the good. Desire was meant to stretch the heart toward communion. Sorrow was meant to awaken compassion. Fear was meant to guard the soul against sin. But the fall bent these movements inward. Anger became self-protection. Desire became hunger for substitutes. Sorrow collapsed into despair. Fear turned inward and began guarding wounds instead of guarding holiness.

When the Spirit enters the passions, He does not crush them. He reorders them. He turns their gaze outward again—toward God and others. Anger touched by the Spirit becomes courage. Desire touched by the Spirit becomes longing for holiness. Sorrow touched by the Spirit becomes compassion for the suffering. Even fear becomes wisdom, reverence, watchfulness. The passions are not extinguished; they are tuned. The Spirit turns noise into harmony. Evagrius called this state apatheia—not the absence of feeling but the transfiguration of feeling into readiness for love. The Spirit restores the passions to their original music.

Yet healing requires more than reordered passions. The conscience itself must be healed. Conscience is not merely a moral barometer or an inner rulebook. It is the place in the soul where truth is meant to speak. It is the interior sanctuary where the voice of God echoes. But a wounded conscience can no longer distinguish the voice of God from the voice of fear or shame or accusation. One person becomes scrupulous, haunted by imagined sins. Another becomes numb, unable to feel anything at all. Another becomes self-condemning, believing that God's voice is harsh simply because the world has been harsh to them. A damaged conscience is like a cracked mirror—it reflects something, but not clearly.

The Spirit heals conscience not by shouting truth over the noise but by quieting the noise. The Spirit convicts without crushing. Jesus described His work beautifully: "He will convince the world concerning sin, righteousness, and judgment." Convince, not condemn. The Spirit's conviction is the sensation of being known entirely and loved entirely at the same time. It is the shocking experience of realising, "Nothing is hidden from God, yet nothing in me has made Him withdraw." This experience heals conscience. The soul learns again to recognise truth without fear. It becomes possible to repent without despairing, to examine oneself without self-hatred, to desire holiness without anxiety.

All the while, the Spirit begins weaving together the interior world—memory, desire, reason, conscience, imagination—into unity. The divided self begins to feel whole again. The scattered pieces of identity slowly gather around a single centre: Christ. Healing is simply this: the Spirit reorders the heart until it becomes one. Not perfect, not unfeeling, not invulnerable—simply one. A heart unified in love becomes a heart capable of God.

As the interior world begins to find its centre again, the person discovers an unexpected truth: healing is not primarily the removal of pain but the restoration of communion. The Spirit heals by returning the soul to relationship—relationship with God, with others, and even with the self. Sin isolates. Wounds isolate. Fear isolates. But the Spirit gathers. Wherever He moves, communion forms. Healing unfolds at the pace of communion becoming possible again.

The relationship most distorted by wounds is the relationship with oneself. Many people live internally divided—one part desperate for holiness, another part clinging to sin; one part longing for trust, another part terrified of being vulnerable; one part longing for connection, another part hiding from rejection. The human person becomes a civil war. The Spirit enters this conflict not as a military commander but as the One who speaks peace into storm-tossed waters. His presence quiets the inner voices that have battled for years. He does not suppress their noise by force; He absorbs it with love. A person who once lived in perpetual interior conflict begins to taste interior stillness.

This stillness is not emotional numbness. It is the quiet that emerges when the soul stops fighting itself. When the Spirit dwells deeply, the self no longer needs to choose between war and escape. The heart becomes a place that can breathe. Only then does deeper healing become possible, because the Spirit can finally address the hidden roots that feed the wounds. The desert fathers understood this well: superficial calm means nothing until the heart's roots are exposed and healed. The Spirit reaches those roots not by digging violently but by softening the soil.

At this depth, the Spirit begins healing the lies that have shaped identity. Every wound carries a lie beneath it. The lie may concern God ("He is distant," "He is disappointed," "He is dangerous"). Or it may concern the self ("I am unwanted," "I am unlovable," "I am irredeemably broken"). These lies are not intellectual conclusions; they are emotional certainties. They become the atmosphere the soul breathes. Healing occurs when the Spirit changes the atmosphere. He introduces a new climate: the climate of truth.

The truth He brings is not an abstract theological proposition. It is Christ Himself. The Spirit speaks Christ into every hidden chamber of the soul. Not merely, "Christ loves you," but "Christ loves *you here.*" Not merely, "You are forgiven," but "You are forgiven *in the place you fear to reveal.*" Not merely, "God is near," but "God is near *in the memory you thought He abandoned."* Healing becomes possible because Christ Himself becomes present where the pain once reigned. The human heart learns that the places it thought were furthest from God are the places God has chosen to enter most deeply.

As truth begins to untangle the roots of wounds, the emotions themselves begin to transform. Many people imagine that healing means the disappearance of difficult emotions. It does not. The Spirit does not erase human feeling; He restores it to its rightful purpose. A healed heart still feels sorrow, but sorrow becomes a river that leads to compassion rather than a swamp that traps the soul. A healed heart still feels fear, but fear becomes watchfulness rather than paralysis. A healed heart still feels desire, but desire becomes a yearning for communion rather than a hunger for substitutes. The passions do not vanish; they become luminous.

One of the most astonishing signs of this healing is the transformation of anger. Unhealed anger is chaotic, unpredictable, self-protective, often destructive. But healed anger becomes protective of goodness. It becomes the courage to name injustice, the strength to defend the weak, the fire to resist temptation. The Spirit does not cool anger into apathy. He transforms it into holy fire—the fire Christ showed when He cleansed the Temple, when He confronted hypocrisy, when He faced evil without fear. Anger becomes a gift again.

Another sign of healing is the restoration of desire. Many people live with desire that has been fractured—desire for intimacy twisted into addiction, desire for belonging twisted into people-pleasing, desire for love twisted into dependency. The Spirit does not suppress desire; He resurrects it. He teaches the heart to desire God first, and then—in God—to desire everything else rightly. A healed desire is not smaller but greater, because only the Spirit can teach the soul to want without clinging, to hope without controlling, to love without fearing loss.

But perhaps the deepest sign of healing is the return of trust.

Wounds destroy trust. They teach the heart that trust is dangerous, that vulnerability leads to pain, that surrender is unsafe. The Spirit restores trust by revealing Himself as the One who never wounds. He reintroduces the soul to the possibility that it is safe to rest in Another. Trust does not return quickly. It returns slowly, like a dawn rising over a long night. But once it rises, the entire landscape of the soul changes.

As trust returns, conscience becomes clear again. A healed conscience is not harsh, anxious, or hyper-vigilant. Nor is it numb, indifferent, or blind. A healed conscience becomes simple—alert to truth, open to grace, unafraid of repentance. The person discovers that the Spirit's guidance is gentle. He does not push; He draws. He does not threaten; He invites. He does not accuse; He reveals. Conscience becomes a place of peace, not panic. Moral discernment becomes an act of love, not a courtroom.

This interior unity—memory redeemed, passions reordered, conscience illumined—becomes the foundation for the Spirit's deepest healing: the restoration of the heart's capacity for communion. The human person was created for relationship with God and others. Wounds disrupt communion; the Spirit restores it. A healed heart can love again—not perfectly, but freely. A healed heart can pray again—not mechanically, but relationally. A healed heart can hope again—not naïvely, but with trust refined by suffering.

Healing is simply the Spirit making the soul whole enough to love.

The Spirit's healing work cannot be separated from discernment. Every wounded heart becomes vulnerable to counterfeit voices—voices that sound like conscience but are really fear, or sound like prudence but are really self-protection, or sound like humility but are really shame wearing a religious mask. Wounded people often mistake these voices for God. The Spirit's first act of discernment is to teach the soul the difference.

Authentic discernment begins with learning the tone of the Spirit. His voice bears a recognisable quality. It is steady, never frantic. It points toward truth without crushing the heart. It convicts without condemning. It clarifies without humiliating. It is a fire that gives light, not a fire that burns indiscriminately. When the Spirit speaks, the heart feels exposed yet safe, known yet not rejected. This is why the Fathers describe discernment as the mother of all virtues: it is the ability to recognise the movements of the Spirit and distinguish them from the counter-movements that mimic Him.

These counter-movements come from many sources. Some arise from the wounds themselves—patterns of fear, defensiveness, shame, or desire that act like emotional reflexes. Some arise from the enemy, who speaks in the language of accusation, distortion, urgency, and despair. Some arise from disordered habits formed over years. Discernment is not a matter of decoding secret messages; it is learning to identify the spiritual "taste" of each movement. The Spirit tastes like peace. The enemy tastes like agitation. Wounds taste like confusion. Only the Spirit brings clarity without violence.

To discern well, the soul must allow the Spirit to illuminate the conscience. Many people imagine conscience as a stern judge or an emotional alarm system. The Spirit reveals it as something far more beautiful: the meeting place of truth and love. The Fathers often describe conscience as a small chapel hidden within the heart—a place where God whispers. But in wounded hearts, that chapel is cluttered. Old fears, internalised accusations, unrealistic expectations, and habits of self-condemnation crowd the space. Before conscience can speak clearly, the Spirit must restore its simplicity.

He restores it first by silence. A noisy soul cannot discern, because it cannot hear. The Spirit does not compete with noise; He waits for quiet. This is why healing always involves some measure of interior stillness—moments where the heart stops rehearsing arguments, stops replaying memories, stops planning defence. Silence is not emptiness; it is the atmosphere where truth becomes audible. When silence deepens, conscience begins to reflect God's light like a polished mirror. The person discovers that what once terrified them—the internal gaze of truth—now brings peace. They can finally see themselves as God sees them.

When conscience becomes clear, the person begins to recognise the Spirit's guidance in daily life. Little promptings—small movements of compassion, caution, courage, humility, generosity—become visible as invitations rather than random feelings. The Spirit shapes virtue not by grand gestures but by thousands of gentle nudges. Healing deepens as the soul cooperates with these nudges. Discernment is not merely knowing good from evil; it is recognising the specific way the Spirit forms Christ within a person's particular temperament and story.

As discernment matures, the person becomes able to confront temptations without being overwhelmed. Temptation loses its power when its source is recognised. The enemy thrives on confusion; the Spirit dissolves confusion by naming it. A person who can say, "This thought comes from fear," or "This impulse comes from old pain," or "This urgency is not the Spirit's voice," has already defeated the temptation. Clarity is half the victory. The Spirit does not remove every temptation. He teaches the person to stand calmly in the midst of them. A healed heart is not a heart without struggle; it is a heart that no longer fears the struggle.

Yet the deepest dimension of the Spirit's healing work is not psychological but relational. He heals the passions not merely by moderating emotion but by reconnecting emotion to love. The passions—desire, anger, sorrow, joy, fear—are like rivers that have overflowed their banks. The Spirit guides them back into their God-given channels. Desire becomes longing for goodness. Anger becomes energy to protect the vulnerable. Sorrow becomes compassion. Fear becomes vigilance. Joy becomes thanksgiving. Every passion is reclaimed for communion.

This restoration culminates in what the Fathers call "purity of heart." Purity of heart is not innocence but integration. It is the condition of a soul whose desires, thoughts, and actions move in a single direction toward God. The healed person does not function in fragments anymore. Their words, choices, desires, and conscience begin to align. They become transparent—not in the sense of being flawless, but in the sense that there is no longer a vast interior gap between who they are and who they are becoming.

A person who reaches even the beginning of purity finds something astonishing: the Spirit begins to heal not only what was broken but what was never fully alive to begin with. There are capacities of the soul—gentleness, courage, creativity, understanding, compassion, spiritual insight—that remain dormant until the Spirit awakens them. Healing is not merely recovery; it is emergence. The person discovers facets of themselves they never knew existed, not because they have reinvented themselves but because the Spirit has revealed the self God always intended.

At this point, a profound humility settles into the heart. The healed person understands that none of this transformation came from self-management or willpower. They see clearly that the Spirit has been the physician, the counsellor, the advocate, the guide. The soul's freedom has not been erased—it has been released to cooperate. Healing becomes a hymn of gratitude.

And yet the Spirit is not finished. The soul that has found peace must now learn how to live that peace in a world that wounds, tempts, and confuses. Healing must become mission. Love must become action. Communion must become witness.

The movement from healing to mission does not begin with external work; it begins with the Spirit strengthening the inner structure of the heart. A healed conscience must become a discerning conscience. A calmed passion must become a virtuous passion. A restored memory must become a memory that blesses rather than binds. The Spirit completes His healing not when wounds vanish, but when wounds become places where grace flows outward to others. The soul does not simply recover; it becomes generative.

To accomplish this, the Spirit grants two gifts essential for the Christian journey: counsel and fortitude. Without these, healing remains fragile, constantly threatened by relapse, discouragement, or confusion. With them, the soul becomes stable, capable of bearing weight—its own and the burdens of others.

The gift of counsel is not a spiritual intuition about future events. It is the Spirit's way of guiding the heart in concrete decisions, especially when emotions, wounds, or fears would otherwise cloud judgment. Counsel is the Spirit whispering: "This is the path of peace." It clarifies choices the way a shaft of light clarifies a dark room—quietly, instantly, without explanation, yet unmistakably. The Spirit does not overwhelm the intellect; He steadies it. He does not bypass human reasoning; He purifies it of distortion.

This gift becomes crucial when old patterns of thought attempt to resurface. A person who has lived under shame easily misinterprets every difficulty as failure. Someone who has lived with fear easily mistakes every unknown as danger. Someone who has lived through betrayal easily distrusts even healthy relationships. The gift of counsel interrupts these reflexes. It helps the soul recognise that the movements of the wounded past are not the movements of God. The Spirit teaches the person to choose paths aligned with truth, not paths shaped by trauma.

Fortitude, meanwhile, is the gift that enables the soul to persevere in healing even when the process becomes painful or slow. Many imagine fortitude as toughness or emotional detachment, but the Spirit's fortitude is different. It is not the refusal to feel pain; it is the refusal to let pain be decisive. It is the courage to move forward even when the heart trembles. It is the strength Christ displays in Gethsemane, where fear does not dictate His obedience. Fortitude enables the soul to remain faithful to the path of healing despite setbacks. The Spirit prevents the person from collapsing back into old habits simply because growth is hard.

As these gifts deepen, the soul begins to notice something remarkable: healing no longer feels like self-focus. The person becomes less concerned with their own wounds and more attentive to the suffering of others. Compassion awakens not as a moral obligation but as an instinct. The Spirit heals inwardly so that the heart may incline outwardly. Only the Spirit can produce this shift, because only the Spirit can transform wounds into wells.

One of the most beautiful fruits of the Spirit's healing work is the restoration of interpersonal trust. Wounds often produce isolation. People hide from relationships, afraid that others will repeat the injuries of their past. The Spirit slowly softens this isolation. He teaches the soul that vulnerability is not a threat when lived in God. The Spirit does not guarantee that every relationship will be safe, but He grants the discernment and courage needed to love wisely. He heals the fear that prevents communion. In this way, interior healing becomes ecclesial: the restored soul re-enters the Body of Christ more deeply, more freely, more joyfully.

This restoration also transforms the person's relationship to time. Wounded hearts often live trapped in yesterday's pain or tomorrow's anxiety. The Spirit teaches the soul how to live now. He anchors the person in the present tense of grace, the moment where God actually meets the soul. This anchoring dissolves despair, because despair is always rooted in a future imagined without God. It dissolves regret, because regret is always rooted in a past remembered without mercy. The Spirit heals time itself by revealing that every moment—past, present, future—rests in the hands of the Father.

As the heart becomes whole, the conscience becomes luminous. The person begins to see with a clarity that is not harsh but tender—an ability to perceive the deeper reality beneath actions, emotions, relationships, and choices. This clarity is not suspicion but second sight. It allows the soul to recognise where God is at work, where human frailty distorts vision, and where the enemy seeks to sow confusion. A healed conscience becomes like a lamp in a dark room—able to reveal without shaming, able to expose without wounding.

At this stage, the Spirit often draws the soul into a deeper surrender. Healing prepares the heart not merely to function well but to belong entirely to God. Many people reach this point and fear what comes next, imagining that surrender will erase their identity. The Spirit reveals the opposite. The more a soul belongs to God, the more that soul becomes itself. Surrender is not loss but unveiling. The healed person discovers their true face.

This unveiling allows the Spirit to complete His most profound work: restoring unity within the heart. Human wounds create fragmentation. A person may have a compassionate nature but explosive anger. A contemplative heart but compulsive habits. Deep faith but deep fear. The Spirit draws all of this into harmony, not by suppressing parts of the self but by integrating them. Anger becomes strength. Sensitivity becomes tenderness. Intelligence becomes wisdom. Creativity becomes praise. The Spirit does not erase the complexity of the soul; He orchestrates it.

As unity deepens, prayer changes. The healed person does not pray merely to survive or to seek relief; they pray because their heart has begun to resonate with God. Prayer becomes the natural breath of the soul. The Spirit, having healed the wounds that once obstructed communion, now draws the person into a stable, joyful intimacy with the Father. Healing leads to union.

At this point, the person discovers a truth they could not have understood earlier: interior healing is a form of holiness. To be healed is to be free for love. To be whole is to be available for God. The Spirit does not heal simply to mend; He heals to sanctify. Every wound touched by grace becomes a doorway through which divine life flows.

Healing reaches its fullest depth when the Spirit restores the soul's interior unity—when mind, heart, memory, imagination, and desire begin to move toward God with a shared rhythm. This state is not perfection, nor is it an emotional plateau. It is harmony: a convergence of the faculties around a single centre, the indwelling Spirit. The person no longer feels pulled apart by competing impulses or contradictory fears. The various layers of the self do not chatter against one another. Instead, the entire interior life begins to echo the prayer of the psalmist: "Unite my heart to fear Your name."

This is the moment when wounds, once sources of shame or chaos, become places of communion. Augustine delights in this mystery when he cries, "In my wounds, Your fingers touch me and heal me." Pain is no longer an obstacle to God but a point of contact with Him. The wound does not vanish; it becomes translucent. Grace shines through it. What once produced isolation now draws the soul into deeper dependence upon divine love. What once crippled the heart now becomes the place where compassion is born.

The Spirit performs this work quietly. He does not dismantle the human personality but sanctifies it from within. The old anxieties may still whisper, but they no longer dominate. The old fears may still appear, but they no longer define. The old temptations may pass by, but they no longer hold the same magnetism. The power of sin weakens not because the soul becomes stronger but because the Spirit has become the soul's strength. Everything that once fractured the interior life now becomes ordered under His light.

As unity grows, something even deeper emerges: the heart becomes teachable. Pride, defensiveness, and self-protection—the walls erected by woundedness—begin to crumble. The soul grows simple, open, receptive. It is the disposition Jesus praises when He says, "Blessed are the pure in heart, for they shall see God." Purity here does not mean moral flawlessness but unbroken attention, a gaze that is no longer diverted by fear or scattered by desire. The healed soul can finally behold God without flinching.

This vision opens the door to true discernment. The Spirit teaches the soul to distinguish His quiet movements from the turbulent movements of the passions. A resentment begins to rise—and the Spirit reveals it as self-protection, inviting forgiveness instead. An impulse toward self-promotion appears—and the Spirit unmasks it as fear of invisibility, inviting humility instead. A temptation whispers its promise—and the Spirit exposes the lie beneath the surface, revealing it as a hunger for intimacy that only God can satisfy. Discernment becomes natural, not because the soul is wise but because the Spirit has become its wisdom.

This is why the healed soul becomes a source of healing for others. Not through advice or analysis, but through presence. Others feel safe near someone whose heart is unified. They sense stability, patience, openness, gentleness—qualities that do not arise from personality alone but from the Spirit's presence. Holiness becomes magnetic. Grace radiates. The person does not broadcast piety; they carry peace. And peace draws the wounded as surely as fragrance draws the weary traveller.

Here the Spirit accomplishes something breathtaking: He makes the soul transparent to Christ. The person becomes a living icon—not a replica, but a bearer of divine light. The treasures of the Spirit begin to manifest: love that seeks nothing for itself, joy that circumstances cannot choke, peace that settles over turbulence like a quiet dawn. Patience, kindness, generosity, faithfulness, gentleness, self-control—these fruits are not human achievements; they are the blossoms of a heart restored to communion. Each fruit is a sign that the Spirit has healed not just symptoms but the roots.

At this stage, obedience no longer feels like external obligation but internal harmony. The soul desires what God commands. The conscience no longer oscillates between guilt and confusion; it becomes steady as a compass pointing north. Hearing God's will becomes less about deciphering signs and more about following the deep peace the Spirit plants beneath each faithful choice. The soul begins to recognise that God's commands are not impositions but invitations into greater freedom.

Freedom—true freedom—is the final fruit of healing. Woundedness imprisons: in fear, in addiction, in resentment, in self-punishment, in habitual sin. The Spirit liberates not by removing responsibility but by restoring capacity. The person becomes able to do the good they love rather than merely avoid the evil they fear. Freedom is not the absence of struggle; it is the presence of grace stronger than struggle. The Spirit transforms the soul from a battlefield into a sanctuary where conflict no longer defines identity.

This sanctuary becomes the dwelling-place of union. A heart at peace with itself can finally rest in God without resistance. Prayer becomes gentle, spontaneous, constant. Love becomes the natural expression of the soul. Suffering becomes the place where the Spirit's strength is felt most intimately. Ordinary tasks—work, parenting, friendship, silence—become sacraments of presence. The Spirit has healed not only wounds but vision. The person sees God everywhere.

And so, healing reveals its true purpose: not comfort, not psychological adjustment, not moral tidiness, but union. The Spirit heals the heart so that the heart may belong to God without fear. He calms the passions so that love may flow unimpeded. He restores the conscience so that the soul may delight in the good. He redeems memories so that nothing in the past can prevent communion in the present. He binds up wounds so that they become wells of mercy.

The Spirit heals because the human heart was made for glory.

Everything broken becomes a place for God to enter. Everything healed becomes a place for God to dwell. The Spirit's final work is not merely to repair but to divinise—so that the soul, once fragmented, once fearful, once wounded, may shine with the very light of Christ.

This is the restoration of unity.

This is holiness as wholeness.

This is healing as participation in divine life.

This is the Spirit completing His work.

19

From Union to Glory

Union is not an ending but a beginning. When the Spirit brings a soul into harmony—when memory is healed, desire is purified, conscience is restored, and the heart learns to breathe with the very breath of God—the result is not stillness but readiness. Everything the Spirit has done in the secret places of the soul begins to press outward, the way fire, once kindled, presses outward into flame. Divine life cannot remain enclosed. It expands. It moves. It searches for the farthest edges of love, because love that stops expanding has ceased to be divine. The Spirit who indwells is the Spirit who sends, and the soul that has been made whole finds that wholeness awakening into mission.

This expansion is not forced. It is the natural movement of communion. To be united to the Spirit is to be caught up in the very dynamism of God. The Father gives Himself; the Son receives and returns that gift; the Spirit is the radiant love that flows between them. When the Spirit dwells within a soul, the soul is drawn into this rhythm. It begins to live from the logic of divine generosity. It begins to discover that holiness is never self-contained. Sanctity is not an inward treasure to be guarded but a living fire to be shared. A healed heart becomes a source of healing; a purified desire becomes a vessel of mercy; a soul at rest becomes a place of refuge for others. This movement from interior to exterior is not a departure from union but its fulfillment.

The saints bear witness to this truth. The more profoundly the Spirit united them to Christ, the more widely their love reached. Francis of Assisi embraced lepers. Thérèse of Lisieux embraced the world from a cloister. Maximus the Confessor embraced suffering to defend the truth. Their lives show a single pattern: when the Spirit makes a person whole, that person becomes a gift. This is not activism and it is not strategy. Mission arises because the Spirit who dwells within is the Spirit of the Son who was sent. The soul in union begins to feel the pulse of this sending. Love becomes restless—not with anxiety, but with longing. The heart seeks those who have not yet tasted the fire that has remade it.

Yet the movement toward mission reveals another truth: love, when it becomes real, becomes vulnerable. A heart reshaped by the Spirit cannot avoid the wounds of the world, because divine love moves toward wounded places. Christ went where suffering was deepest; the Spirit who united Him to the Father is the same Spirit who unites the Christian to Christ. The soul that lives in the Spirit will inevitably find itself drawn into places where compassion demands courage. This is not a detour from union but the cost of it. Love that shares God's tenderness must share God's vulnerability. The heart becomes capable of endurance not through its own strength but because the Spirit breathes Christ's own perseverance within it.

This is why suffering is woven into the life of the Spirit-filled person. It is not punishment. It is participation. The Spirit does not lead the soul away from the world's pain but through it, the way He led Christ from Gethsemane to Calvary, not abandoning Him but empowering Him. The Spirit consoles not by removing affliction but by infusing meaning. He illuminates suffering from the inside. He makes the heart capable of bearing weight that would otherwise crush it. Consolation is not the easing of sorrow; it is the discovery of God within sorrow. When the Spirit consoles, the soul perceives, perhaps dimly but truly, that nothing suffered in faith is ever wasted. It becomes part of the mysterious exchange of love by which Christ redeems the world.

This movement toward suffering prepares the soul for another revelation: the Spirit who heals is also the Spirit who judges. Judgment is often imagined as the interruption of divine mercy, but in truth it is the consummation of it. The Spirit's fire purifies the soul in this life; at the end of life, that same fire becomes fully unveiled. The Spirit reveals all things as they truly are—not to condemn but to liberate. Whatever cannot endure divine love burns away; whatever yields to love shines. This is why the Fathers speak of judgment as illumination. The light that once purified in hiddenness will purify openly, completing the work begun in baptism, sustained in prayer, nourished in the Eucharist, and carried through every movement of grace.

The soul that has yielded to the Spirit knows this fire already. It has tasted purification; it has tasted union. It has felt within itself the burning away of what is false and the rising of what is true. Judgment, then, is not foreign. It is familiar. It is the final flame of a fire that has been growing quietly within. The Spirit who has been forming Christ in the soul now prepares to reveal that Christ fully. This is not destruction but consummation—the moment when the human heart becomes entirely transparent to divine life.

The horizon widens further still. The Spirit's work is not confined to individual souls but stretches across the whole arc of history. The same Spirit who hovered over the waters at creation now hovers over the destiny of the world. The movement from chaos to order, from darkness to light, from formlessness to beauty, repeats on the scale of the cosmos. Salvation history is the story of the Spirit guiding creation toward transfiguration. The resurrection of Christ is the first revelation of what the Spirit intends for all flesh; Pentecost is the down payment; the Church is the vessel; the sacraments are the channels; the saints are the proof. Everything leans toward a future in which the Spirit will fill all things with God.

Union in this life is therefore only a beginning. It is a seed. Glory is the blossom. The Spirit's indwelling makes the human person capable of eternity, capable of communion, capable of bearing a weight of glory that would annihilate the unprepared soul. The Fathers call the Spirit the "arrabon," the pledge, the guarantee. Eternity begins now, in hiddenness, as the Spirit breathes within the soul. But the fullness of what He breathes will only be revealed when Christ appears and creation itself is set free from decay. The Spirit who unites us to God now will unite heaven and earth then.

Glory, then, is not a sudden interruption but the natural flowering of everything the Spirit has been doing from the beginning. When He hovered over the waters, He was already preparing for the day when He would hover over the New Creation. When He breathed life into Adam, He was already preparing for the day when humanity would breathe the atmosphere of eternity. When He sanctified Israel, anointed kings, inspired prophets, overshadowed the Virgin, descended upon the Church, and indwelt the hearts of the faithful, He was not moving in different directions. He was moving along one uninterrupted path—the path that leads creation back into God. The Spirit is the Alpha and the Omega of divine action. His descent in Genesis is the first note of a symphony whose final movement resounds in the Book of Revelation.

This is why the soul that has known union begins to sense a new horizon: life with the Spirit is not merely about becoming holy; it is about becoming ready. Ready to be sent. Ready to love without fear. Ready to suffer without losing hope. Ready to see God. The Spirit prepares the heart to endure glory, because glory is not passive spectacle—it is participation in divine life. Glory is communion made visible. Glory is love bearing fruit that the world cannot ignore. Glory is the human person fully alive, which is to say, fully aflame. The Spirit forms that flame in secret until the soul becomes capable of carrying its light into the world.

Once the soul reaches this point, the movements of the Spirit take on a new quality. His work is no longer only interior. It becomes incarnate in the world. The heart overflowing with divine life becomes a sign, a presence, a sacrament of God's love in a broken age. Mission is the natural consequence of union. It is not the ascent of the zealous but the overflow of the transfigured. A soul united to Christ cannot remain silent about the One who has healed it. Love longs to be shared. Truth longs to be spoken. Mercy longs to find the wounds that need it. The Spirit pushes the soul outward the way fire pushes heat outward—freely, expansively, without measure.

Yet the world is not neutral to this fire. Divine love encounters resistance. Holiness provokes contradiction. The Spirit's presence in a believer disrupts darkness by revealing it. The closer a soul draws to God, the more clearly it sees the world's wounds—and the more deeply the world's wounds press upon the soul. This is why suffering is not an accident of mission but the seal of it. The Spirit does not lead the Christian around the cross but into it, because the cross is not simply a place of death. It is the place where love reaches its furthest expression. The Spirit who united Christ and the Father in the Passion now unites the Christian to Christ in every trial. In persecution, in misunderstanding, in loneliness, in loss, the Spirit whispers the same truth He whispered to Christ: that love is stronger than death, and fidelity is stronger than fear.

This companionship of the Spirit in suffering is not a side theme of the Christian life; it is the crown of it. For it is here, more than in ecstasy or insight, that union reveals its depth. Joy teaches the soul to rejoice in God; suffering teaches the soul to cling to Him. In joy, the Spirit fills; in suffering, the Spirit anchors. In joy, the Spirit expands the heart; in suffering, the Spirit fortifies it. The believer discovers that the Spirit's consolation is not fragile warmth but steadfast presence. Consolation is the assurance that one is never alone in the fire. Christ dwells in the suffering Christian by the Spirit, transforming affliction into a hidden participation in redemption.

From this interior transformation, a new vision of reality emerges. The Spirit who heals the heart also disentangles the mind. He enables the believer to see the world not through the fog of fear or self-interest but through the clarity of truth. Judgment, in this sense, begins long before death. Every moment of Spirit-given clarity, every purification of motive, every deepening of humility is a small unveiling of truth. The Spirit reveals who we are and who God is—and this unveiling is the same movement that will reach its fullness at the end of time. The fire that purifies us now is the same fire that will purify creation. Judgment is not the interruption of grace but its completion.

Viewed in this light, the Last Things are not remote doctrines but the horizon of the spiritual life. The Spirit who dwells within is already drawing the soul toward its destiny. The resurrection is not an abstract hope; it is the future shape of every Spirit-filled body. The new heavens and new earth are not poetic images but the cosmic fulfillment of the Spirit's creative work. Just as He once brought form out of chaos, He will bring transfiguration out of decay. Just as He once breathed life into dust, He will breathe immortal glory into the bodies of the redeemed. Humanity was made for this. Creation was made for this. The Spirit presses history toward this moment with unrelenting gentleness.

The soul that has been healed, illumined, and united begins to desire this fulfillment—not out of impatience with the world but out of longing for the world's true completion. The Spirit teaches the heart to pray with the Bride, "Come, Lord Jesus," not simply as a cry for rescue but as a cry for consummation. The Spirit awakens a desire for the world to be transfigured as the soul has been transfigured. He expands hope until it includes all creation. He bends the soul toward a future where nothing remains wounded, nothing remains hidden, nothing remains unfulfilled. The Spirit who sanctifies now will glorify then. The fire that purifies now will illuminate then. The love that indwells now will reign then.

This is the threshold on which the Christian stands. The Spirit has healed the heart and united it to God. Now He prepares it for the final movements of divine love: mission, suffering, revelation, and glory. The soul does not advance alone; it advances with the One who has breathed life into it since the beginning. Everything the Spirit has done so far—creating, shaping, cleansing, restoring, illuminating, uniting—has been preparing the soul to participate in the fullness of God's plan. Part IV is not a new story but the unveiling of the story that has been unfolding since Genesis. The Spirit who began over the waters now leads the soul toward the horizon where God will be "all in all."

IV

The Spirit Who Consummates (Glory)

20

The Spirit and Mission: Love to the Ends of the Earth

Mission does not begin with the Church looking out at the world. It begins with God looking out from eternity. The human impulse is always to imagine mission as an activity—something the Church initiates, organises, or evaluates. Scripture shatters that illusion. Before the apostles ever lifted their eyes to the horizon, the Father had already spoken the eternal Word, and the Word had already turned His face toward creation in unending love, and the Spirit had already been the infinite bond of that love who would one day be poured upon flesh. Mission begins not in strategy but in the Trinity. The Father sends the Son; the Son breathes the Spirit; the Spirit forms the Son's Body and draws all creation back toward the Father. Only when this divine movement is understood can the Church understand her own.

This is why the New Testament never speaks of mission as an idea. It speaks of mission as a sending. The risen Christ says to His disciples, "As the Father has sent me, so I send you," and then, to make clear the nature of this sending, He breathes on them. The gesture is not symbolic. It is ontological. The breath that moves from His mouth is the Spirit of the new creation, completing in the apostles what was begun in Adam. The first mission was creation; the final mission is re-creation. In both cases the Spirit is the divine breath animating the work. Whenever Christ sends, He never sends without giving His own breath. The Church does not act *for* Christ at a distance; she acts *in* Christ because she breathes with His Spirit.

Pentecost reveals this truth in its purest form. The Spirit does not descend as instruction or command. He descends as fire. Fire cannot be contained. Fire expands by its very nature. Fire creates light around itself and spreads warmth beyond itself. That is why the Fathers insist that Pentecost is not the beginning of the Church's activity but the beginning of the Church's being. The Spirit falls, the Church begins to burn, and that burning becomes witness. No one at Pentecost had a strategy. No one drafted a mission statement. They simply caught fire. The Spirit Himself became the movement, the speech, the courage, the beginning of a new world.

The fire did not come upon individuals in isolation. It came upon the gathered body, forming them into one. Mission is always born in communion. The Spirit does not ignite solitary flames scattered in the dark; He builds a furnace, a single heart whose heat radiates outward. When Acts says, "And there were added that day three thousand souls," it is describing not a mass conversion campaign but a gravity. The Spirit-filled Church becomes luminous, and those who dwell in darkness begin to see. The Spirit's presence creates attraction because He is the beauty of God made visible in human lives. Mission is the overflow of beauty.

This beauty is not sentimental warmth. It is the radiance of the crucified and risen Christ. When the Spirit fills the apostles, He does not erase the wounds of Christ from their memory; He makes those wounds the centre of their proclamation. The blood shed on Calvary becomes the fountain of life announced in Jerusalem. The death that appeared to end everything becomes the beginning of everything. Mission, therefore, is not the triumphal march of religious enthusiasm. It is the humble disclosure of a love strong enough to die. The Spirit empowers witness precisely by joining believers to the sacrificial love of Christ. He gives courage not by inflating human confidence but by anchoring the heart in the victory already won.

The earliest Christians understood mission in these terms. Their boldness did not arise from persuasive techniques but from union with the living Christ. Fear vanished not because circumstances changed but because the Spirit within them was greater than the hostility around them. "We cannot but speak of what we have seen and heard," Peter and John declare—not because they had memorised a message, but because the message had entered their bones. Witness is not recitation; witness is participation. Mission is the Spirit bearing testimony through human voices He has set aflame.

This participation reveals another dimension of mission: its direction. Mission does not aim simply to instruct the ignorant or correct the wayward. It aims to draw humanity into communion. The Church is not an organisation expanding its influence; the Church is the Body of Christ expanding its life. Every act of mission is an invitation into a relationship—the relationship the Son has with the Father in the Spirit. The goal is not recruitment but transfiguration. The Spirit who sends is the Spirit who indwells; He draws souls not toward ideology but toward the fire of divine life.

Because mission is communion expanding, it always flows through charisms. Charisms are not religious talents; they are the concrete ways the Spirit extends the love of Christ through the members of His Body. One teaches with a wisdom not his own; another consoles with compassion not her own; another serves with a strength not their own. Each charism is a spark from the one fire. Each contributes to the furnace of love God is building in the world. Mission becomes distorted when charisms are treated as personal properties or marks of status. They exist to bind, not divide; to heal, not elevate; to draw together, not set apart. The Spirit gives gifts to create communion, and communion to sustain mission.

Every movement of mission, therefore, must be interpreted as the unfolding of Pentecost. The Spirit who descended on the apostles has not withdrawn His fire. He continues to widen the circle of love. He continues to send the Church to the margins not as coloniser but as companion, not as propagandist but as witness, not as competitor but as servant. Mission is not the Church conquering the world; it is the Spirit gathering the world into Christ. The apostles did not leave the Upper Room to impose theology; they left because the fire would not let them remain. Where the Spirit burns, silence becomes proclamation. Where the Spirit moves, fear becomes boldness. Where the Spirit breathes, the Church becomes truly herself.

Mission is not what the Church does after she has prayed; mission is what the Church becomes when she has prayed. Christ did not say, "Wait until you are ready." He said, "Wait until you are clothed with power." The Spirit is that clothing—light that becomes courage, fire that becomes speech, love that becomes mission. The apostles received the Spirit and saw the world differently, not because their minds had been expanded but because their hearts had been enlarged. The Spirit does not give strategies; He gives vision. He does not supply methods; He supplies love. Mission is the shape love takes when it refuses to remain still.

Mission unfolds wherever the Spirit widens the heart. The apostles do not begin preaching because they suddenly feel responsible for the world; they begin because the Spirit has filled them with the love of Christ, and that love presses outward. "The love of Christ impels us," Paul writes, and the verb is violent—love pushes, urges, compels. This compulsion does not arise from anxiety or duty but from the interior weight of divine charity. The Spirit pours this charity into the heart until it cannot be contained. Mission is the overflow of a heart that has discovered it belongs not to itself but to Christ.

This is why Christian mission never begins with correcting errors. It begins with revealing a Person. The Spirit always moves first through witness, not argument. He arranges encounters, opens paths, softens the soil of hearts. He prepares long before the missionary speaks, and He continues long after the missionary departs. The entire world is the Spirit's field, the entire Church His instrument. The apostle's task is simply to cooperate with the movements already unfolding. In this sense, mission is less an initiative than a response. The Spirit is the protagonist; the believer is the one carried along.

To understand the nature of this carrying, one must understand the biblical word *parrhesia*. It is often translated as "boldness," but its true meaning is freer and deeper—speech unchained, a heart supported by the Spirit so fully that truth can be spoken without fear. Parrhesia is not bravado; it is a confidence rooted in the awareness that the Spirit Himself testifies. When the early Christians stood before councils or kings, they did not rely on their rhetorical skill; they relied on the One within them who knows the Father and reveals the Son. Boldness is not a human virtue; it is a divine gift. The Spirit speaks, and the disciple becomes its echo.

This boldness is always marked by charity. The Spirit never makes a person harsh. His fire burns, but it burns without scorching. Christ's mission is love offered even when rejected, and the Spirit forms that same gentleness in His witnesses. Martyrdom—whether the shedding of blood or the slow martyrdom of fidelity—is the highest expression of mission because it reveals a love stronger than fear. The Spirit strengthens the martyr not by numbing the pain but by uniting the heart to Christ, so that love becomes greater than life. The witness becomes transparent. Humanity becomes the lantern;

divinity becomes the flame.

Yet the Spirit's work in mission is not limited to speech or heroic sacrifice. He is also the quiet architect of communion, shaping the Church into a sign of God's kingdom. Every time Christians forgive, reconcile, serve, or share their goods, a new glimpse of divine life appears. The early Church's unity was not a social achievement; it was the visible sign that the Spirit had created a new humanity. The world saw a community where Jew and Gentile, slave and free, rich and poor ate at the same table, prayed with one voice, and called each other brother and sister. This was not an ideology; it was the Spirit's architecture. Communion is mission because communion reveals God.

This communion is never merely internal. The Spirit sends outward what He has gathered inward. The same love that unites believers compels them to seek the lost, tend the suffering, and announce hope. Mission is the Church exhaling what she has inhaled. She breathes in the Spirit, and she breathes out charity. Without the Spirit, the Church's efforts collapse into activism, fatigue, or triumphalism. With the Spirit, even the smallest gesture becomes charged with divine meaning. A word spoken, a meal shared, a wound tended, a prison visited—each becomes a place where Christ Himself draws near through His Body.

The Spirit shapes mission also by placing within believers a sense of divine urgency. Not haste, not panic, but the awareness that love is always timely. Christ speaks of the harvest not to impose pressure but to reveal generosity—the fields are ready because the Father desires His children. Mission is not an emergency; it is an invitation. The Spirit knows the hour for each soul. He knows when to prompt a question, when to open a memory, when to awaken conscience, when to console, when to unsettle. He knows when silence will speak more loudly than exhortation. The missionary is not a strategist but a listener—listening to the Spirit within and the Spirit working in the other.

In this way the Spirit prevents mission from becoming ideological. Ideology seeks to conquer; the Spirit seeks to liberate. Ideology imposes; the Spirit invites. Ideology reduces people to problems; the Spirit reveals them as mysteries. This is why all true mission is marked by reverence. The Spirit teaches the Church to bow inwardly before every soul, recognising that each person stands on ground where God is already present. Mission becomes an act of wonder. The evangeliser kneels before the beauty the Spirit is preparing, even if that beauty is still hidden beneath wounds, fears, or sin.

Such reverence flows naturally into discernment. The Spirit not only empowers mission; He guides it. Paul's missionary journeys are shaped less by planning than by listening. The Spirit forbids certain paths, opens others, and directs him toward those whom God has prepared. He teaches through dreams, visions, inner movements, and the communal judgment of the Church. Mission is never a solo venture; it is the Church listening together to the voice of her Lord. Discernment is the art of cooperation—of discovering how the fire already burning in the heart of God is meant to touch the hearts of the world.

Mission is therefore never merely geographical; it is always relational. A heart inflamed with divine love becomes a bridge between heaven and earth. Where that heart goes, Christ goes. Where that heart speaks, Christ speaks. Where that heart rests, Christ rests. Mission is the sacrament of presence—Christ made present by the Spirit through the lives of His people. The Christian does not carry Christ as one carries a message; he carries Christ as one carries breath. The witness does not point to a distant truth; he becomes transparent to the Truth dwelling within. The Spirit is not simply the fire behind mission; He is the fire within the missionary.

Mission always begins with an encounter, and the Spirit is the master of encounters. The apostles move through the world not as entrepreneurs of the sacred but as men carried along by currents they did not generate. Every conversion in Acts bears this signature. Philip is drawn to the Ethiopian by an inner nudge, and the story unfolds like a liturgy: a question, a Scripture, a revelation, a baptism, and then Philip is taken away as swiftly as he arrived, leaving the man rejoicing. Paul is directed to Macedonia not by strategic analysis but by a nocturnal vision, and Lydia's heart opens "as the Lord gave her grace to listen." The Church is born in moments like these—moments orchestrated by One who sees farther and loves deeper than any missionary ever could. The Spirit does not wait for perfect vessels; He simply seeks willing ones.

This willingness is purified over time, because mission is always contested. Wherever the Spirit advances, resistance arises—not only from the world but from the human heart itself. The missionary soon discovers the truth Jesus spoke: "Without Me you can do nothing." Fatigue, disappointment, rejection, misunderstanding—these do not simply challenge the missionary; they reveal the need for continual dependence on the Spirit. Mission becomes a kind of school where pride is broken, illusions are stripped away, and the soul learns to rely not on its eloquence or energy but on a deeper strength. Ratzinger often notes that the Church evangelises most fruitfully when she evangelises from weakness. The Spirit delights in working through those who know they are insufficient, because insufficiency makes room for grace.

This is why the Spirit forms missionaries not only through moments of triumph but through seasons of silence. Elijah on Horeb learns this truth in the sound of sheer silence, discovering that God does not always arrive in wind, fire, or earthquake. The missionary who expects constant visible results will lose heart; the missionary who expects God to be faithful even in obscurity becomes unshakeable. The Spirit trains His witnesses to see beyond appearances, to trust that He is sowing seeds even when the soil looks barren. Mission is not measured by numbers but by fidelity.

When the Spirit matures this fidelity, a new kind of joy appears. It is not the passing exhilaration of success, nor the sentimental thrill of novelty. It is the quiet joy of watching Christ revealed in another person. Luke notes that the early Church was "filled with joy and with the Holy Spirit," and the two are inseparable. Joy is the echo of the Spirit's presence. Wherever joy is absent, mission becomes a burden. Wherever joy abounds, mission becomes the natural expression of a heart aligned with God. This joy is not naive; it knows the cost of love. It is the joy of the Cross, the joy that "for the sake of the joy set before Him, Christ endured." A missionary shaped by this joy does not flee suffering, because he recognises that suffering is often the ground where the Spirit performs His deepest work.

The Spirit also guards mission from distortion by rooting it in truth. Love without truth collapses into sentimentality; truth without love hardens into ideology. The Spirit is the Spirit of truth and the Spirit of love, and therefore He binds the two together in perfect harmony. The missionary does not invent doctrine; he hands on what he has received. He does not reshape the Gospel to suit cultural expectations; he allows the Gospel to reshape the culture. Yet even as he speaks truth boldly, he does so with the tenderness the Spirit produces. Truth becomes luminous, not abrasive; it wounds only to heal; it judges only to liberate. When truth is spoken in the Spirit, it carries the resonance of Christ's voice—firm, piercing, and yet filled with mercy.

In the same way, the Spirit purifies mission from self-reference. A missionary who secretly seeks validation or admiration will ultimately betray the Gospel. But a missionary who has learned to disappear so that Christ may appear becomes a vessel through whom God works freely. This self-forgetfulness is not humiliation; it is freedom. The Spirit teaches the heart to rejoice more in the salvation of another than in its own accomplishments. Augustine describes the missionary as one who "loves the truth he preaches and loves the person he preaches to, for Christ dwells in both." When the Spirit forms this double love, the missionary becomes a sacrament of divine presence.

This sacramental quality is important, because mission is not merely about the transmission of information; it is about the communication of life. The Spirit does not simply enlighten the mind; He warms the heart, strengthens the will, and awakens desire. A person may hear the Gospel many times, yet remain unchanged until the Spirit touches them in the depth where words alone cannot reach. The missionary cooperates with this hidden work by living a life that reflects what he proclaims. The world is converted not only by preaching but by holiness—a holiness that makes the invisible visible. Francis of Assisi, Thérèse of Lisieux, Mother Teresa—these saints evangelised through radiance. Their words mattered, but their lives mattered more. The Spirit made their hearts transparent, and through the transparency others saw God.

This transparency gives mission its universal scope. The Spirit is never provincial. He is the Lord and Giver of Life, moving across continents, cultures, and histories with the same aim: to gather all things in Christ. This universality is not a political programme; it is the fruit of divine charity. The Spirit does not homogenise cultures; He sanctifies them, preserving their particular beauty while freeing them from the chains that bind. Pentecost is the reversal of Babel—not because languages dissolves into one, but because diversity becomes harmony. Mission respects this harmony. It does not demand cultural self-erasure; it seeks the conversion of hearts. And when the heart is converted, culture is healed from within.

The Spirit therefore shapes a missionary spirituality marked by humility, fidelity, joy, reverence, and universality. This spirituality is not reserved for apostles or religious; it belongs to every baptised person. Every vocation participates in mission: the mother raising children in faith, the father living integrity in his labour, the parishioner visiting the sick, the young man resisting temptation, the elderly woman offering her loneliness for the salvation of souls. The Spirit turns ordinary lives into missionary vessels. Wherever love is offered in Christ, mission takes place.

The deepest truth about mission emerges in the way the Spirit shapes time. The apostles are not sent into a neutral world; they are sent into a world already stirred, already prepared, already awaiting the Word. The Spirit always arrives before the missionary. He is the hidden guest in every conversation, the quiet restlessness in every heart, the whisper that precedes the human voice. The missionary does not plant Christ in barren soil; he uncovers Him where grace has already begun to germinate. There is no missionary field untouched by the Spirit, because the Spirit is the One who "prepares the Bride for the Bridegroom." Mission is therefore an unveiling rather than an invasion.

This unveiling often occurs in surprising ways. The Spirit's paths are neither linear nor predictable. A persecutor becomes an apostle. A jailer becomes a brother. A Samaritan woman becomes an evangelist to her village. A dying thief becomes the first to enter paradise. The Spirit creates openings where logic sees only barriers. He brings the Gospel to those the Church least expects, and sometimes through those the Church least expects. In this way, mission becomes an exercise in wonder. The missionary learns to expect the unexpected, because he recognises that grace is always more creative than human plans.

This creativity is rooted in love. The Spirit is the Love of the Father and the Son, and therefore all His works bear love's signature.

When the Spirit sends, He sends out of love; when He convicts, He convicts for love; when He gathers, He gathers into love. Mission is not activism; it is the outward movement of divine charity. A missionary who is not rooted in love will eventually wound those he intends to heal. But a missionary whose heart has been purified by the Spirit becomes a living extension of Christ's compassion. The Gospel becomes credible not primarily through argument but through the tenderness of those who bear it.

Tenderness does not mean weakness. The Spirit gives courage—parrhesia, that boldness which astonishes even the apostles themselves. Peter, who once trembled before a servant girl, now stands unshaken before the Sanhedrin. Paul, who once breathed threats, now breathes mercy into hostile cities. Francis Xavier crosses oceans; Isaac Jogues returns to the very tribe that tortured him; Maximilian Kolbe steps forward into a death cell for the sake of another. These acts are not heroic by human effort; they are the fruit of a love that fears nothing because it belongs entirely to God. The Spirit makes the heart spacious, capable of bearing the weight of the world's need without collapsing into despair.

This spaciousness is essential, because mission always encounters suffering. To proclaim Christ is to enter the drama of salvation, which means entering the places where darkness resists the light. Missionaries face hostility not because they are political, but because the Gospel confronts the idols of every age. It exposes false gods, unmasks lies, and liberates consciences that evil would prefer to keep bound. This unveiling provokes opposition. Yet the Spirit sustains His witnesses with a consolation the world cannot give. Not the comfort of ease, but the comfort of presence—the assurance that Christ is near, that the Father sees, that suffering offered in love becomes a seed of resurrection.

The Spirit's presence in suffering is among His most mysterious works. He does not remove the cross; He makes the cross fruitful. He transforms anguish into intercession, weakness into strength, defeat into witness. Missionaries through the ages testify that their most powerful moments of evangelisation were born not from eloquent speeches but from silent fidelity in hardship. The world believes strength is persuasive; the Spirit knows holiness is irresistible. A life surrendered in suffering speaks a language the heart understands before the mind can interpret it. It reveals the Gospel in its purest form: love enduring unto the end.

Through all of this, the Spirit protects mission from despair by fixing the missionary's gaze on Christ's victory. The resurrection is not merely an event in the past; it is the atmosphere in which mission takes place. Every proclamation assumes that Christ lives; every act of charity assumes that death is defeated; every moment of fidelity assumes that history is moving towards a consummation already guaranteed. The missionary does not fight for a fragile victory; he witnesses to an established one. This confidence is not triumphalism; it is the serenity that comes from knowing the outcome of the story. The Spirit anchors mission in this serenity.

This serenity, in turn, gives rise to gratitude. Mission is not a burden but a privilege—the privilege of participating in the divine generosity that flows eternally between Father, Son, and Spirit. When the missionary sees a heart awakened, he recognises he has witnessed a miracle. When he sees repentance, he rejoices as heaven rejoices. When he sees faith arise where once there was indifference, he marvels at the artistry of God. Gratitude becomes the atmosphere of mission, purifying motives and sustaining perseverance. A grateful missionary is one who recognises that the Spirit has done everything, and that his role has been simply to cooperate with that grace.

In this gratitude, mission attains its most luminous form: it becomes worship. Evangelisation is not an activity separate from prayer but an extension of prayer. The missionary carries the presence of God into the world because the Spirit has made his heart a temple. He speaks because he has listened; he gives because he has received; he loves because he has been loved. The rhythms of contemplation and mission are not opposed; they are two breaths of the same Spirit. The inward breath draws the soul into God; the outward breath carries God into the world.

When a missionary lives in this rhythm, the distinction between mission and life dissolves. Every action becomes a space for grace: a smile, a conversation, a gesture of forgiveness, a moment of patience, a silent prayer for a stranger. Mission ceases to be something one does and becomes something one is—a living witness to the God who dwells within. The Spirit no longer merely sends; He shines. The missionary becomes transparent, and Christ becomes visible.

This is the ultimate shape of mission: not conquest, but communion. The Spirit draws humanity into the embrace of the Father through the Son, gathering the scattered fragments of the world into one Body. Mission is the Spirit's way of extending this embrace until it reaches the ends of the earth. And when the final heart has been touched, when the final soul has been awakened, mission will resolve into the eternal praise of the redeemed. The Church that once travelled will finally rest, and the Spirit who once sent will now fill all things with glory.

21

The spirit in suffering: Consolation and martyrdom

Suffering has always stood as the one experience capable of silencing every human philosophy. Arguments fail before it. Explanations feel hollow beside it. Even theology hesitates when a soul is bent under the weight of anguish. There are places in the human heart where words cannot enter because pain has already taken all the space. Yet it is precisely here—where human strength collapses and understanding dissolves—that the Holy Spirit descends with a nearness so delicate and so hidden that many never recognise Him. The Spirit does not approach suffering from above, as one who observes and evaluates. He approaches from within, as One who already inhabits every cry, every fear, every loneliness, every trembling. He comes not with solutions but with presence, and His presence becomes light inside the darkness.

Christ promised this presence in the language of intimacy: "I will not leave you orphans; I will come to you" (Jn 14:18). The One through whom He comes is the Spirit. In Scripture, the Spirit is not primarily the giver of ecstasy or enthusiasm, but the *Parakletos*—the One called alongside, the Defender, the Advocate, the Companion in distress.

The ancient Christian ear heard not "comforter" in the soft modern sense, but One who stands with the sufferer, strengthening, stabilising, empowering. Consolation in the Spirit does not numb pain; it makes the heart able to bear it without collapsing. He does not shield the believer from the Cross; He upholds the believer while the Cross is embraced.

The Fathers often say that the Spirit is the love between the Father and the Son. If this is true, then suffering brings the believer into the most radiant furnace of divine life. For what is suffering in Christian terms, if not love under pressure? Love refusing to withdraw even when wounded. Love choosing fidelity even when it costs. Love moving outward even when every instinct calls it inward. Where love becomes costly, the Spirit becomes visible. Where suffering threatens to turn the heart inward on itself, the Spirit breathes outwardness again. He expands the heart precisely where pain tries to constrict it. The interior spaces suffering seems to destroy become, under His touch, the very capacity for deeper communion.

This is why the Spirit does not remove the Cross. Removal would relieve pain but hinder transformation. The Cross is not sacred because it hurts; it is sacred because it reveals the truth of love. And love's truth is revealed only when love is tested. The Spirit's role in suffering is not to make the Cross disappear but to make it luminous—to fill it with the same love with which Christ embraced His own Cross.

This was already foreshadowed in the Passion. Scripture reveals that Christ offered Himself "through the eternal Spirit" (Heb 9:14). This single line is the key to all Christian suffering. The Passion is not the Son alone, nor the Father imposing suffering upon the Son. The Passion is a Trinitarian event. The Father receives the sacrifice; the Son offers Himself freely; and the Spirit sustains that offering from within the humanity of Christ. The Spirit is the flame inside the sacrifice, the strength inside obedience, the fire that makes Christ's suffering not merely endured but *given*. Without the Spirit, the Cross would be only tragedy. Through the Spirit, the Cross becomes redemption.

The same Spirit who strengthened Christ strengthens His disciples. This is why the earliest Christian witnesses understood martyrdom not as heroic bravery but as the work of the Spirit. In Acts, the first martyr, Stephen, does not die in rage or fear. He dies "full of the Holy Spirit." He sees the glory of God; he forgives his killers; he surrenders his spirit to Christ. None of these gestures express human capacity. They express divine presence. Stephen is not simply imitating Christ—he is participating in Christ through the Spirit. His death reveals the same movement of love Christ displayed at Calvary because it is animated by the same Spirit.

As persecution intensified in the early centuries, the Church learned to recognise the marks of the Spirit in the dying faithful. Martyrs often entered the arena not with panic but with peace—some even with joy. Accounts record faces luminous with serenity, bodies at rest, songs rising in the midst of violence. This joy is not psychological denial. It is not natural courage. It is the Spirit's joy, the joy Christ promised: "My joy will be in you, and your joy will be full" (Jn 15:11). The Spirit's joy is not the suppression of fear but its transfiguration. It is the interior proof that death has been defeated from within.

The Fathers frequently describe martyrdom as a continuation of Pentecost. The same fire that fell upon the Apostles now descends upon the suffering believer. Martyrdom becomes a second outpouring of flame—not a flame that consumes, but a flame that illuminates. The martyrs do not burn; they shine. Their blood does not simply fall to the ground; it becomes seed. Tertullian's line—"the blood of the martyrs is the seed of the Church"—is not rhetoric. It is pneumatology. The Spirit fructifies suffering. The Spirit makes death fertile. The

Spirit uses what the world destroys to build the Kingdom. What hatred attempts to silence becomes, in the Spirit, proclamation.

This is why persecution has always been the engine of evangelisation. Not because Christians are heroic masochists, but because the Spirit manifests Himself with unparalleled clarity when the believer is stripped of every earthly support. In ordinary times, the Spirit works quietly, hidden within the fabric of daily life. But in persecution, His presence intensifies, becomes visible, becomes radiant. The world recognises something in the persecuted Christian that it cannot explain. Why do they forgive? Why do they refuse hatred? Why do they possess peace stronger than violence? Why do they face death with songs rather than curses? To see a martyr is to see the Spirit.

The global Church continues to witness this same mystery. The places of greatest persecution become the places of greatest growth. The Spirit pours Himself out where the Cross is heaviest. In Africa, where Christians suffer violence and loss, the Church grows with extraordinary vitality. In parts of Asia, where faith must be whispered or hidden, communities multiply underground with apostolic fervour. In the Middle East, where ancient Christian families face danger and displacement, the Spirit preserves fidelity with supernatural endurance. History testifies to this pattern again and again: ancient Rome, Japan under the Tokugawa shogunate, the underground Church in Korea, believers under communism in Eastern Europe. The Spirit turns attempted destruction into new creation.

Wherever Christians suffer, the paradox intensifies: suffering produces fruit, hatred generates unity, persecution reveals holiness. Observers looking upon persecuted believers often convert not because of arguments, but because of beauty—the beauty of forgiveness, peace, gentleness, fidelity. They encounter the "attraction of holiness," the Spirit shining through wounds. The martyrs' radiance becomes its own gospel.

THE SPIRIT IN SUFFERING: CONSOLATION AND MARTYRDOM

The Spirit's presence in suffering does not stop at endurance or even at joy. It becomes mission. The Spirit draws observers not by spectacle but by revelation—by unveiling something divine in those who suffer with love. This is the Spirit's missional logic: suffering becomes the theatre where the victory of Christ is displayed before the eyes of the world. Christians do not seek this stage, but when it is placed beneath their feet, the Spirit fills it with a light the world cannot extinguish. Martyrdom becomes a proclamation made not by speech but by being. Love stronger than fear becomes visible, and the Spirit uses that visibility to draw souls.

This is why Christian evangelisation in its earliest centuries was inseparable from persecution. The Church expanded not by cultural dominance or political favour but by the moral authority of those who suffered in the Spirit. The Roman authorities executed Christians to silence the movement. Instead, the Spirit made their deaths the loudest homily the world had yet heard. Crowds came to watch executions expecting fear and despair; they found serenity and forgiveness instead. These scenes became invitations. Men and women left the arena silent, unsettled, unable to explain what they had just seen. Something in them recognised a truth too beautiful to deny. The Spirit used the martyrs' witness to open their hearts, and through them, new communities were born.

The early Church Fathers never tired of pointing to this paradox, because it revealed the Spirit's character. The Spirit is the One who turns loss into gain, weakness into strength, death into life. The Spirit always moves outward, always expands communion, always builds the Church. Therefore, persecution becomes an instrument in His hands. The more the Church is pressed, the more the Spirit flows through the cracks. The more the world tries to extinguish the flame, the more the flame spreads. Fire, when pressed, does not shrink; it leaps.

In the writings of Ignatius of Antioch, we find a soul who understood this mystery with startling clarity. He does not seek death out of fanaticism. He does not desire suffering for its own sake. Rather, he desires union with Christ in the Spirit. He sees martyrdom as the moment when the Spirit completes the configuration of the disciple to the Master. "Let me be the wheat of God," he writes, "and let me be ground by the teeth of the beasts, that I may be found the pure bread of Christ." This is not grim resignation. It is spiritual maturity. It is the recognition that the Spirit brings the believer into Christ's offering, making his life—and even his death—Eucharistic.

The martyrs' serenity is part of this Eucharistic mystery. They are not consumed by hatred, nor paralysed by terror. They stand or kneel or fall with a composure that confounds onlookers. Roman officials accused them of madness. But the Church understood the truth: the Spirit was bearing witness through them. The Spirit was making visible the interior life of Christ. The radiance on their faces was not psychological calm but the reflection of divine light. Many accounts describe martyrs whose faces shone as though lit from within. This was the Pentecostal fire made visible in human features.

Such radiance is not romantic exaggeration. Even in modern times, similar testimonies persist. When Vietnamese martyrs were executed in the 19th century, witnesses spoke of an unearthly peace on their faces. When Christians in the Middle East faced death in recent years, recordings and testimonies revealed a calm, even joy, that defied human comprehension. This is the same Spirit, acting in the same way, across centuries and continents. The Spirit's joy is not bound to historical era or cultural context. It is the fruit of love made perfect in weakness.

The global pattern is unmistakable. Where Christian suffering increases, faith does not shrink. It intensifies. It deepens. It multiplies. In Africa today, communities devastated by violence still

THE SPIRIT IN SUFFERING: CONSOLATION AND MARTYRDOM

worship with a vibrancy that astonishes missionaries. In parts of Asia where Christianity must remain hidden, the Spirit gathers secret churches in homes, cellars, remote forests—communities that grow despite imprisonment, harassment, and surveillance. In the Middle East, where ancient Christian roots run deep, small and persecuted communities remain steadfast, guarding the flame of faith with a fidelity that can only be explained by grace.

This is not a sociological phenomenon. It is a pneumatological one. The Spirit moves freely where worldly power is weak. The Spirit thrives in places where Christians rely on Him entirely because they have nothing else. The Spirit turns attempted destruction into new creation because He is the Giver of life and the One who renews the face of the earth. When the earth is scorched by violence, He makes it fertile again.

The paradox extends further. Persecuted Christians often radiate not only courage but forgiveness. The world expects retaliation. Instead, it encounters mercy. Forgiveness offered in the midst of suffering is perhaps the most powerful proof of the Spirit's presence. It is not natural. It is supernatural. It is Christ's forgiveness made visible again and again through His members. When the world witnesses this forgiveness, it encounters a love it cannot explain and a strength it cannot imitate by willpower alone. This is why the Spirit uses suffering as evangelisation. It reveals love in its purest form—love that cannot be reduced to psychology, culture, or strategy. Love that can only come from above.

History records numerous persecutors who became believers after witnessing the serenity and love of the condemned. Guards converted. Magistrates converted. Soldiers converted. Spectators converted. The Spirit spoke through wounds more powerfully than through words. The Church fathers understood this as the logic of the Spirit: the truth of the Gospel is not proven by argument alone, but by a life that cannot be explained without grace. The persecuted Christian becomes a living apologetic. The Spirit writes the Gospel on the body of the martyr, and the world reads it.

Yet suffering is not limited to persecution. The Spirit is present in every human crucible: illness, poverty, loneliness, betrayal, fear, failure, grief. In these places, the Spirit's action is no less real and no less profound. The difference is not in the quality of suffering but in the openness of the heart. When the believer offers his suffering to God, the Spirit transforms it. When he closes himself, the Spirit waits. The Spirit does not force Himself into the inner life. He descends when invited, and when He descends, suffering is reshaped. It may still hurt, but it is no longer fruitless. It becomes prayer, intercession, transformation, purification.

If suffering can become prayer, it is because the Spirit makes it so. The Spirit does not merely hold the believer during pain; He draws that pain upward into the life of Christ. Every wound, every tear, every hidden anguish becomes, in His hands, material for communion. The human heart, left to itself, cannot interpret suffering. It sees only loss. It feels only threat. But the Spirit interprets suffering from within the mystery of Christ's own Passion, and this interpretation is not intellectual—it is experiential. The Spirit does not give explanations; He gives participation. He draws the believer into the place where Christ's sacrifice was offered, and there, suffering becomes transformed.

This is the meaning of Paul's astonishing line: "I rejoice in my sufferings... and fill up what is lacking in Christ's afflictions" (Col 1:24). Nothing is lacking in Christ's redemption. The only thing "lacking" is our participation in it. The Spirit supplies this participation by uniting the believer to Christ's self-offering. Christian suffering becomes redemptive not because the believer adds to Christ's work, but because the Spirit weaves the believer's love, endurance, and surrender into

THE SPIRIT IN SUFFERING: CONSOLATION AND MARTYRDOM

the tapestry of the Cross. The Cross is not a past event; it is a living mystery, and the Spirit makes this mystery accessible in every age.

The early Church understood this profoundly. Martyrs did not die alone. They died in the Spirit. They died inside the flame of divine love. Their suffering was not merely endured; it was offered. Their blood did not simply fall; it was poured out. Christian martyrdom is not suicide, nor stoicism, nor spectacle. It is sacrament: an outward sign of inward grace, an embodied proclamation of the Spirit's presence. Through martyrdom, the Spirit reveals the full extent of His power: the ability to make love victorious where violence should have triumphed, to make serenity bloom in the heart of terror, to make death the gate of life.

This same mystery unfolds in less dramatic forms of suffering. Chronic illness, unfulfilled longing, financial hardship, mental anguish, family breakdown—these experiences reveal the same pattern when lived in the Spirit. The believer who suffers with Christ and in the Spirit becomes a vessel of divine compassion. His suffering becomes intercession for others. Her endurance becomes light for those who watch. Their pain becomes a hidden offering that the Spirit carries into the heart of the Trinity. Very often, the most powerful witnesses in the Church are those whose names will never appear in a martyrology. They are parents who persevere through grief, spouses who remain faithful through hardship, priests who continue to serve through exhaustion, the elderly who pray through loneliness, the sick who unite each day's pain to Christ. The Spirit dwells in these lives with a tenderness that does not often make history books but makes saints.

The Spirit's presence in suffering also exposes the poverty of human self-sufficiency. The world's logic insists that strength is measured by control, and suffering is the collapse of control. The Spirit reveals a different logic: strength is measured by love, and suffering is the place where love is tested and proven. When someone suffers with fidelity, it becomes clear that something more than human endurance is at work. The Spirit shows His power not by removing vulnerability, but by filling vulnerability with divine life. In this way, the weak become the strongest, the poor become the richest, and those who seem defeated become the ones through whom God renews the world.

This renewal often unfolds invisibly. The Spirit loves hiddenness. He performs His deepest work in silence, beneath the surface, beneath emotion, beneath understanding. Many believers think they have been abandoned in suffering because they feel no consolation. Yet it is precisely in this absence of feeling that the Spirit works most profoundly. The "dark night," described by John of the Cross, is not the Spirit's withdrawal but the Spirit's purification. He removes sensible comforts not to punish but to untether the soul from reliance on emotion. He teaches the soul to love God for God's sake, not for the consolations God gives. This is the highest form of love, the love Christ Himself displayed when every consolation was stripped away at Calvary.

In this night, the Spirit becomes the breath within the believer's breath. He sustains the heart without the heart realising it. He prays within the soul even when the soul cannot form words. Paul's line in Romans 8 is not poetic exaggeration: "The Spirit Himself intercedes for us with groanings too deep for words." These groanings are not emotional expressions. They are divine movements within the human heart, the Spirit praying where the believer cannot, strengthening where the believer collapses, carrying the believer when he can no longer walk.

The Spirit also acts in the conscience during suffering. Pain exposes the interior fault lines of the soul. It reveals attachments, fears, motives, illusions. The Spirit gently illuminates these places—not to condemn, but to heal. In suffering, many realise they have been trusting in false securities. They discover that their hearts cling to things incapable of sustaining them. The Spirit uses suffering to unmask these illusions, not harshly but mercifully. He removes idols by showing their fragility. He restores truth by revealing love's solidity. In this light, suffering becomes not only a place of endurance but of revelation. The Spirit reveals the soul to itself so that the soul may be healed.

This healing is not always dramatic. Often it is subtle, gradual, slow. The Spirit's work in suffering is more like the soft shaping of river water than the blows of a sculptor's hammer. He sands down pride, fear, resentment, self-pity. He deepens patience, magnanimity, gentleness, compassion. He widens the heart. He makes room for God. Over time, the believer emerges from suffering not hardened but softened, not bitter but wise, not diminished but enlarged. The Spirit turns the crucible into a sanctuary.

Perhaps the most beautiful fruit of the Spirit in suffering is compassion. Those who suffer deeply in the Spirit become capable of consoling others with a tenderness that cannot be fabricated. They know the terrain of pain, but they also know the Presence who walks there. Their words carry weight. Their empathy carries grace. Their presence becomes healing. Pain has taught them what human strength cannot, and the Spirit has sanctified what pain revealed. In this sense, suffering becomes the school of divine compassion. The one who suffers in the Spirit becomes a vessel of the same consolation he once received, and through him, others encounter God's mercy.

The Spirit's work in suffering reaches a distinctive climax in the mystery of martyrdom, for martyrdom is not simply the Church's most dramatic witness but its most luminous. In martyrdom, suffering and mission converge. The disciple becomes transparent to the Spirit in a way that is rarely possible in ordinary circumstances. The world sees a human being stripped of every earthly protection—no weapons, no defence, no influence—and yet discovers in them a strength, peace, and joy utterly inexplicable. This is not the triumph of human courage but the manifestation of divine life. Martyrdom is the Spirit revealing Himself with a clarity that leaves the world without excuses.

This is why the earliest Christians regarded martyrs not as spiritual elites but as the mature fruits of Pentecost. The same fire that rested upon the Apostles in Jerusalem descended upon the martyrs in Rome, Alexandria, Carthage, Antioch. They were "burning ones," not because flames consumed them but because divine love filled them. Their serenity was not the absence of fear but the presence of the Spirit whose joy no torment could extinguish. Martyrdom, in this sense, is Pentecost extended into the body: fire not on the head but in the heart, radiance not around the apostles but around the condemned.

The ancient accounts preserve this radiance with astonishing detail. When Polycarp stood in the arena, witnesses recorded that his face shone "as though filled with light." When Perpetua and Felicity went to their execution, the crowd saw joy on their faces—joy, not because they sought death, but because the Spirit filled them with the certainty of Christ's nearness. Even Roman officials, accustomed to brutality, marvelled at the peace emanating from those they condemned. They recognised in these Christians a composure foreign to the human condition, a serenity that resisted every attempt to intimidate or corrupt. That serenity was the Holy Spirit.

The visible joy of martyrs is one of the clearest signs of the Spirit's presence. Human strength may endure suffering for a time, but it cannot produce joy in the midst of it. Joy belongs to the Spirit alone. The Spirit gives courage, but He also gives radiance. He gives endurance, but He also gives light. The martyrs' joy is the ultimate contradiction to the logic of violence. Violence seeks to dominate through fear. Joy dissolves that fear from within. Joy proclaims a kingdom that cannot be conquered by force. Joy reveals a life that death cannot touch. When the world encounters this joy, it sees the Spirit—not the person—standing before it.

This is why martyrdom has always been the seed of evangelisation. Tertullian's famous line was not poetic exaggeration. It was sober observation. The blood of martyrs is seed because the Spirit makes it seed. The Spirit uses death to give birth. He uses destruction to generate new life. The early Church exploded in growth not because Christians were persuasive diplomats or skilful organisers, but because pagans saw the Spirit in the martyrs. They saw faces filled with light. They saw forgiveness where revenge was expected. They saw men and women singing hymns as they were torn apart. These are not moral achievements. They are divine manifestations. The Spirit preached through their bodies.

This same pattern continues today in the global Church. It is one of the most striking features of Christian history that the faith spreads most rapidly in places where it is most fiercely opposed. In Africa, where many Christians face violence or threat, the Church grows with astonishing vitality. In Nigeria, believers who bury their dead on Saturday often worship with dancing and rejoicing on Sunday, because the Spirit sustains their courage with divine fire. In China, where the Church has long operated underground, communities thrive under hardship with a depth of fidelity that cannot be manufactured. In the Middle East, where ancient Christian communities face hardship unimaginable to the West, the Spirit strengthens them with a supernatural endurance that preserves identity, tradition, and faith.

This is not sociological irony; it is theological certainty. The Spirit multiplies faith when suffering is greatest because suffering is the place where human self-reliance collapses, and grace becomes everything. Persecuted communities do not survive by clever strategy. They survive because the Spirit holds them together. He knits them into communion. He fills them with courage stronger than their fear. He gives them hope that transcends loss. This is why Christian communities in trouble often shine with a purity that is absent in comfortable churches. Their faith is not diluted by compromise. Their unity is not eroded by trivial disputes. Their worship is not reduced to performance or preference. The Spirit Himself has become their life.

Persecution often brings forth a paradox that cannot be rationalised: those who suffer most often display the deepest love. The world expects suffering to make people hard, fearful, or resentful. Instead, persecuted Christians frequently radiate forgiveness. They pray for their enemies. They remain open-hearted. They refuse to retaliate. This forgiveness is not the fruit of human nobility but of divine life. It is Christ's forgiveness flowing through them by the Spirit. This supernatural forgiveness becomes its own form of martyrdom—a dying to self, a crucifixion of pride, a victory of love over hatred. The Spirit makes this possible.

Observers encounter this forgiveness as revelation. It is not normal. It is not natural. It does not fit human patterns. Something divine becomes visible. Many persecutors throughout history converted after witnessing such forgiveness, not because of theological debate but because they encountered the Spirit in the Christian they tormented. The heart that refuses hatred is the clearest icon of the Trinity, for the Spirit is the Love that binds Father and Son. When that Love appears in the world through a suffering believer, it strikes the heart with a conviction no argument can rival.

To see a Christian suffer with love is to see a window opened into eternity. It is to witness heaven touching earth. The Spirit turns suffering into revelation, not by glorifying pain but by glorifying love. Martyrs are not advertisements for hardship; they are revelations of divine love's power. They show what the Spirit can make of a human life surrendered wholly to God. And they show the world a love it cannot destroy.

Yet even as the Spirit shines most visibly in martyrdom, His work is not confined to moments of public witness. The Spirit's deepest labour often unfolds in the hidden places of the soul where no one but God sees. Martyrdom is the summit, but suffering lived in secret fidelity is the long ascent that prepares the heart for such heights. The Spirit works not only in extraordinary trials but in the ordinary agonies of human life: the quiet heartbreak of unfulfilled longing, the slow erosion of health, the weight of financial strain, the wounds carried from childhood, the griefs that never quite heal, the loneliness that lingers even in company. If martyrdom is the trumpet blast, these are the steady notes of the Spirit's interior symphony.

In these hidden sufferings, the Spirit forms saints. He does not simply grant endurance; He forms the soul according to Christ's own heart. He infuses patience where impatience once ruled. He draws forth gentleness from places previously hardened by self-protection. He awakens compassion in those who once felt only resentment. He gives clarity where confusion once clouded perception. This transformation is rarely dramatic, and often unnoticed by the one being transformed, because the Spirit works from within. His movements are quiet, like the slow dawning of light or the soft deepening of roots.

This interior transformation is not sentimental. It is a participation in Christ's kenosis—the self-emptying of the Son who became obedient unto death. The Spirit who filled Christ with obedient love in Gethsemane fills the believer with the same love in every act of surrender. Sometimes surrender means offering one's life; sometimes it means offering one's will, pride, fears, illusions, or attachments. The Spirit reveals that suffering is not a test of survival but an invitation to communion. The believer who listens to the Spirit in suffering does not merely endure—it is the believer who begins to love more deeply, trust more completely, and hope more fiercely.

Indeed, the Spirit reveals the deepest truth of Christian suffering: suffering is not the opposite of love but its proving ground. Love that avoids suffering is fragile. Love that survives suffering becomes strong. Love that transforms suffering becomes holy. The Spirit teaches the heart that suffering, when lived with Christ, becomes an altar—an interior place where love is purified and offered. On this altar, the believer places not only pain but also fear, loss, and uncertainty. The Spirit lifts these offerings to the Father, joining them to Christ's own sacrifice, and in doing so, He fills the soul with divine life.

This divine life manifests itself not only in endurance but in peace. The peace the Spirit gives is not escape from suffering but harmony within it. It is a peace that coexists with pain, a peace that does not depend on circumstances, a peace rooted in the unshakeable fidelity of God. This peace is the fruit of communion, not the absence of conflict. It is a peace that often confounds those who witness it. Many believers in hospital beds, war zones, or places of persecution radiate a peace stronger than their physical frailty. This is the Spirit's peace—a peace Christ promised when He breathed the Spirit upon His disciples: "My peace I give to you; not as the world gives" (Jn 14:27).

The Spirit's peace also reveals something crucial: suffering does not have the final word. The Spirit is the pledge of resurrection. He is the foretaste of glory. He is the down payment of the new creation. In suffering, He does not only console; He anticipates. He whispers the promise of things not yet seen. He makes hope real, not by denying the Cross but by carrying the believer through it. The Spirit transforms suffering by setting it within the horizon of eternity. "The sufferings of this present time," Paul writes, "are not worth comparing with the glory that is to be revealed" (Rom 8:18). This is not stoicism. It is vision. It is the Spirit giving the believer Christ's own perspective on suffering.

This perspective becomes most radiant at the moment of death. Death is the final suffering, the ultimate stripping away. Yet Scripture describes the Spirit as "the guarantee of our inheritance" (Eph 1:14)—the One who accompanies the believer into the Father's presence. The early Christians believed that the Spirit bears the soul at death, just as He bore Christ through death into resurrection. Many martyrs spoke of dying "in the peace of the Spirit," as though death were not an extinguishing but a passage into fuller light. Even in ordinary Christian deaths, witnesses often describe a serenity that defies explanation. The Spirit completes His work by conforming the believer to Christ even in the final surrender.

What emerges from all of this is a stunningly coherent vision: the Spirit transfigures suffering from the inside. He does not glamorise it. He does not romanticise it. He does not turn Christians into masochists or fatalists. Instead, He turns suffering into communion, communion into offering, offering into mission, and mission into glory. The Spirit does not waste a single tear. He does not ignore a single wound. He does not overlook a single act of fidelity. He is the divine Artist who paints holiness on the canvas of a wounded heart.

This divine artistry is why the Church venerates martyrs and honours the suffering faithful. It is not because pain is good, but because the Spirit makes of pain something beautiful. In martyrs, He makes suffering luminous; in the hidden faithful, He makes it fruitful. In all, He makes it a path to union.

The chapter finds its deepest synthesis in a single truth: the Spirit is the One who turns suffering into offering. Without Him, suffering remains a closed circle, a descent into self. With Him, suffering becomes an ascent—a movement into the life of Christ, a participation in the world's redemption, a revelation of love stronger than violence, and a foretaste of the new creation. Where the Spirit is, suffering does not end in despair. It ends in glory.

And so the believer who suffers is never alone. The Spirit stands beside him as Paraclete, dwells within him as Consoler, strengthens him as Advocate, guides him as Wisdom, purifies him as Fire, and unites him to Christ as Love. The Spirit who sustained Jesus in His Passion sustains every disciple in theirs. The Spirit who made the martyrs radiant makes every act of faithful suffering a quiet miracle. The Spirit who raised Christ from the dead will raise the believer into the same glory.

For suffering, in the Spirit, is not the story's end.

It is the place where God begins to write the next chapter.

22

The Spirit and the Last Things: Judgment and Mercy

The final things are often spoken of with fear, yet Scripture approaches them with a vocabulary of light. The last day is not described as a cosmic ambush but as an unveiling, an *apokalypsis*—a revelation of what has always been true, now shown without distortion. When the prophets speak of judgment, they do not describe a moment in which God becomes different. They speak of a moment in which everything else becomes transparent. What lies hidden is laid bare, not to shame, but to heal; not to terrify, but to reveal; not to crush, but to clarify. And at the heart of this unveiling stands the Holy Spirit, the One whom the Fathers call the "Light of the soul," the "Fire of God," the "Eyes of the Father," the "Gaze of Love."

From the opening pages of Scripture, the Spirit is the One who brings order from chaos and light from darkness. At the world's beginning, the Spirit hovers over the waters, preparing creation to receive the Word. At the world's end, the Spirit will hover over all creation once again, preparing it for glory. What He accomplishes in the soul during a lifetime—illumination, purification, sanctification—He will accomplish for the entire human race at the end of time.

Judgment is, in this sense, the Spirit's final act of truth-telling, the moment the divine artistry is seen without veil.

To speak of judgment through the Spirit, then, is to move away from courtroom metaphors and into the language of revelation. Judgment is the moment the Spirit shines so fully that nothing untrue can survive the light. It is not the collision of two wills—God's against ours—but the encounter between God's truth and our freedom. Truth does not humiliate; truth liberates. The Spirit reveals, not to crush, but to heal; not to annihilate, but to consummate. As Ratzinger writes, "Judgment is above all the moment of definitive truth." And truth is always the atmosphere of love.

At the heart of this final revelation is one decisive reality: the Spirit is always the Spirit of Christ. He reveals Christ, forms Christ, illumines Christ, draws all things into Christ. The Last Day is not a day when the Father acts apart from the Son or the Son acts apart from the Spirit. It is the day when the Spirit reveals the Son in glory and all humanity sees itself in that light. Christ is the measure; the Spirit is the light in which that measure is seen. Christ is the truth; the Spirit is the radiance of that truth. Christ is the face of God; the Spirit is the gaze that lets us behold that face. Therefore judgment is not a threat but a theophany—an encounter with the One who is Truth made flesh.

The Scriptures use the language of fire to describe this encounter, not because God delights in destruction, but because nothing expresses purity and truth as powerfully as flame. Isaiah speaks of the Spirit as "a spirit of judgment and burning," a fire that cleanses Jerusalem. Malachi describes the Lord as a refiner's fire, separating dross from gold. Paul writes that each person's work will be tested "as through fire," not to condemn, but to reveal what has substance and what is straw. Hebrews declares that "our God is a consuming fire," not to terrify, but to proclaim that God's love is so pure, so radiant, so holy, that it transforms everything it touches.

The Fathers understood this fire as the presence of the Spirit Himself. Fire is not merely an image of divine wrath; it is the nature of divine love. St. Basil describes the Spirit as "the all-consuming fire who purifies." Gregory of Nyssa sees purgation as the soul's painful but liberating encounter with divine light. And St. Isaac the Syrian expresses the mystery with unparalleled depth when he writes, "Hell is the love of God misunderstood." For the saints, the fire of judgment is nothing less than the presence of the Spirit experienced according to the soul's condition. The open heart experiences the fire as warmth, illumination, joy. The closed heart experiences it as anguish, not because the Spirit changes, but because the soul resists.

The fire is one; the experience is twofold. The Spirit is one; love is one; truth is one. Yet how the soul meets that love depends on the freedom of the heart. The purpose of divine fire is always purification. The Spirit burns only what is not love. The aim is not destruction but transfiguration. His fire reveals what is genuine, burns away what is false, and strengthens what is holy. This is why Scripture says that those tested by fire "will be saved"—even if they pass "as through fire." Salvation is the fruit of being purified by love.

This vision changes everything about how Christians understand judgment. Judgment is not arbitrary sentencing. Judgment is not divine anger unleashed. Judgment is the final encounter with truth as love. Judgment is the moment when we see ourselves as we truly are in the light of God's unchanging mercy. In this sense, the Last Things are not about the end; they are about the revealing of purpose. Humanity is destined for divine life. Judgment unveils the degree to which we have allowed the Spirit to accomplish that destiny within us.

Every moment of our life has prepared for this unveiling. In every sacrament, the Spirit has healed and illumined. In every act of repentance, the Spirit has purified. In every act of love, the Spirit has conformed us to Christ. Judgment is simply the revelation of what the Spirit has done—and what we have allowed Him to do. The soul sees the story of grace written in its depths, and it sees, with painful clarity, every place where grace was resisted.

Yet even this pain belongs to mercy. The Spirit does not wound; the Spirit reveals the wounds we cause ourselves by refusing love. He exposes them only to heal them. Nothing in divine judgment contradicts divine tenderness. The Spirit is the Love poured out in our hearts, and His final act is to show the soul the truth of that love with unflinching clarity. The revelation may burn, but it burns with the brightness of healing.

Christ Himself is the measure of this revelation. We will see Him as He is—and by that sight we will see ourselves. The Spirit reveals Christ not as judge in the worldly sense, but as the One who stood among us as mercy incarnate. Judgment is the soul standing beneath the gaze of the Crucified and Risen One. Every sin will be seen in light of the One who forgave from the cross. Every refusal of love will be seen in light of the One who offered Himself without reserve. Every missed opportunity will be seen in light of the One who never withheld grace.

The Spirit reveals all of this not to condemn, but to draw the soul into truth.

The Spirit's revelation at the moment of death—the particular judgment—is the soul's most intimate encounter with truth. It is not the entrance into a tribunal but the unveiling of one's life in the gaze of the Holy Trinity. The Church has always taught that at the moment of death the soul stands before Christ. Yet this encounter unfolds in the light of the Spirit, for it is the Spirit who enables the soul to see with divine clarity. What we call "judgment" is nothing other than the Spirit removing every veil: the veil of denial, the veil of pride, the veil of self-deception, the veil of fear. The Spirit gives the soul the capacity to behold its life as God sees it.

In that moment, nothing external is added to the soul—no new information, no new accusation. What occurs is an act of divine illumination. St. John of the Cross expresses this succinctly: "In the evening of life, we will be judged on love." Not on success or failure, not on reputation or achievement, not on how we compared ourselves to others, but on love—what we received, what we offered, what we rejected. Love is the measure because love is the nature of God, and the Spirit is the Love poured into the human heart. The particular judgment is the Spirit showing the soul the truth of its capacity for love.

The soul sees the whole landscape of its journey—every moment of grace accepted, every grace ignored; every wound healed, every wound clung to; every act of mercy given, every act withheld. The Spirit reveals the story of the soul not with cold judgment but with an overwhelming gentleness that makes the truth undeniable. Even the painful parts are shown with a strange sweetness, because the soul finally understands them in light of God's unwavering love. The pain comes not from divine severity but from recognising how often love was offered and refused.

This recognition leads directly into the mystery of purgation. Purgatory is frequently misunderstood as a place of punishment, a spiritual waiting room of torment. But the tradition—both East and West—insists that purgation is fundamentally the Spirit's final act of mercy. If the soul dies in friendship with God yet still bears wounds, attachments, distortions of love, the Spirit completes His work through a healing fire. Paul's words in 1 Corinthians echo with gentle assurance: "He will be saved, but only as through fire." Salvation is assured; the fire is purifying, not destructive.

The Fathers often describe this process using the imagery of gold in the furnace. Gold is not punished by fire; it is perfected. The impurities melt away; the nature remains. So too with the soul. Nothing the Spirit burns is part of our true identity. The fire touches only what does not belong—resentment, pride, vanity, fear, self-love, illusions. The Spirit removes these burdens because they cannot enter glory. Heaven is communion. Anything that isolates or distorts the heart must be healed or surrendered. Purgation is therefore the Spirit preparing the soul for full participation in divine life.

This healing can be painful only because we resist love. Pain is the friction between divine mercy and human attachment. St. Catherine of Genoa writes with startling clarity that the souls in purgation "would cast themselves into a thousand hells rather than appear before God with a single stain." As the Spirit reveals God's holiness, the soul's longing to be pure intensifies. The pain is not inflicted from without; it rises from the soul's desire to be wholly God's. Purgation is longing turned into transformation.

This final work of the Spirit also reveals something essential: salvation is not merely forgiveness. Salvation is healing, restoration, deification. The Spirit will not permit the soul to enter communion half-healed, half-bound, half-loving. Divine love is not content with partial gift. The Spirit completes sanctification because divine love desires full union. Purgation is not God delaying heaven; it is God ensuring that heaven can be fully received.

Yet the revelation of the Last Things does not belong only to the individual. Scripture also speaks of a day when the Spirit will unveil the truth for all creation—the general judgment. The Christian imagination often caricatures this as a vast courtroom scene. But the language of the Gospels and the Fathers moves in a different direction. Christ returns in glory, and everything is seen in His light. The Spirit brings to completion what began in the Upper Room. Pentecost was the Spirit descending into human hearts; the Last Day is the Spirit descending upon all creation.

This universal illumination accomplishes several things simultaneously. First, the Spirit reveals the hidden communion that binds all believers together. Every act of love, every prayer, every sacrifice, every hidden offering that shaped salvation history becomes visible. The saints are seen in their true radiance. The poor in spirit are revealed as kings. The meek are shown as conquerors. The martyrs shine with the fire that sustained them. The entire tapestry of redemption becomes visible—not as isolated stories but as a single symphony conducted by the Spirit.

Second, the Spirit reveals the consequences of sin—the real consequences, the relational consequences. Every wound inflicted becomes visible not for humiliation but for truth. Nothing is lost, nothing is trivial, nothing is without meaning. The sins we dismiss as "small" are seen in their ripple effects across the lives of others. Every refusal of grace is understood not as a private moment but as a fracture in communion. This revelation does not shame; it clarifies. The soul sees what love would have accomplished had it been welcomed. This is judgment as illumination.

Third, the Spirit reveals Christ in glory. The Last Day is not primarily about humanity but about the triumph of Christ. Everything is drawn into the light of the Lamb. His wounds shine. His mercy overwhelms. His kingship is established not through domination but through the radiance of love stronger than death. The Spirit is the fire of this revelation. He is the clarity in which Christ is known and adored.

This unveiling is not the suspension of mercy but its triumph. Judgment is the moment when mercy is finally seen for what it is: the burning fire of divine love.

To say that judgment is the triumph of mercy is to enter the very heart of Christian revelation. Scripture never presents mercy as a soft alternative to truth, nor truth as a rigid counterweight to mercy. In the Spirit they are one reality, just as the light from the sun and the warmth it gives cannot be separated. What we call "judgment" is simply this one reality—the encounter with truth-filled mercy and mercy-filled truth. It is the moment when everything false falls away and only the Real remains. The Spirit is the One who accomplishes this unveiling because He is the communion of Father and Son poured into the world, the Love in which all things are meant to be held.

This explains why fear-based images of judgment distort the Gospel. God does not suddenly become severe at the end of history. The severity belongs not to God's heart but to truth itself when it meets a heart that has fled from it. The Spirit does not abandon the sinner; the sinner abandons the Spirit. Divine fire does not change into something else; the soul's disposition toward that fire determines whether the flame illuminates or burns. Gregory Nazianzen said it plainly: "The same fire that enlightens the soul of the pure is the fire that burns the soul that is not." The Spirit is one; love is one; the experience becomes two only because human freedom can welcome or reject.

Here lies the sobering beauty of divine judgment: the Spirit respects the dignity of human freedom even in the final unveiling. He does not override the will; He reveals the truth. That truth is mercy. Mercy is offered, not forced. The tragedy of the Last Things is not God's refusal to forgive; it is the possibility of the human refusal to be healed. Lewis captured it in a single line: "The doors of hell are locked on the inside." Hell is the soul's final insistence that it will not be opened to love.

Yet this refusal must never be imagined as a one-time impulse, a sudden whim at the end of life. The final "no" to the Spirit is the solidification of a thousand smaller refusals woven through a lifetime. Hell is simply the soul's decision, carried to its end, to remain closed.

God does not drag the soul into isolation. The soul walks into isolation because it insists on self-definition without love. And the sorrow of hell is not that God ceases to love, but that divine love, experienced by a heart hardened against it, becomes anguish. Isaac the Syrian's insight is not a poetic exaggeration; it is metaphysical truth: "Hell is the love of God misunderstood."

Still, the aim of Christian eschatology is not to dwell on loss but to unveil the victory of divine love. The Spirit's work in the final judgment is not to increase fear but to bring joy to completion. Judgment is the consummation of everything the Spirit has been doing throughout salvation history. What He whispered in conscience, He now proclaims in clarity. What He began at Baptism, He brings to perfection. What He ignited at Pentecost, He now reveals in full fire. Judgment is the completion of the Spirit's pedagogy: the long schooling in love that leads the human person into communion.

This becomes even clearer when we consider the resurrection of the dead. Paul's words in Romans 8:11 shine with eschatological splendour: "The Spirit who raised Jesus from the dead will give life to your mortal bodies." The resurrection is not a bolt of external power; it is the final flowering of the Spirit's indwelling. The same Spirit who hovers over creation at the beginning, the same Spirit who overshadowed Mary, the same Spirit who descended upon the Church at Pentecost, is the Spirit who will breathe new life into every body laid in the dust. Resurrection is the victory of the Spirit.

This gives the body eternal dignity. The Spirit does not save the soul *from* the body but the soul *with* the body. The Christian hope is not disembodied bliss; it is glorified embodiment. The risen body is not a shadow of earthly life but its transfigured fulfilment. Christ's risen body—radiant, wounded, unbound by decay—is the sign of what the Spirit intends for all humanity. Judgment, therefore, is not the final sorting but the final transformation, the moment the Spirit restores creation to harmony by restoring the human person to glory.

This restoration is not only individual; it is cosmic. Paul writes that "creation itself groans for the revealing of the sons of God" (Rom 8:19). The Spirit's work in the world is not completed until creation shares in the liberation of the children of God. At the Last Day, the Spirit gathers all things—visible and invisible—into the light of Christ. The harmony lost in Eden returns, not as an echo of the beginning but as the fulfilment of the entire history of grace. The new creation is not a return to simplicity; it is the transfiguration of complexity through divine love.

When Christ returns in glory, the Spirit reveals this truth universally. What has been accomplished secretly in the soul is now displayed openly in the cosmos. This is why the final cry of Scripture is not a warning but an invitation: "The Spirit and the Bride say, 'Come.'" These are the last words the Bible gives us—the Spirit calling creation back to the Father through the Son. Judgment is not the divine "No" but the divine "Come." It is the summoning of all creation into the banquet of divine life.

There is extraordinary consolation in this. The Spirit's final word over the world is not destruction but communion. The Bride does not tremble at His coming; she calls for Him. And the Spirit prompts her cry. The end of history is a love story, not a tragedy. The Spirit who hovered over the waters in Genesis hovers over the world again, now to draw all things into consummation. His work is not to terrify but to fulfill. His fire is not to scorch but to transfigure. His judgment is not to reject but to reveal.

Understood in this light, eschatology becomes a celebration of divine fidelity. The Spirit finishes what He begins. His work in creation, in Israel, in Christ, in the Church, and in the soul reaches its final crescendo in the Last Things. Everything moves toward union. Judgment and mercy are not two paths but one reality: love unveiled.

THE SPIRIT AND THE LAST THINGS: JUDGMENT AND MERCY

To understand the Last Things through the Spirit is to recognise that divine judgment has a single purpose: the healing of creation through the revelation of truth. Truth is the atmosphere of love, and when it fills the cosmos without obstruction, everything false collapses. The final judgment is not the insertion of something foreign into the story of salvation; it is the culmination of what the Spirit has already been doing in secret. Throughout Scripture, the Spirit forms a people capable of receiving truth without fear, for only in truth can love be lived. When the Spirit descends upon all creation at the Last Day, this quiet interior formation becomes cosmic in scale.

One of the most beautiful affirmations of the Christian tradition is that the Spirit does not merely reveal truth but makes truth lovable. The human heart often resists truth because truth exposes our wounds. But the Spirit is the Comforter, and His comfort does not numb the wound; it illumines it with tenderness. This tenderness is what the soul encounters in judgment. Even the painful revelations come wrapped in a strange sweetness, because the soul sees itself through the eyes of mercy. This is why the saints could approach death with serenity: they trusted that the Spirit who had guided them in life would guide them in truth.

The final judgment, then, must never be imagined as a moment of divine humiliation. God does not expose the soul to embarrass or crush; He exposes to restore. The Spirit reveals the truth of our lives not as a prosecutor but as a physician. In His light, the soul sees what must be healed, what must be relinquished, what must be forgiven. Nothing in this revelation is arbitrary. Everything is ordered toward love. Even the disclosure of our failures is ordered toward communion. We see how sin wounded our own souls and the souls of others, not to drown in regret, but to grasp how deeply God desires our healing.

This brings us to the mystery of the damned—an anguished but necessary part of Christian revelation. The Church has never taught that God wills any soul to be lost. Scripture is clear that God "desires all to be saved" and that Christ died for all. The Spirit works tirelessly in every heart, pressing upon conscience, stirring desire, awakening repentance, offering grace. Hell exists not because divine mercy fails but because human freedom can resist the Spirit absolutely. The tragedy of hell is not that God ceases to love, but that the soul ceases to let love in.

The Fathers speak of this with profound sobriety. Gregory of Nyssa sees the soul's refusal as a "hardening" that renders it incapable of receiving God's light with joy. Maximus the Confessor describes the final state of the unrepentant as the soul's insistence on defining love according to its own terms. Lewis, echoing patristic intuition, imagines hell as a place where the soul clings to its own illusions, even when truth stands before it. The Spirit does not cast the soul away; the soul withdraws because love, experienced without surrender, becomes unbearable. Hell is not divine cruelty. Hell is the collision between divine love and human refusal.

Yet even here, the Spirit remains the Lover of souls. The tradition insists that the Spirit never stops loving, never stops yearning, never becomes the enemy of the damned. Divine love is eternal, and the Spirit is eternal Love. The anguish of hell arises precisely because love persists. A heart shut to love experiences that persistence as torment. Isaac the Syrian's insight holds: "Those in hell are scourged by the scourge of love." The pain is not inflicted; it is experienced. The fire is not different; the heart is.

Still, this is not the focus of Christian hope. The Church never meditates on hell to foster fear but to safeguard freedom. Love cannot be coerced. The Spirit draws; He does not drag. The entire architecture of salvation is structured around consent—Mary's fiat, the apostles' surrender, the saints' yes. The Last Things respect this architecture. Judgment reveals, but it does not force. The final state of the soul is the mature flowering of the choices it has made, the loves it has cultivated, the desires it has welcomed or resisted.

Turning from refusal to fulfillment, we arrive again at the central promise of Scripture: resurrection. Without the resurrection of the body, the story of the Spirit remains incomplete. Resurrection is the Spirit's masterpiece. It is the moment when divine life saturates the human body so fully that decay becomes impossible. The Spirit does not simply animate the body; He glorifies it. The risen body is not merely restored; it is transfigured. Its wounds become windows of glory. Its limitations become capacities for communion. Its mortality becomes participation in the eternal life of God.

Christ's risen body reveals the destiny of all humanity. His wounds shining like jewels, His presence unbound by time or space, His humanity radiant with divine energy—this is not an exception but the pattern. Paul insists that Christ is the "first fruits" of those who have fallen asleep. The Spirit who raised Him from the dead will raise us also. Judgment, therefore, is not the ending of a story but the threshold of a new one. The Spirit's fire does not consume creation; it prepares it for glory.

The resurrection also reveals that salvation is not escape but consummation. Creation itself awaits the unveiling of the children of God, longing to share in the freedom of the Spirit. At the Last Day, the Spirit does not only raise the dead; He renews the cosmos. Heaven and earth meet. The city of God descends. The world becomes sacramental. Nothing is thrown away; everything is transformed. This is the promise of the new creation: the Spirit will finish what He began in Genesis.

And at the climax of this transformation stands a single cry: "The Spirit and the Bride say, 'Come.'" The last word of the whole Bible is not judgment but invitation. The Spirit calls the world to Christ, and the Bride—the Church—echoes His voice. Judgment is the moment when this call becomes final, not because God ceases to invite, but because the world has reached the horizon of history. The Spirit does not whisper here; He proclaims.

The cry, "Come," is astonishing in its simplicity. It is not the cry of a world collapsing, nor of the Church in despair, nor of a God issuing threats. It is the cry of longing. The Spirit who descended at Pentecost with tongues of fire now speaks with the full voice of eternity, summoning creation into communion. The Bride, purified and made radiant, echoes the call—not out of fear, but out of love. The end of history is an act of desire. God desires us. The Spirit desires our transformation. The Bride desires her Bridegroom. Judgment unfolds within this mutual longing.

This is why Christian eschatology is ultimately a contemplation of beauty. The Last Things are not a terrifying interruption of life but the unveiling of its meaning. Human beings have always sensed that history strains toward something, that time itself carries promise and pressure. The prophets speak of this with urgency: the Day of the Lord is coming. Yet they describe it not as the collapse of creation but as the birth of something new. Jesus calls these pangs "the beginnings of the birth agonies." The Spirit is the midwife of new creation. Judgment is labour. Glory is the child born.

The Christian imagination is free to contemplate this without fear because the end belongs to the Spirit. The Spirit who hovered over the waters of Genesis hovers again over the waters of history. The Spirit who overshadowed Mary overshadows the world at its consummation. The Spirit who filled the Upper Room fills creation with fire. Salvation history is bracketed by the same presence: the creative fire of the Spirit at the beginning, and the consummating fire of the Spirit at the end. The Spirit is the Alpha and the Omega of the world's transfiguration.

This gives profound coherence to the Christian life. Every sacrament, every act of charity, every prayer offered in weakness, every moment of repentance, every victory over sin, every hidden sacrifice, every tear shed in hope—all of it participates in the final revealing. Nothing is wasted. The Spirit weaves every moment into the tapestry of judgment. The story the soul sees at the moment of death is the same story the world sees at the Last Day: the victory of divine love woven through the fragility of human freedom.

The Spirit's role in this final unveiling cannot be emphasised strongly enough. Eschatology is not merely Christological; it is profoundly pneumatic. Christ is the One who judges, but the Spirit is the light in which judgment becomes visible. Christ is the measure; the Spirit is the radiance in which the measure is revealed. Christ is the truth; the Spirit is the transparency that allows truth to be seen and adored. At the end of history, humanity beholds the Trinity in the splendour of divine love because the Spirit makes this vision possible.

This vision brings consummation. Judgment is not a transaction but a transformation. The soul becomes capable of God. The body becomes capable of glory. Creation becomes capable of eternity. Everything that resists love is removed; everything that welcomes love is perfected. This is the meaning of divine justice: the right ordering of all things in love. Justice and mercy are not two acts but one. Mercy heals; justice restores; both arise from the Spirit who is Love.

Christian tradition often speaks of the "Beatific Vision," the final gaze into the face of God. The Spirit is the One who grants this sight. Human eyes cannot see God unless divinised. Human hearts cannot bear the weight of glory unless purified. Human minds cannot grasp the splendour of truth unless illumined. The Spirit accomplishes all of this. He does not simply prepare us for the Beatific Vision; He inserts us into it. The Spirit is the One through whom we see the Son and, in the Son, behold the Father. The Last Things are not an appendage to Christian doctrine; they are the consummation of Trinitarian life in the creature.

Even the resurrection of the body flows from this vision. A soul divinised by the Spirit must receive a body worthy of glory. The risen body is capable of communion at a depth unimaginable now. It is capable of receiving and radiating divine light. It is capable of joy without measure. Paul hints at this mystery when he says, "What is sown in weakness is raised in power." Weakness was never the final word; power is. Mortality was never the final word; immortality is. Corruption was never the final word; glory is. The Spirit is the author of this victory.

From here the chapter turns naturally to its final contemplation: the Last Day as the triumph of communion. Heaven is not a private bliss or an eternal solitude. Heaven is the endless exchange of life within the Trinity, shared with the redeemed. The Spirit makes this communion possible not only within God but within humanity. The multitude standing before the throne in Revelation shines with the unity of the Spirit. Each saint retains their uniqueness, yet all share the same fire. Diversity does not fracture communion; it magnifies it. Every face reflects the light of the Lamb. Every voice contributes to the harmony of worship. The Spirit is the Music of the new creation.

In that world, judgment is remembered not as fear but as dawn. The fire that burned became the fire that illumined. The truth that wounded became the truth that healed. The unveiling that exposed became the unveiling that transfigured. Everything that entered judgment emerged either healed or revealed for what it chose to become. Everything the Spirit could purify, He purified. Everything He could heal, He healed. Nothing good is lost; everything true endures. Love has the last word because the Spirit is the last fire.

This is why the final page of Scripture ends not with threat but with invitation. The Spirit calls. The Bride echoes. Christ answers. And the world, healed and restored, enters the life for which it was made.

Judgment is the doorway; mercy is the threshold; glory is the home.

The Spirit finishes what He began. Creation ends as it began: in the breath of God.

23

The Spirit of the New Creation: All Things Made New

Everything in this book has been leading here. The Spirit who hovered over the waters in the beginning, the Spirit who overshadowed the Virgin in Nazareth, the Spirit who descended at Pentecost, the Spirit who has walked with creation through every valley of sin, exile, repentance, illumination and sanctification—this same Spirit now stands at the threshold of eternity. The final chapter of salvation history is not written in the ink of catastrophe but in the fire of transfiguration. Revelation does not end with ruin; it ends with radiance. Christ does not simply return to judge; He returns to glorify. And the one who accomplishes this glorification is the Spirit, the Giver of Life.

John's vision opens with a proclamation that shakes the foundations of the universe: *"Behold, I make all things new."* The speaker is Christ, yet the one who effects this newness is the Spirit. The entire book of Revelation culminates in this declaration, not as a poetic flourish but as the deepest truth of eschatology. Newness is not a cosmetic change. It is not the world being wiped clean like a chalkboard and replaced with a sterile alternate reality. Newness is the world becoming what it was always meant to be. Newness is creation receiving the fullness of divine life. Newness is the Spirit finishing what He began.

The Scriptures teach that the end of history is not annihilation but transfiguration. "A new heaven and a new earth" does not mean "a different heaven and a different earth." It means heaven and earth *renewed*. Made whole. Filled with glory. Purified by fire, not destroyed by it. The early Christians knew this well. They were not waiting for escape; they were waiting for fulfillment. The world is not a failed experiment God abandons. It is the garden God cultivates until it becomes a city of eternal communion. The Creator does not give up on His handiwork; He perfects it. And the One who perfects is the Spirit.

Christian imagination has often feared the Last Day. Yet the biblical imagination does not tremble. It stands in awe. The final unveiling is not the shattering of the cosmos but the shattering of illusions. It is not the collapse of creation but the collapse of everything that cannot live in communion. The world passes through fire, yes—but it is the fire of the Spirit, the same fire that descended at Pentecost, the same fire that purified Isaiah's lips, the same fire that burns in the heart of the Trinity. In that fire, all that is false is burned away; all that is true shines.

The Spirit is the Lord and Giver of Life. This title reveals the centre of the final chapter: the resurrection of the body. Resurrection is not an accessory to the Christian faith. It is its heart. Without resurrection, salvation is incomplete. Without resurrection, death still reigns. Without resurrection, the Spirit's mission is unfinished. But resurrection completes everything. It is the Spirit's masterpiece.

Paul's words to the Romans echo with eschatological music: "The Spirit who raised Jesus from the dead will give life to your mortal bodies also." The power that rolled away the stone, the love that lifted the crucified Lord into indestructible life, the fire that filled His risen body with glory—that same Spirit will pass through every human grave. Not as a symbol. Not as comfort. As power. As life. As glory.

The risen Jesus is the revelation of what humanity is destined to become. His glorified body is not a ghost, not a vision, not a hallucination. It is a body irradiated with the Spirit. His wounds shine because suffering has been turned inside out. His presence moves freely because the Spirit is not bound by decay. His humanity is fully itself because the Spirit elevates, never erases. Everything broken becomes whole. Everything heavy becomes light. Everything mortal becomes immortal.

That is the future of every believer. Not disembodied existence. Not a merely spiritual afterlife. But a body made capable of God.

The Fathers speak of the risen human as "pneumatic"—Spirit-filled, Spirit-shaped, Spirit-animated. Not that matter disappears, but that matter becomes radiant. The Spirit does not abolish the body; He glorifies it. What was fragile becomes strong. What was limited becomes expansive. What was opaque becomes luminous. The resurrection is the Spirit's final declaration that creation is good, and that God will not rest until goodness is clothed in glory.

But resurrection is not an isolated miracle. It happens within the larger transformation of the world. Paul speaks of creation groaning, waiting for the revealing of the sons of God. Creation is not passive in the drama of salvation. It suffers under sin. It bends under the weight of disorder. It longs for healing. The Spirit's presence in the Church is a down payment for this cosmic renewal—a first taste of what the world itself will experience. When humanity is glorified, creation follows. The world is bound to humanity in a shared destiny.

The fire of the Last Day—so often misunderstood—signals not destruction but purification. The world passes through the Spirit's flame and emerges transfigured. The prophets describe the new creation with bold imagery: deserts blooming, lions resting with lambs, tears wiped away, darkness dissolved in everlasting light. These are not sentimental images; they are symbols of a world healed of violence, healed of decay, healed of fragmentation. A world saturated with the presence of the Spirit. A world no longer subject to entropy but lifted into the eternal energy of God.

The culmination of this transformation is the New Jerusalem. John's vision is not of a return to Eden but of a city where nature and grace are perfectly married. The city descends from heaven; humanity does not build it by its own effort. It is gift. It is grace. It is the Spirit's construction, brick by living brick, through every act of charity, every sacrifice, every liturgy, every martyr's witness, every humble yes to God. The New Jerusalem is the Bride made radiant.

And within it there is no temple. The Spirit fills everything. God is the temple. The Lamb is the light. Humanity walks in glory. Diversity is not erased but perfected. Every people, every culture, every redeemed personality shines with unique splendour. The Spirit does not create uniformity; He creates communion.

The absence of a temple in the New Jerusalem is not a lack; it is the fulfilment of everything the temple symbolised. The whole city becomes a dwelling-place of God because the Spirit fills all things. What Israel tasted in the Holy of Holies becomes the air every redeemed soul breathes. The veil is gone forever. The separation between sacred and secular dissolves. There is no "outside" to God's presence. The Spirit, once given in measure, now floods creation without restraint. The whole world becomes liturgy. The whole cosmos becomes communion.

In this world made new, humanity stands radiant. This is the completion of theosis—the journey traced throughout this book. The Spirit who restored the image, healed the faculties, illumined the mind, purified the heart, and united the soul to Christ now brings the entire human person, body and spirit, into full participation in divine life.

Glory is not an accessory; it is the fulfilment of human nature. "The glory of God is man fully alive," said Irenaeus, and the saints in the new creation are the living proof. They are fully alive—alive with the life of God, alive with the energy of the Spirit.

This radiance is not uniform. Glory never flattens individuality. Instead, the Spirit perfects the distinct beauty of each soul. One saint reflects God through contemplative stillness. Another through active love. One through gentleness, another through boldness, another through childlike trust. In the new creation, these differences do not divide; they harmonise. The Holy Spirit is a master of diversity. Just as He animated the early Church with many gifts but one love, so He crowns humanity with many splendours but one glory. The communion of saints becomes a living icon of the Trinity—many persons, one fire.

The risen humanity in this city is the humanity Christ manifested after Easter. They are visible, touchable, fully themselves, yet transformed beyond decay. Their senses are heightened, their desires purified, their wills made strong. They see God, not in fleeting glimpses but in sustained vision. They love without effort. They worship without fatigue. They rejoice without decline. This is not fantasy. It is the destiny of those who have allowed the Spirit to shape their lives. In the new creation, the dignity of human freedom finds its perfection. The soul freely surrenders to God, not as a duty but as its greatest delight.

All of this revelation rests on a foundational truth: the new creation is not merely the restoration of Eden. It is the consummation of everything Eden hinted at. The garden becomes a city because human history, culture, and creativity are not erased but redeemed. Human labour is not discarded; it is transfigured. Every good we built in the present life—every act of mercy, every beauty crafted, every truth lived, every relationship nurtured—finds fulfilment in the new world.

Nothing good is lost. Nothing given in love disappears. The Spirit gathers all of it into eternal significance.

This is why the eschatological vision cannot be reduced to spiritual abstraction. The Spirit does not save souls out of the world; He saves the world through the souls He has transformed. Matter is not an obstacle to glory; it is the vessel of glory. Human bodies rising in splendour are not an afterthought; they are the proclamation that creation itself is destined for union with God. The Spirit's task is not finished until everything earthly becomes capable of heaven.

Paul's words ring with this reality: "The creation waits with eager longing for the revealing of the sons of God." Creation itself has been dragged into the drama of salvation. It suffered when humanity fell. It groans under the weight of sin. It longs for liberation. And it will share in redemption. The renewal of the world is not optional; it is promised. When the sons and daughters of God are revealed in glory, creation exults. Rivers rejoice. Mountains dance. Nature, once wounded, is healed. The Spirit who breathed life into the first garden breathes eternal life into the final city.

This is not naïve optimism. It is the Gospel's deepest hope. The Spirit is not content with partial victory. He does not redeem souls but abandon bodies. He does not sanctify individuals but forget creation. He does not restore hearts but ignore history. Everything He touches He makes new. Everything He begins He completes. The Spirit is the great Finisher. He is the One who carries all things toward their fulfilment.

What emerges from this vision is a profoundly relational understanding of heaven. Heaven is not an isolated bliss reserved for individuals floating in private contemplation. Heaven is communion. Heaven is the human race, healed and united, participating in the eternal exchange of love within the Trinity. Heaven is the Father pouring His love into the Son, the Son offering Himself to the Father, and the Spirit drawing redeemed humanity into that divine embrace.

In heaven, the Spirit is the atmosphere of existence. He is the breath of the redeemed, the joy of the saints, the unity of the Church, the radiance of the Lamb, the song of creation. Every heartbeat echoes His presence. Every face shines with His light. Every movement is an act of worship. Every desire flows toward God with total freedom. The Spirit is not one gift among many; He is the life of the age to come.

This is why the new creation cannot be thought of as static. The Fathers speak often of *epektasis*—the eternal movement of the soul into greater and greater depths of God. Glory is not a plateau; it is an ascent without end. The Spirit draws the redeemed into an ever-deepening participation in divine life. There is no boredom because there is no exhaustion. There is no limit because God is infinite. The soul expands forever, delighted forever, discovering forever. Eternity is not endless time but endless love.

The new creation, then, is the Spirit's final masterpiece. It is the world aflame with the beauty of God, the human person radiant with eternal life, the cosmos resonating with divine harmony. It is everything creation was meant to be when the Spirit first hovered over the waters—but now complete, glorified, made new.

If the new creation is the Spirit's masterpiece, then its centrepiece is the vision of God. This is the moment theologians have struggled to describe for centuries, for the simple reason that human language cannot capture what the Spirit enables the redeemed to behold. Scripture calls it seeing "face to face." Augustine calls it "the full possession of truth." Aquinas calls it "the beatific vision"—the intellect elevated beyond all natural capacity through the Spirit. The Eastern Fathers describe it with their favourite word: light. Uncreated light. The light of Tabor. The light of the burning bush that did not consume. The light Moses glimpsed on Sinai. The light that blinded Paul on the road to Damascus. The light that fills the soul in the new creation.

This light is not merely visual. It is personal. It is the radiance of the Father shining in the face of Christ, made visible by the Spirit. The redeemed do not simply witness divine glory; they participate in it. The Spirit makes their minds capable of understanding God without error, their wills capable of loving God without hesitation, their hearts capable of receiving God without fear. The beatific vision is the fulfilment of the anthropology traced throughout this book: the image healed, the likeness restored, the faculties purified and perfected. The Spirit does not merely show God; He renders the soul able to behold God.

This is why the new creation is not a reward but a revelation. It unveils what humanity was created for from the beginning. Adam and Eve were made to walk with God without shame. Israel was chosen to reflect God's holiness. The prophets were sent to awaken desire for the divine presence. Christ came to open the way into that presence. The Spirit was given to transform the human person into a dwelling place of God. Heaven is the unveiling of all these mysteries in their final form. It is the Spirit finishing what He began in Genesis.

The redeemed do not lose their identity in this vision. They become more themselves than ever before. This is one of the paradoxes of the new creation: in beholding God, the human person discovers the truth of their own being. Sin fractured identity; glory restores it. Sin scattered the self; the Spirit gathers the self into unity. Sin obscured purpose; the Spirit clarifies purpose. In this vision, personality does not dissolve—it blossoms. The saints remain distinct, their stories intact, their struggles remembered, their triumphs crowned. Grace does not erase history; it transfigures it.

In the new creation, the soul sees the pattern of its earthly life with clarity. Every moment of surrender becomes radiant. Every act of love becomes immortal. Every sacrifice becomes treasure. Every wound becomes a window for glory. Suffering is not forgotten but reframed. The cross becomes the seed of splendour. No tear is wasted. No prayer dies. No act of mercy disappears. The Spirit gathers every thread of a life lived in faith and weaves it into eternal significance.

This is why the new creation is called a "city." Cities are woven from stories, relationships, histories, cultures. The heavenly city gathers into itself the goodness of human history purified by the Spirit. Everything holy in human civilisation—beauty, art, music, culture, science, virtue, friendship—finds a place within the New Jerusalem. Earth is not discarded; earth is offered. Grace does not eliminate nature; grace perfects it. The world becomes sacrament because the Spirit fills it.

From this vantage point, it becomes clear why the Spirit has worked with such relentless patience throughout salvation history. The Spirit has been preparing not only individuals but humanity as a whole for communion. The Spirit has been forming a people capable of living together in love. Heaven is not simply the union of God and the soul; it is the union of humanity with itself in God. Every division healed, every hostility dissolved, every wound reconciled—this is the work of the Spirit. The communion of saints is not a poetic image; it is the social form of divinisation. The Spirit makes unity possible.

In this unity, love is the law. Not the fragile love of fallen desire but the strong, self-giving love of the Trinity poured into the human heart. In heaven, love is effortless because it is natural. All fear is gone. All insecurity gone. All envy gone. All comparison gone. The Spirit crowns every soul with a dignity that cannot be threatened. Love becomes the atmosphere of existence. Each person becomes a gift to every other. Heaven is the human race learning to love the way God loves.

This love is dynamic. Just as the Spirit is eternally dynamic within the Trinity—proceeding, giving, uniting—so the redeemed participate in this movement. Heaven is not static contemplation but infinite ascent. Gregory of Nyssa describes this as *epektasis*—the soul stretching into God forever, never exhausted, never stationary, always entering deeper joy. The Spirit draws the redeemed into an endless discovery of divine beauty. No day in eternity repeats the previous one. No gaze at God exhausts His splendour. No act of love reaches its limit. Glory expands forever.

This is why the new creation is described not as the end but as the beginning. The last chapter of the Bible feels like the first chapter of something greater. The voice saying, "Behold, I make all things new," does not close a book; it opens an eternal story. The Spirit is the author of this story. He leads the redeemed through the infinite landscapes of divine life. Eternity is not the cessation of story but the flowering of story.

And so, the final vision of this chapter must bring us back to the threshold of Revelation, where John sees the river of life, clear as crystal, flowing from the throne of God and of the Lamb. This river is the Spirit. He flows through the city, giving life to everything He touches. He nourishes the tree of life, whose leaves are for the healing of the nations. He fills the streets with light. He animates the worship of the saints. He makes God all in all.

The river of life that flows through the New Jerusalem is one of Scripture's most evocative images of the Holy Spirit. Water has always been the Spirit's sign: the waters of creation stirred by His breath, the flood that cleansed the earth, the Red Sea parted by His power, the water from the rock in the wilderness, the flow from Ezekiel's temple vision, the living water promised by Jesus to the Samaritan woman, the streams of grace in Baptism. But in Revelation the imagery reaches its fulfilment. This water is not symbolic; it is the life of God Himself. It pours from the throne of God and of the Lamb, because the Spirit proceeds eternally from the Father and the Son, and in the new creation He pours without measure.

This river does more than sustain life—it creates life. It is the pulse of the new cosmos. Everything touched by this water becomes luminous. The trees lining its banks bear fruit without ceasing, echoing the fullness of life the Spirit gives. Their leaves are "for the healing of the nations," because in the Spirit every wound finds its cure. The ancient divisions that tore humanity apart—violence, prejudice, pride, hatred—are healed by the life-giving flow. In the new creation, the Spirit does not simply end conflict; He creates communion. Nations retain their identities, but those identities harmonise under the Spirit's fire rather than clash. Cultural diversity becomes a choir of glory.

This scene corrects two common errors. The first is the notion that heaven is an escape from earth. Revelation shows the opposite: heaven descends to earth. The second error is the assumption that heaven is the afterlife of individual souls. But the new creation is not a private paradise. It is a world renewed, a community glorified, a cosmos set free. Salvation is social because the Spirit's life is communion. God is not solitude; God is Trinity. Therefore the final world cannot be solitude. It must be communion.

This brings us to one of the most profound mysteries in the entire biblical vision: the absence of night. "There shall be no more night," says John, "for the Lord God will be their light." Night, in Scripture, symbolises fear, ignorance, sin, and death. To say that night is gone is to say that everything opposed to communion has been overcome. No more fear—because love has driven it out. No more ignorance—because the Spirit illumines all things. No more sin—because the will is wholly aligned with divine love. No more death—because the Spirit has filled the body with everlasting life.

The Spirit is the light that makes night impossible. Not a created light, like the sun or stars, but the uncreated light of God. This is the light that shone from Christ at the Transfiguration. It is the radiance that filled the tomb on Easter morning. It is the fire that burned in tongues over the apostles' heads. In the new creation, this light is not momentary. It is perpetual. The redeemed live in a world suffused with glory. Every corner illuminated. Every face transfigured. Every moment a hymn of praise.

In this world, worship is not an activity; it is existence. The saints do not gather occasionally to give glory to God—they *exist* within glory. Every thought is doxology. Every movement is liturgy. Every desire is communion. The Spirit is the breath of this worship, drawing humanity into the eternal exchange between Father and Son. Worship becomes second nature because humanity's true nature has been restored. Sin distorted desire; the Spirit healed it. In the new creation, desire flows naturally toward God, effortlessly, joyfully.

It is this effortless communion that reveals the final beauty of the Spirit's work: freedom. In the fallen world, freedom often feels like a burden—choices, temptations, divided desires, conflicting loves. But in the new creation, freedom becomes pure delight. The redeemed are not constrained to love God; they *want* to love God. They do not fear losing Him; they rejoice in possessing Him. Their wills are stable, their minds clear, their hearts spacious. Freedom is fulfilled because it is finally anchored in love.

This transformation shows why the Spirit had to purify the human person throughout earthly life. The heart cannot leap into eternal communion unless it has learned to let go of idols. The will cannot embrace unending love unless it has surrendered its compulsions. The mind cannot behold divine beauty unless it has been cleansed of falsehood. The Spirit's entire work of sanctification—conviction, repentance, illumination, virtue, prayer, charity—was preparing the person for this freedom.

And freedom, once fully awakened, expresses itself not only in worship but in joy. Joy is the Spirit's signature. Already in this life, joy appears whenever the Spirit is near—Mary's Magnificat, the apostles singing in prison, the early Church sharing possessions with gladness. But in the new creation, joy is no longer intermittent. It is the rhythm of existence. The redeemed rejoice without interruption because nothing obstructs the flow of divine life. Joy is not an emotion here; it is the state of the soul bathed in the fire of love.

This joy extends not only inward but outward. In the new creation, relationships reach their perfection. Friendships become bonds of pure charity. Families are reunited in harmony. The communion of saints becomes a living network of unbroken affection. No memory carries shame. No relationship bears resentment. Everything is reconciled. The Spirit who forged unity in the early Church now creates unity without fracture across the entire redeemed humanity.

This is why Scripture describes heaven as a wedding feast. The imagery is not sentimental. It reveals the consummation of longing, the arrival of joy, the satisfaction of desire. The Spirit has been preparing the Bride—the Church—for this union throughout history. Every sacrament was a rehearsal; every liturgy was a foretaste; every act of love a preparation. In the new creation, preparation becomes fulfilment. The Bride is ready. The Lamb receives her. And the Spirit fills the union with splendour.

This is also why the new creation is described as a kingdom. Not a kingdom of domination or hierarchy, but a kingdom of peace, justice, and truth—because the Spirit reigns. Where the Spirit reigns, peace is perfect, justice is fulfilled, love is complete. The kingdom Jesus preached is not a metaphor. It is the final order of reality. The Spirit establishes this order and sustains it eternally.

To stand within this kingdom is to stand within the fullness of God's intention for humanity. All of history, with its agonies and triumphs, its failures and repentances, its longing and its hope, converges here. The Spirit is not simply the one who accompanies humanity on its journey; He is the One who guides history toward consummation. Every prophecy, every covenant, every sacrament, every whisper of grace has been leading toward a single horizon: a world made new. The new creation is the revelation of God's fidelity through the Spirit.

It is here that the Trinity's work appears in perfect harmony. The Father speaks the eternal Word; the Son becomes incarnate, dies, rises, and stands as the Lamb upon the throne; and the Spirit, proceeding from both, fills creation with the life of God. The Spirit reveals the Father's plan and the Son's glory. He completes what the Father wills and the Son accomplishes. If the Incarnation is the beginning of the new creation, then the Spirit's descent at Pentecost is its ignition, and the Spirit's fire at the end of history is its completion. This final chapter reveals the Spirit's identity as the Finisher, the One who brings history into its divine rest.

The Fathers often spoke of salvation in three great movements: creation, redemption, and consummation. All three are the work of the Trinity. But each bears the distinct imprint of one divine Person. The Father creates; the Son redeems; and the Spirit consummates. This does not mean division of labour—it means the revelation of divine communion. The Spirit's work at the end of time is not separate from the Son's victory but its unfolding. The Lamb who was slain is the centre of the new creation, but it is the Spirit who makes His victory visible in every corner of the cosmos.

This is why the final vision of Revelation shows the Lamb and the Spirit shaping the world together. The kings of the earth bring their glory into the city. The nations walk by the Lamb's light. The river of the Spirit flows from the throne of God and the Lamb. Everything—nature, humanity, angels, creation—is drawn into this radiant communion. The city shines "with the glory of God," and this glory is nothing other than the Spirit filling the redeemed with divine life. The Father is seen. The Son is adored. The Spirit is glorified.

And creation becomes transparent to the Trinity.

The absence of suffering in this world is not a denial of the significance of earthly suffering. On the contrary, the new creation reveals that every sorrow was a seed planted for future glory. Paul's words echo with renewed clarity here: "The sufferings of this present time are not worth comparing with the glory that is to be revealed." This is not stoicism. It is not naïve optimism. It is revelation. When the Spirit heals the wounds of the world, the scars do not disappear; they shine. Just as Christ's resurrected wounds are now sources of beauty, so the wounds of the redeemed become testaments of grace.

Every injustice endured becomes a crown. Every sacrifice becomes treasure. Every grief becomes a doorway into consolation. Nothing is forgotten, nothing erased, nothing trivialised. Every pain has been gathered by the Spirit, transfigured, woven into the destiny of glory. The new creation is not a satisfaction that replaces sorrow; it is a fulfilment that redeems it. Suffering is not undone—it is completed.

This is why the saints speak of heaven as a place of rest. Not rest as idleness but rest as fulfilment. The restless heart finds its home because its desires, purified by the Spirit, finally match its destiny. Augustine's confession—"Our hearts are restless until they rest in You"—is not poetic longing. It is anthropology. The new creation is the home for which every human heart was made. It is the reunion of the soul with its origin and its goal. The Spirit is the one who gives this rest, because He is the Love in which the human person lives and moves and has its being.

Yet rest is not stagnation. Heaven is rest and movement simultaneously. Rest because desire no longer wars with itself; movement because desire expands endlessly toward God. The Spirit enables both. He secures the soul in divine love, and He propels the soul into deeper participation in that love. Heaven is stability and ascent, peace and exultation, stillness and song. Eternity is movement in love.

This endless ascent reveals the inexhaustibility of God. The redeemed never reach a point at which they have "seen" all there is to see or "known" all there is to know. Divine beauty is boundless. Divine truth infinite. Divine goodness immeasurable. The Spirit draws the soul into this mystery without end. Every moment brings new splendour, new joy, new depth. Love increases forever. Communion deepens forever. Glory expands forever. The Spirit ensures eternity is not an endless loop but an endless blossoming.

It is this perpetual newness that reveals the heart of the Spirit's identity. The Spirit is the One who makes all things new—not once, not occasionally, but perpetually. Newness is His signature. Wherever He is, life unfolds. Wherever He breathes, glory expands. Wherever He rests, love intensifies. The new creation is the world finally able to receive Him without measure. The Spirit fills all things, and all things flourish.

In this flourishing, God is all in all. This is the final line of the entire Christian story. The Father, who spoke creation into existence; the Son, who redeemed it through His life, death, and resurrection; and the Spirit, who sanctified every moment of history—all dwell in perfect communion with redeemed humanity. Nothing lies outside this communion. No darkness remains. No sorrow lingers. Heaven is the universe fully opened to God, radiant with divine presence.

And yet the Scriptures end not with silence but with a cry. The cry of the Spirit. The cry of the Bride. "Come." It is the cry of longing fulfilled and yet still longing, because love always desires more love. It is the cry of history completed and eternity beginning. It is the cry of the Church who sees her Bridegroom coming. It is the cry of the Spirit who has led creation from breath to fire to glory.

The Scriptures end with an invitation because the new creation is not a wall but a door. It is not a sealed empire of the saved but an open embrace offered to the world by the Spirit and the Bride. "Come," they cry—not in desperation, not in fear of missing something, but in the overflowing abundance of divine love. The Spirit who hovered over the waters at the dawn of time now stands at the edge of eternity, summoning creation into glory. The Bride—the Church—echoes this summons because she has been fashioned by the Spirit into the voice of Christ in the world. The final act of salvation history is a harmony: the Spirit calling, the Church responding, Christ drawing near.

This cry reveals the heart of the eschaton. The end of history is not primarily judgment (though judgment is included), nor destruction (for nothing truly good is lost), nor escape (for creation is redeemed). The end of history is invitation. It is the Spirit calling humanity to the marriage feast of the Lamb. It is the Bride, finally perfected, longing for union with her Bridegroom. It is the yearning of creation itself, healed of all groaning, now exulting in new life. The cry "Come" is the sound of the world finding its meaning.

In the final vision, John beholds something astonishing: God dwelling with humanity. Not visiting. Dwelling. Permanently. Intimately. Tenderly. "Behold, the dwelling place of God is with men, and He will dwell with them." This is the reversal of Eden's exile. This is the undoing of every distance introduced by sin. This is the healing of every wound that made intimacy fearful. The Spirit, who dwelt in the tabernacle, who filled the temple, who overshadowed Mary, who descended at Pentecost—now fills the entire world. There is no corner left untouched by His flame.

In this world radiant with divine indwelling, humanity becomes what it was always meant to be: a living icon of the Trinity. The Father's love shines in every face. The Son's glory is reflected in every body. The Spirit's fire burns in every soul. The redeemed do not merely live alongside God; they participate in the exchange of divine love. Heaven is Trinitarian communion extended to creatures. It is the Spirit drawing every redeemed heart into the eternal rhythm of giving and receiving that flows between Father and Son.

This communion does not erase individuality; it perfects it. The saints shine with unique splendours. Each life becomes a facet of divine beauty. The redeemed do not lose themselves—they find themselves. Everything true in them is intensified, everything false burned away, everything wounded healed, everything noble fulfilled. The new creation is personal. Salvation is not absorption into an impersonal divine ocean; it is fellowship with the living God. The Spirit ensures that each human person becomes fully, gloriously themselves in God.

The particular beauty of this final state is its harmony. No rivalry. No jealousy. No insecurity. No suspicion. All relationships, once marked by misunderstanding and distance, now become transparent with love. The communion of saints is not sentimental imagery—it is the social fullness of theosis. Humanity, once divided, becomes one people, one body, one bride. The Spirit creates a unity that does not erase difference but elevates it. Every redeemed culture, personality, and vocation converges in a single symphony. The city of God is not monochrome; it is a mosaic lit from within.

Standing within this communion, creation itself becomes sacramental. The redeemed do not float in ethereal abstraction; they inhabit a world. A real world. A resurrected world. A world in which mountains shimmer with divine splendour, rivers run with living water, trees bear fruit for healing, and every blade of grass is lit with the presence of God. Matter itself becomes transparent to glory. The universe becomes the cathedral of the Spirit. Every horizon shines. Every moment is holy. Every breath is praise.

It is here that the deepest truth of the new creation becomes visible: the Spirit finishes what He began.

The breath that stirred the primordial waters now fills the cosmos with life.

The fire that descended at Sinai now burns in every redeemed heart.

The overshadowing that made the Word flesh now overshadows creation to make it divine.

The flame that descended at Pentecost to birth the Church now descends to consummate the world.

The Spirit is the great Artist of salvation history. Every movement of the story—creation, covenant, prophets, Incarnation, Church, sanctification, judgment—leads toward this final canvas. In the new creation, the tapestry of salvation is revealed. Nothing was random. Nothing was wasted. Everything was guided by the quiet compulsion of divine love.

And the final word of Scripture—indeed, the final word of this entire book—is the Spirit's own: "Come." This word is the summation of divine desire. God desires humanity. God desires union. God desires communion. And the Spirit is the desire of God made visible, audible, tangible. The Spirit is the longing of the Trinity for creation and the longing of creation for the Trinity.

The Bride answers with the same word—"Come"—because the Spirit has shaped her heart into a mirror of Christ's own desire. Love calls to Love. Fire calls to fire. Glory calls to glory. And the Lamb, hearing this cry, responds: "Surely I am coming soon."

Between these two words—"Come" and "I am coming"—the whole mystery of salvation is held. The cry of the Spirit. The cry of the Church. The promise of the Son. The love of the Father. And the world transfigured in their embrace.

This is the new creation.

This is the home of redeemed humanity.

This is the consummation of the Spirit's work.

The Spirit finishes what He began.

24

Conclusion

Creation began with breath. Redemption unfolded through fire. The Church was born in wind and flame. Every page of Scripture, every sacrament that touches the flesh, every healing of a human heart, every whisper of holiness in the quiet interior of a soul—all of it has been the work of the Holy Spirit. The entire story you have walked through in this book is not a sequence of ideas but a single movement: the Spirit drawing creation toward glory. Nothing in the Christian life stands apart from Him. Nothing in salvation history moves without Him. Nothing in you can become what God desires except by Him.

Looking back, the Spirit has been the hidden protagonist of the entire journey. At the beginning He hovered over the waters, the silent architect of beauty. In Israel He raised judges, inspired prophets, filled kings, and kindled longing for the Messiah. In Christ He overshadowed, anointed, strengthened, and raised. At Pentecost He descended as flame, and the world became charged with a new kind of light. In the sacraments He breathes, consecrates, forgives, transforms. In the soul He purifies the heart, illumines the mind, binds us to Christ, heals our wounds, strengthens our virtues, and leads us into the fire of divine life. At the end of all things, He will raise the dead and transfigure creation.

Every movement in salvation—from Genesis to Revelation, from dust to resurrection glory—has been the work of the Spirit who fashions all things toward the Father's design through the Son.

Yet for many Christians today, the Spirit remains the great forgotten Person. Faith feels dry. Prayer feels mechanical. The moral life feels like a burden carried alone. The Scriptures feel distant, the sacraments feel routine, and the interior life feels like a landscape of distraction. We assent to the faith, but we do not feel alive with it. We speak of God, but the words do not burn.

Modern Christianity often suffers from a spiritual anaemia not because Christ is distant but because His Spirit is unwelcomed. Not consciously rejected—but unopened, uninvited, unrecognised. We try to live the Christian life as though it were a matter of willpower rather than participation in divine life.

Deep within, every believer knows the ache:

"There must be more than this."

That ache is the Spirit Himself, stirring desire for the life He longs to give.

Life in the Spirit is not an enhancement of Christianity—it *is* Christianity. Everything else is the shadow; life in the Spirit is the substance. This conclusion is not a summary of what has been said. It is a final invitation into the life that every chapter has been pointing toward: the life of holiness, communion, mission, and glory that unfolds when the Spirit is welcomed as the daily breath of the soul.

To live in the Spirit is to awaken to the truth that God is no longer outside you, above you, or beyond you. He dwells within you. He prays in your prayer. He strengthens your weakness. He purifies your desire. He illumines your darkness. He binds you to Christ so deeply that the life of Christ becomes your own. The Spirit does not visit occasionally; He inhabits, transforms, and re-creates.

CONCLUSION

The Fathers loved to say that the Christian life is not an imitation but a participation. The Spirit does not teach you to mimic Christ. The Spirit joins your life to Christ so that His virtues, His desires, His compassion, His courage, and His purity begin to breathe through your humanity. This is what Paul meant when he cried, "It is no longer I who live, but Christ who lives in me." This is what Basil meant when he described the Spirit as the One who makes the soul radiant. This is what Seraphim of Sarov meant when he said that the entire aim of the Christian life is "the acquisition of the Holy Spirit."

Life in the Spirit is not a mystical elite experience. It is the ordinary vocation of every baptised soul. It is the normal Christian life—so normal, in fact, that anything less is the abnormality.

Yet to live in the Spirit is not passive. Love never is. The Spirit always moves, invites, prompts, stirs, wounds gently, heals deeply, and strengthens quietly. But He never forces. Life in the Spirit is a relationship—a friendship, a communion, a breathing together.

And so the final movement of this book must be practical. Not practical in the shallow sense of a checklist or technique, but practical in the spiritual sense of how to *live* the truths that have been unveiled. The whole ascent of purification, illumination, union, and glory becomes daily life when approached through four simple movements, each carrying the weight of the entire mystical tradition.

The first is purification. This is the Spirit's work of reordering the heart, of healing the disordered loves that divide our attention and distort our desires. Purification is not self-condemnation but surrender. It takes shape in humility, repentance, honest confession, patient endurance, and trust. In purification we give the Spirit permission to touch the hidden places in us—the grudges, wounds, sins, resentments, fantasies, fears—that we have long guarded from His light. The Spirit never humiliates. He heals. Purification is simply the act of letting Him do what He came to do: burn away whatever is not love.

The second is illumination. Illumination is not brilliant insight or theological cleverness. Illumination is learning to see with Christ's eyes, to hear with Christ's heart, to interpret reality as Christ does. The Spirit does this in Scripture, where words become living encounters. He does this in silence, where the soul begins to listen rather than speak. He does this in the Eucharist, where Christ's presence reshapes perception. He does this in discernment, where the Spirit teaches the heart to recognise His movements and refuse the counterfeits that mimic His voice. Illumination is nothing other than the Spirit placing Christ's mind within the believer.

The third is union. Union is the Spirit's greatest joy. It is the goal toward which He moves every moment of the Christian life. In union, Christ's virtues grow in the soul not as external ideals but as interior habits. Courage, patience, purity, generosity, gentleness, fortitude, fidelity—these do not appear by effort alone; they bloom because the Spirit breathes divine life through the human faculties. Union is not emotional ecstasy. It is the steady, quiet awareness that Christ lives in you and that you live in Him.

The fourth is mission. Mission is not activism, strategy, or pressure. Mission is what happens when divine love overflows. A heart purified, illumined, and united with Christ cannot help but radiate Him. The Spirit pushes outward. He draws others in. He gives words to those who fear speaking, courage to those who fear suffering, compassion to those who fear love. Mission is the natural expansion of a Spirit-filled heart into the world.

Everything in the Christian life fits somewhere within these four movements. They are not stages to complete but rhythms to breathe.

And beneath them all is the Spirit—the fire at the centre of the soul, the quiet presence who makes holiness possible, who turns faith into vision, who transforms suffering into offering, who prepares the heart

CONCLUSION

for glory.

The Spirit has never stopped doing what He did in Genesis. He still hovers over chaos—cosmic and personal. He still brings order, awakens beauty, creates life, and shapes the image of God into likeness. He still breathes. He still burns. He still raises the dead.

Your life is His canvas. Your soul is His dwelling. Your destiny is His glory.

To live daily in the Spirit is to allow these four movements—purification, illumination, union, and mission—to become the quiet rhythm of your soul. Not as tasks. Not as achievements. As the natural breathing of a heart drawn into God. The Spirit is not asking you to become extraordinary in your own strength. He is asking you to become *available*. Holiness never begins with effort; it begins with openness. The Spirit is the breath of divine life, and breath does not force itself. It flows wherever it finds space.

Perhaps the most important truth to remember is this: every desire for God already carries the signature of the Spirit. You do not long for holiness on your own. You do not yearn for prayer on your own. You do not ache for freedom, purity, peace, or meaning on your own. The Spirit Himself stirs these movements in you. He is the origin of every good impulse. Before you lifted your heart, He was already lifting it. Before you sought God, He was already seeking you. Every beginning of love is His.

This is why the spiritual life never needs to begin with anxiety. You are not trying to build a ladder to heaven. You are responding to the One who has already descended into your depths. The Spirit is not above you pulling; He is within you drawing. His work is not distant; it is intimate. He teaches you the rhythms of holiness the way a mother teaches a child to breathe—gently, patiently, with constant presence.

In the ordinary moments of your life, the Spirit is already at work.

When your conscience pricks with that small discomfort that says, "This is not who you are," the Spirit is purifying. When a line of Scripture suddenly pierces with unexpected beauty, the Spirit is illuminating. When you feel forgiveness softening a wound you thought would never heal, the Spirit is uniting. When you find strength to love when you would rather withdraw, the Spirit is sending. The entire Christian life unfolds through these quiet movements.

Yet the Spirit's presence does not mean that life becomes painless or simple. He does not remove suffering; He transforms it. He does not erase wounds instantly; He heals them from the inside out. He does not prevent weakness; He fills weakness with Himself. To walk in the Spirit is not to escape the human condition but to discover God within it.

This is why the saints could suffer without losing hope. They did not possess superhuman resilience. They possessed divine companionship. The Spirit prayed in their prayer, wept in their tears, strengthened their resolve, purified their motives, and lifted their gaze. What looked heroic from the outside was simply cooperation from within. Grace does not make suffering painless; it makes suffering fruitful. It turns the human heart into an altar. It turns each cross into communion. The Spirit does not explain pain; He inhabits it.

If you want to live in the Spirit, begin small. Begin human. Begin where you are, not where you believe you should be. The Spirit's favourite place to work is the place you least expect to see grace—the impatience you can't shake, the habit you can't break, the fear you can't name, the wound you can't forget. He enters not when you are polished but when you are honest. If you simply whisper, "Come, Holy Spirit," the entire weight of divine love responds. The Spirit delights in being invited.

Set aside moments of silence—not long, not elaborate. Just enough space for the heart to lower its defences. In that silence, say nothing.

CONCLUSION

Breathe. Let the Spirit breathe with you. You will begin to notice subtle movements: a softening, a calming, a clarity that was not present before. This is not imagination; it is communion. Rest there. You are not producing prayer. You are receiving presence.

Approach Scripture the same way—not as a text to analyse but as a place to encounter the One who speaks. Before you read, pray, "Spirit of truth, open my heart." Then listen. Sometimes a verse will shimmer with meaning; sometimes it will simply sit in the heart like a warm stone. Both are grace. Let the Word shape you. Let it carry you. Scripture is the Spirit's language.

In the sacraments, expect transformation. In confession, do not rehearse shame; offer your wounds. The Spirit is the One who purifies. In the Eucharist, do not rush; linger in gratitude. The Spirit is the One who unites. In anointing, marriage, and holy orders, trust that the Spirit consecrates human weakness into channels of divine strength. God never touches without transforming.

In your relationships, let the Spirit lead you toward gentleness. Love that costs nothing is not Christ's love. The Spirit will stretch your patience, deepen your compassion, sharpen your attention to others. This is His artistry—He turns ordinary human encounters into places of divine presence. When you show mercy, it is Christ showing mercy in you. When you forgive, you join the divine forgiveness that sustains the world.

In moments of temptation, do not panic. Call upon the Spirit. You will discover that desire for God burns deeper than desire for sin. Grace is stronger than habit. You might fall; you might fall often. But every fall is a place where the Spirit waits to lift you. Holiness is not never falling; holiness is rising with Him. The Spirit is patient. His work in you is slow, tender, and unwavering.

In moments of mission, remember that the Spirit sends before He commands. You do not bring Christ to others; Christ brings you.

Your words do not convert hearts; His Spirit does. What matters is not eloquence but fidelity. Spirit-filled mission often looks small: a conversation, a gesture, a decision to hope when others despair. Yet these are the seeds the Spirit loves. He sows through you more than you ever see.

To live in the Spirit is to become light—not by shining your own brilliance but by reflecting God's. This is why the saints appear luminous. They did not purify themselves, illuminate themselves, unite themselves, or sanctify themselves. They cooperated. They opened the door. The Spirit poured Himself through them, and the world saw God.

Life in the Spirit will make your life beautiful—not in the sense of ease, but in the sense of radiance. The Spirit shapes a person into something the world cannot explain: gentle yet strong, humble yet courageous, prayerful yet active, wounded yet hopeful. This is what glory looks like on earth. You become a living icon, a place where heaven touches the world.

The Spirit does not want to visit you now and then. He wants to make your life His dwelling place. He wants to craft in you the beauty He imagined from the beginning. He wants to finish in you the work He began in Genesis: bringing order from chaos, light from darkness, and life from dust.

You were made for this life. Everything in Scripture, everything in the Church, everything in the sacraments, everything in the saints' stories, everything in the long movements of salvation history has been steering you toward this one truth: you are created, redeemed, indwelt, and destined for the Spirit.

Creation is not a past event; it continues in you. The Spirit who hovered over the waters now hovers over the waters of your heart, waiting for the word of surrender that allows Him to bring order from chaos once more. Redemption is not distant history; it is Christ's life pressed into your life through the Spirit. Sanctification is not moral self-improvement; it is Christ's holiness unfolding in you because the Spirit breathes where you cannot. Glory is not a future unknown; it is the trajectory of your existence because the Spirit who raised Jesus from the dead will raise you too.

Everything begins in Him. Everything continues in Him. Everything returns to Him.

The Spirit is not a guest in your life; He is the atmosphere of your life. He is the breath beneath every prayer, the fire beneath every virtue, the light beneath every truth recognised, the tenderness beneath every healing, the strength beneath every sacrifice. When you feel courage that is greater than your fear, that is the Spirit. When you feel peace you cannot explain, that is the Spirit. When you feel conviction without condemnation, that is the Spirit. When you feel moved to love someone who has wounded you, that is the Spirit. When you find the strength to take one more step when you believed you had nothing left, that too is the Spirit.

This is why the saints often appear impossibly radiant. They do not become holy by technique. They become holy by relationship. They live inside the Spirit's embrace. They walk through the world with the quiet certainty that God moves in them even when He seems silent. Their joy is not emotional enthusiasm; it is the Spirit's flame. Their purity is not repression; it is freedom. Their courage is not bravado; it is participation in Christ's own strength. Their peace is not detachment; it is communion. Their generosity is not self-sacrifice for its own sake; it is divine love overflowing.

This is the life the Spirit desires for you.

He does not love you in theory. He loves you personally, attentively, fiercely, gently. He knows the specific wounds that have shaped your fears, the anxieties that constrict your choices, the habits that drag you down, the past that still echoes in you. He knows the burdens you carry and the hopes you barely dare to express. The Spirit never sees you abstractly. He sees you with divine precision. And He desires to restore your life with divine artistry.

Your wounds do not repel Him. They attract Him. Where you feel least capable of holiness is where He is most ready to work. Where you feel least lovable is where He is most ready to love. Where your soul feels tangled, He begins to untie. Where your heart feels cold, He begins to warm. Where your mind feels clouded, He begins to illumine. Where your strength fails, He becomes strength.

This is what it means to be a Christian: not to perform for God, but to live from God. Not to carry your life toward heaven with your own muscles, but to allow heaven to carry you through the Spirit who dwells within you. Christianity without the Spirit becomes moralism. Christianity with the Spirit becomes life—abundant, radiant, free.

Life in the Spirit is not exceptional. It is natural. It is what your humanity was designed for. You are most human when you are most surrendered to Him. You are most alive when you let Him breathe through you. You are most yourself when the Spirit shapes your heart into Christ's image. Your identity is not defined by failure but by belovedness. Your destiny is not determined by weakness but by grace.

Listen carefully: the Spirit is already working in you more than you realise. The fact that you read this book is a sign that He is stirring desire. The fact that you want holiness is proof that He is already near. The fact that you feel the ache for God is the Spirit praying within you. You do not need to manufacture the spiritual life; you need only respond.

Your life in the Spirit begins again every morning. Begin with a simple posture:

"Spirit of God, I am Yours.

Lead me today."

CONCLUSION

Do not ask for perfection. Ask for presence. Ask for awareness. Ask for willingness. The Spirit will shape the day from within. He will give you clarity where you feel confusion. He will give you peace where you feel tension. He will give you courage where you feel temptation. He will give you tenderness where you feel anger. He will give you humility where you feel pride. He will give you mercy where you feel resentment. And when you fail—and you will—He will lift you again with the same patience that raised the saints one thousand times.

Allow your life to breathe these simple rhythms:

In temptation:

"Spirit, strengthen me."

In confusion:

"Spirit, enlighten me."

In sorrow:

"Spirit, comfort me."

In fear:

"Spirit, be my courage."

In prayer:

"Spirit, pray in me."

In love:

"Spirit, love through me."

If you whisper these words with sincerity, the Spirit will do the rest. Holiness is not your achievement. It is your surrender.

And so we arrive at the final vision—the one that has been rising slowly beneath every chapter of this book. Your life does not end in death. Your story is not small. Your destiny is not fragile. The Spirit who hovered over the waters at the dawn of creation, the Spirit who descended upon Christ, the Spirit who ignited the Church, the Spirit who enters your heart at baptism, the Spirit who strengthens you in every sacrament, the Spirit who purifies, illumines, and unites—this same Spirit will one day raise you from the dead.

Your body will be made new. Your heart will be made whole. Your wounds will shine. Your desires will burn with perfect clarity. You will be filled with divine life. And the Spirit will complete in you what He began before the world existed.

This is where all things are going:

toward glory,

toward communion,

toward the face of the Father,

through Christ,

in the Spirit.

And on that final day, when all things are made new, when the Spirit completes His work in creation, when the Bride stands radiant before the Bridegroom, when the wounds of history have been healed and the tears of the world have been wiped away, a single cry will rise:

"The Spirit and the Bride say, Come."

Until that day, let your whole life become a reply.

"Come, Holy Spirit."

About the Author

Matthew Sardon is a Catholic writer based in Melbourne, Australia, formed by the depth and breadth of the Church's spiritual heritage. His path has taken him through years of study, prayer, and immersion in both the Roman and Byzantine traditions, giving him a single, integrated Catholic vision rooted in Scripture, nourished by the Fathers, and shaped by the Church's unbroken life of worship.

His work centres on biblical theology and exegesis — exploring how the ancient Word speaks with living power — but it also engages the pressing questions of the modern world. In an age marked by confusion and restless searching, he writes to help readers find clarity, refuge, and strength in the Church's tradition: the wisdom that has shaped saints, sustained families, and offered meaning to every generation.

Alongside his theological works, Matthew creates children's stories that open young hearts to faith and wonder through simple narrative and timeless imagery. Whether speaking to adults or children, he writes with the same purpose: to reveal how grace transforms the human heart and how the truths of the faith illuminate every corner of ordinary life.

When not writing, he serves in his local Catholic community, continues his theological studies and formation for ministry, and spends time with his family — seeking to live the beauty he teaches, one act of love at a time.

You can connect with me on:

🌐 https://matthewsardon.com

www.ingramcontent.com/pod-product-compliance
Lightning Source LLC
Chambersburg PA
CBHW060103230426
43661CB00033B/1403/J